MW01634301

The WOMAN'S GUIDE TO BUSINESS TRAVEL

The
WOMAN'S GUIDE TO BUSINESS TRAVEL

Penelope Naylor

HEARST BOOKS
New York

Library of Congress Cataloging in Publication Data

Naylor, Penelope
    The woman's guide to business travel.

    Includes index.
    1. Women in business.   2. Travel etiquette.
    3. Business travel.   I. Title.
HD6095.N28   910'.24042   81-6497
ISBN 0-87851-303-5   AACR2

Contents

Acknowledgments

I wish to thank those women (and a few men) who have shared their experiences and contributed their insights to this book, in particular Heather Hanley, Suzan Couch, Patricia Miller, Roxane Rauch, Ronny Reed, Christine Jones, Debra Lieberman, Cynthia Moss, Narsai David, Peter Verstappen, Connie Froeb, Carolyn Kenmore, Katy Morgan, Marion Haller, Elizabeth Howe, Phyllis Guest, Marie Toder, Deb Loveless, Rae Barlow, Luke Kahlich, Lisa E. Smith, my editor Wendy Rieder, and most especially, my sister-in-arms, Chrisjean Whitten.

I would also like to thank *W* for permission to reprint a quote from Zandra Rhodes; the *OAG Pocket Flight Guide* for permission to reprint a sample listing; *The Official Airline Guide—Worldwide Edition* for permission to quote from page 10 (copyright ©1980, Official Airline Guides, Inc., Oak Brook, Illinois 60521); American Airlines for permission to reproduce a sample air ticket; the symbols are from *Handbook of Pictorial Symbols* by R. Modley, 1976, Dover Publications, Inc., New York.

Introduction

A lot has been written recently on the subject of women business travelers, some of it constructive and helpful, but much of it distorted by a lingering ambivalence toward the needs and attitudes of contemporary women.

On the one hand there are the breathless exponents of the exclamation point, the "Gee Whiz!" school who seem excited (and not a little surprised) to find themselves actually out there on their own: "Just get up and do it gals! Get yourself to the airport! And don't forget to pack a few premoistened towelettes in your briefcase!"

On the other hand there are the aggressive/defensive "Don't-Mess-with-Me-I'm-an-Independent-Business-Traveler" types who can sling a suitcase or change a flat tire with the best of the boys, but are noted neither for their balanced perspective nor their sparkling wit.

Somewhere in between, one would assume, are the rest of us, the competent, aspiring professionals who work hard for a living and for whom business travel is not only an obligation but an integral, often rewarding, part of our professional lives. The old voices—the ones that address us with such saccharine stupidity, or, conversely, hand down their iron dialectic with such a deadening thud—are missing the point. Perhaps it's time to start redefining the reality.

According to the U.S. Travel Data Center in Washington, D.C., approximately 21 percent of all business travelers in the United States are women, which means there are over three million of us. We account for as much as 24 percent of the airlines' frequent traveler market, and as much as 30 percent of all business-traveler bookings in U.S. hotels. By Eastern Airline's computations, women currently make at least 28 million business trips a year and contribute $2 billion to the airline industry. Western International Hotels calculates that business women spend 32 million nights annually in U.S. and Canadian hotels, adding hundreds of millions of dollars to hotel coffers. Most remarkable of all is the rate at which our numbers have recently skyrocketed. *The Wall Street Journal* reported that back in 1974, just 1 percent of all business travelers were female.

The new statistics tell us that we are no longer unique enough to warrant any more exclamations: In the United States an average of more than 11,500 women set off on business-related journeys every working day of the year. But statistics have a way of painting an incomplete, even artificial, picture. They don't show us what the individual traveler experiences when she's alone in an often indifferent, sometimes hostile, world. And they don't point out that the world has had only a few years of sustained experience in which to learn how to deal with her.

What does the woman business traveler want?

In 1979, the Cornell School of Industrial and Labor Relations sponsored a seminar to try to answer that question and came to the general conclusion that, aside from concern about safety and cleanliness, women business travelers didn't really want anything substantially different from traveling businessmen. In her inimitable fashion, Anne Meara of the comedy team of Stiller and Meara put it all in a nutshell. "Why are you writing a book for women business travelers?" she asked me. "What are we, cripples?"

We're not cripples. Nor do we need to be treated in some superficially feminine manner by having bottles of nail polish remover included as standard gear on airplanes. But we do need to be recognized for who we are, and treated with courtesy and respect. We need to have good travel-related services to back us up so we can get our jobs done professionally, and, most importantly, we still need to readjust and strengthen our attitudes toward ourselves so that we can define for others how they should deal with us.

There appear to be a lot of residual insecurity and doubt in the minds of many women business travelers. There are too many negatives in current books and articles. We are too often cast in the passive role of victims who don't act but get acted upon. We are told of the "difficulties" of traveling on our own, and of the "misunderstandings'' and ''humiliations'' that occur (usually in reference to somebody else's mistaken idea of our sexual availability). We are advised to ''modify'' our behavior to reduce the frustration of our would-be suitors. In addition to being ''fair game'' if we show ourselves publicly, we are ''set upon'' if we linger, and are warned about the ''dangers'' lurking in hallways and elevators, not to mention those dens of iniquity, the hotel bars. We're told of the ''unnerving glares'' and ''insults'' that will be directed at us when we're eating alone in a restaurant. We're even advised to call ourselves ''Doctor'' when reserving a table to disguise the fact that we're merely female.

I don't buy it. The problems are real, and some adjustments are in order. It's the attitudes that are wrong. We're not cripples. Neither are we victims or prisoners. Why should we presuppose guilt and assume that we're the ones who have to change? The suppression of our natural energies and interest in life in order to create some inoffensive, neuter persona for public consumption will neither break down the barriers and change things for the future, nor allow us to have any fun.

One article written for women business travelers contained pointers on how to ''cope'' with life on the road. If you know what you're doing, you don't cope. You control.

This book is for you and women like you who travel for business, whether you log thousands of miles from Maui to Mauritania or are about to attend your first convention in Dubuque.

The idea of this guide is to familiarize you with all the professional, technical, and personal aspects of business travel. The more you know, the more effectively you can control your trip.

Part 1 is concerned with the nitty-gritty of travel: from airline ticketing to car rentals and expense accounts. Part 2 contains almost everything the international business traveler needs to know. Part 3 deals with your personal preparations. Part 4 takes you from the airport to your hotel. And, Part 5 provides tips on doing business, and getting the most enjoyment out of life in the process.

Most of the material is presented chronologically, starting with the first preparations for a trip and ending with a proposed weekend escape. You can read selectively, turning directly to those sections that interest you most. If you're looking for specific information, you'll find it listed in the index. To make your business travel easier, the appendix contains: a chart on international electric currents; conversion tables for temperature, lengths and distances, weights and measures, and clothing sizes; a glossary of travel terms; airport codes and mileage to various cities; offices and agencies to aid the traveler; and a directory of toll-free numbers to call for car rental and hotel bookings.

Throughout, you'll also run into assorted reminiscences and editorial opinions—an author's prerogative—which have been included to give the dry subject of business travel a more human perspective.

In compiling these chapters, I have tried to present a balanced set of alternatives to most travel situations, drawing on the vast knowledge of my friends and professional associates. Chrisjean Whitten, who speaks seven languages and has traveled for business to two-thirds of the countries on the globe, has contributed immeasurably by sharing her solid advice and rich experiences. In many respects, this book is her book.

"The world may not be ready for us," she once told me, laughing, "but we're ready for the world."

Penelope Naylor

Part 1

BEFORE YOU GO

1

Travel Planning like a Pro

It doesn't always go the way you think it's going to go.

A young woman I'll call Marta Collin, manager of agency sales for one of the leading car rental companies, is flying to Acapulco to represent her company in an international trade show. Marta has made dozens of trips like this before. This time she will be carrying 200 pounds of sample materials, and she will be making all the arrangements for a $10,000 display booth to be shipped to Acapulco from New York. In addition, she is scheduled to meet her boss's pregnant wife who will be waiting in the lobby of the Acapulco Princess Hotel for Marta to arrive with the hotel vouchers. Nonetheless, Marta makes her travel plans calmly, with professional ease.

According to her plan, Marta will fly from New York to Los Angeles for business, then connect with a morning flight to Acapulco. She arrives on schedule in Los Angeles with a large trunk, four heavy cartons, and seven enormous suitcases filled with trade materials, looking, as she puts it, like a carpetbagger.

At the airport, Marta learns that all flights to Acapulco have been canceled because of an air controllers' slowdown. If she hurries, she can catch a flight to Mexico City via Guadalajara, then try to get to Acapulco from there. She buys a ticket, grabs a porter, and races to the Aeronaves de Mexico departure gate.

The plane arrives in Guadalajara. The passengers are instructed to disembark for an indefinite delay. In the departure lounge, Marta tries to call her office.

"New York!" she shouts over the airport din into the receiver.

"Eh?" says the operator.

"New York! *New York!*" repeats Marta, but just then a voice over the loudspeaker announces that the flight to Mexico City is about to resume. Marta slams down the phone and races back through the crowded departure lounge onto the plane. In her absence, other passengers have been boarded. Someone has taken her seat and no other seats remain. After a half hour of argument, the passenger who has taken Marta's seat is bumped and Marta sits down, causing no small amount of ill will among the other passengers.

Marta arrives in Mexico City an hour after she was supposed to have met her boss's wife in Acapulco. There are no flights to the coast. Someone suggests that, if she hurries, she can catch a bus from a terminal on the other side of town.

Marta gets her trunk, seven suitcases, and four cartons through customs and deposits them outside by the taxi stand. The first three drivers refuse to take her. The fourth, a smiling man with an old black Dodge that has balled fringe framing the windshield and a plastic icon of the Virgin of Guadalupe dangling from the rearview mirror, loads up her bags. As they drive through the sprawling city, Marta sits anxiously on the edge of the worn flannel seat, crying "bus station" over and over, like a litany.

It is now about 1 P.M., Marta has missed the 12:30 bus. The next available seat is on the midnight bus, which arrives at 6 A.M. Marta checks her bags, which are soon incarcerated behind a fence, and places a telephone call, barely able to hear her own voice over the cacophony of the loudspeaker, to the local branch manager of her company in Mexico City.

His name is Alfonso, and he is not in the office. "Siesta," explains the *telefonista*. Marta waits an hour, then calls again. Alfonso has not returned. Finally, after three hours, Alfonso returns, refreshed, from his siesta.

"Where are you?" he asks.

"At the bus terminal," Marta answers.

"Which bus terminal?"

"The *bus* terminal!" she cries, ready to take the phone cord and strangle the nearest person, or herself.

Alfonso claims he cannot come to pick her up because there are several bus terminals in Mexico City, and he does not know where she is. She must take a taxi to his office. After bribing the clerk, who has refused to release her bags from the fenced enclosure, Marta climbs into another taxi and drives to the car rental office. Alfonso is not there.

An hour later, Alfonso, still yawning, returns. On the office phone, Marta contacts New York. No one know where her boss's wife is, and she learns that the $10,000 display booth is stuck in Houston because of the strike. Since there are no rental cars available, Alfonso books Marta a room at El Presidente Hotel and informs her that he will have a chauffeur pick her up at 9:30 the next morning to drive her to Acapulco.

At 9:30, the chauffeur hasn't arrived. At 10:30, Marta calls Alfonso to see what has happened. Alfonso has not yet come in. At 11:00, Alfonso calls to assure her that the chauffeur is on his way. At 11:30, Marta returns to her room to wait. At 1:45 the hotel hostess calls to tell her that a strange-looking man is wandering around the lobby with her named scribbled on a tattered piece of cardboard. Warily, Marta goes down. The man, whose name is Ricardo, has not shaved for several days. He is not wearing a shirt and there are holes in his stained and dusty pants. Parked in front of the hotel is a World War II-vintage Jeep, painted pink, with underlayers of camouflage.

Marta and Ricardo set off for Acapulco. Ricardo drives with his foot pressed flat on the accelerator as they careen over the treacherous mountain turns. Marta desperately has to urinate, but she's afraid to ask Ricardo to stop. "He could have been a rapist," she says, her large brown eyes wide with horror. "He could have been taking me to the woods. To his brother-in-law's house. He could have had relatives everywhere!"

Six hours later and a day and a half late, Marta arrives in Acapulco.

"It was like an Italian feast," she recalls. "People started running around crying, 'She's arrived!' while I stood in the lobby of the Acapulco Princess, surrounded by my baggage, with tears running from my eyes. My boss's pregnant wife, who had been given a room, embraced me, weeping, 'We all thought you had died.' "

The $10,000 display booth never arrived in Acapulco. Marta hired three local workers and attempted to build a replacement. "It was the ugliest thing you ever saw," she describes, "kind of a tepee made out of little sticks and painted with watercolors that looked as if they had been made from the residue of fruit.

"But I was lucky to get to the convention at all," she continues.

"One guy tried to get from Mexico City to Acapulco on a horse."

Experience has almost nothing to do with it. *Anything* can go wrong on a business trip. At least Marta Collin didn't have to leave for the airport at 5 A.M. in a downpour with her doorman on strike and all the taxi drivers in the city at home or in bed. Or have her suitcase lost en route (U.S. airlines lose about three million pieces of baggage every year). Or get bumped from an overbooked hotel in a crowded foreign city where the haughty desk clerk mumbles something vague in French but might as well be speaking Tupi-Guarani.

No amount of careful planning can protect you totally from the vagaries of life on the road. That doesn't mean you shouldn't plan. The success of every business trip depends on a smooth-flowing use of your energy and time. The more carefully you prepare your trip—misadventures not withstanding—the better your chances of achieving your objectives on the road.

A REALISTIC USE OF TIME

Time is the essential ingredient of the business travel experience—a fluid state of forward motion that determines what you can accomplish, where, and how. You need time to make your travel connections, time in the air and on the road, time checking into your hotel and arranging your business appointments, time getting to those appointments and attending meetings, time to organize your materials, do your paperwork, and keep in touch with your home office. You need time to sleep and eat, do your hair, arrange your clothes, catch your breath, and exchange a few words with another human being so you don't feel like an aspirated automaton.

You also have to allow contingency time for all those schedule-disrupting delays, at least one of which is bound to occur: the long wait in the taxi line, the delayed flight, the 30-minute wait over the crowded airport, the hot and dirty traffic jam.

Plan your time schedule generously. Permit yourself enough time to do your job thoroughly and still maintain your health and composure on the road. That doesn't rule out efficiency: The perfect business trip is one that allows you to accomplish your business objectives in the smallest amount of time, and still provides you with enough flexibility to make you feel comfortable.

Map Sources

Planning a successful, efficient business trip takes homework, especially if you are going to be away several days. Your travel adviser or company travel manager can only provide you with the basics.

Know the city you're going to. Buy a city map at your local bookstore. This may not be easy, as maps of distant cities are not always available. For U.S. and Canadian destinations, check the **Hagstrom** series (mostly limited to the Northeastern states), **Hammond, Rand McNally,** and **National Geographic.** Or buy a copy of the *Rand McNally North American Road Atlas* or a *Gousha/Chek-Chart* (published by the Times Mirror Company, 2001 The Alameda, P.O. Box 6227, San Jose, California), and make do with the city map insets. Automobile Association of America members can request special strip maps plus some city maps published by the AAA (see Chapter 5).

For international map series, look for the excellent **Michelin** city and country maps, the German **Falk Plan** city maps (to European cities), the **Hallwag** maps and the *Hallwag Road Atlas* (Europe). The British mapmaker **Bartholomew** also publishes a series of world maps.

If you are unable to find maps of esoteric destinations in your local map or book store, contact:

> **The Hammond Map & Travel Center**
> 10 East 41st Street
> New York, New York 10017
> (212) 679-3870

This is Hammond's only retail outlet, and it contains the largest map selection in New York City. Hammond sells a wide variety of domestic maps, the Falk and Hallwag series, plus hard-to-get maps produced locally in such places as Bogotá, Colombia, and Guatemala. Also available at Hammond is the expensive (about $20), but well-produced *AA Concise Road Book of Europe,* with legible city maps (published in the United Kingdom and distributed in the United States by W.W. Norton & Company). Hammond will fill both mail and phone orders. For orders under $10, you must pay in advance. For orders over $10, you will be billed, or you can charge your purchase to your American Express, Visa, or Master Card account.

Another great place for maps and guidebooks is:

> **The Complete Traveller**
> 199 Madison Avenue
> New York, New York 10016
> (212) 679-4339

This unique bookstore concentrates solely on travel books, maps, and bilingual dictionaries—everything for the complete traveler. They carry the Falk Plan city maps of European cities, as well as many other maps, and will fill mail and phone orders.

Many maps, especially of secondary U.S. cities, and cities in South America and the Orient, are almost impossible to get away from the destination. Make a point over the course of your business traveling career to pick up maps wherever you go and keep them on file.

Once you have your guidebooks and maps, try to estimate how long it will take to get from the airport to the downtown area in optimum conditions. Then add 50 percent more time if you'll be en route during rush hour. *Travel & Leisure* magazine recommends an addition of 45 minutes to get through the airport traffic during peak travel seasons (summer and holidays) and as much as 75 extra minutes at the beginning and end of high season weekends.

Next, estimate how much time you'll need to set up or confirm your business appointments once you're at your destination. Then figure out how many appointments you'll have to make, where they're located, and how long it will take to get to each. In most grid-designed U.S. cities, you can usually tell the approximate location of your appointments by the address (142 *East* 72nd Street, or Albemarle Street *NW*). Now you're prepared to plot your intinerary fairly accurately on your map. Be aware of local distances by checking the map scale. New York is crowded and compact. In Houston, the distances between business centers are immense, and in Miami, it sometimes seems impossible to get around.

Once you've pinpointed the location of your business calls, try to make your appointments in one area at a time. There's no more inefficient use of time than having to race back and forth across a city from one meeting to another. And once you know where you'll need to be, you can start to think about the most conveniently located hotel.

Multiple-City Trips

If your trip is a multi-city marathon involving a lot of hard traveling, you must be careful to correctly estimate how much time you'll need in each destination. How much time do you need per call? And how much traveling time in between?

In her experience, my friend Chrisjean Whitten has found she needs approximately one hour per call (which includes a 15-minute contingency for waiting), plus time getting from one place to another. On this schedule she estimates she can average five calls per city per day. Since she is often obliged to be on the road for three weeks or more at a time, she develops only the basic structure of her trip in advance. She has her travel agent book all her flights and hotels, start to finish. But she sets up her business appointments only one week at a time.

Instead of trying to construct an ironclad itinerary before she goes, with insufficient accommodation for delays, changed appointments, missed flights, and acts of God, Chrisjean builds a loose schedule that permits enough flexibility to deal with the best—and worst—of possibilities. Once on the road, she gets on the phone every Monday morning and arranges all the following week's appointments in the next city. If she gets seriously behind schedule, she can avoid the difficult business of rescheduling an entire trip's worth of meetings. She needs to adjust only those appointments, flights, and hotel reservations that are affected.

Chrisjean also suggests that you make your business appointments yourself. You're the best judge of how much time you'll need for each call, and, frequently, it takes some artful selling to get the appointment in the first place.

Before calling your travel agent, be sure you know how much time you'll need in each city. Chrisjean never tells her travel agent, "I want in on Tuesday and out on Thursday," but rather, "I'll need eight working hours in this city, four working hours in the next," and so forth. This way, the travel agent can use his or her professional judgment to build the most efficient schedule.

You can also build in an accommodation for delays by traveling during nonbusiness hours. If your plane is stacked up over O'Hare for two hours in the evening, you might not get your nine hours of beauty sleep, but at least you won't throw off the next day's schedule.

Remember to leave plenty of time for your travel agent to plan your itinerary. The longer the trip, the more time the agent will need to figure it out, book and confirm it, and write up your documents. Trips of three weeks or more often take a full week to construct and verify. Give your agent time to do it accurately.

Last but not least in planning your itinerary is the time you factor in for yourself. You need breaks for food and resuscitation during the day, plus enough time to relax, find a bit of diversion, and get organized. Long term, you do yourself and your company a tremendous disservice by running yourself ragged and limiting your effectiveness.

TRAVEL ADVISERS

Picking the right adviser is like picking the right psychiatrist—the criteria are totally subjective, and the chemistry has got to be just right.

If your company does not have a corporate travel manager, start looking now for someone who can facilitate your travel plans. Shop around, checking out various travel agencies and airline reservations offices.

When you try out an airline rep or travel agent, explain to him or her that you will have a considerable amount of business traveling to do in the coming year. Say that you would like to establish a working relationship. You want an agent who can become familiar with your needs, work habits, type of business and travel preferences (seats on planes, types of hotel rooms and rental cars).

The perfect travel agent should be: (1) convenient to where you work; (2) trustworthy and meticulous in all circumstances; (3) part of a sophisticated agency that can handle complicated bookings in obscure destinations; (4) equipped with multi-access computers that get instant readings from the major hotel chains and airlines; (5) willing and able to get you the best deals and discounts; and (6) personally knowledgeable about the world.

This ideal travel agent should also be someone who cares immensely about your comfort and convenience every step of the way. Someone who doesn't mind booking a 16-city, 10-country itinerary for you, and then, when you hit a snag and have to delay the trip a few days, cheerfully does it all over again. Someone who is vitally concerned about every little detail on your ticket, who double-checks every ''RQ'' and ''OK'' with a magnifying glass. Someone who knows something about every destination you've ever had to go to (including details such as which hotels at a destination have tennis courts and whirlpools). And someone who, incredibly, can calmly make order out of chaos when it comes to the air fares.

Such a person does not exist. Nevertheless, ask your traveling professional associates for recommendations, and keep looking. There are incredibly pleasant, helpful men and women behind the counters of travel agencies and airline ticket offices who do their difficult jobs with great enthusiasm, interest, and professionalism, often for an unfairly small return for their effort.

Chrisjean Whitten, whose monstrous itineraries are enough to frighten away the fainthearted, has finally found a wonderful travel agent in a nearby American Express office who knows her and the nature of her work, is interested in solving her travel problems, and takes a professional initiative when it comes to building functional itineraries. It wasn't easy. Chrisjean looked for months before finding someone she could count on.

Currently there are about 15,000 travel agencies in the United States, and the number is growing every day. All reputable agencies are accredited members of ASTA (American Society of Travel Agents) and/or IATA (International Air Transport Association), and they usually have a sticker or plaque in the office to indicate membership. Travel agents, as you probably know, earn their revenues on a commission basis from the airlines, hotels, rental car companies, and other travel services they represent. They do not receive payment from you, except for long-distance telephone calls, cables, or other out-of-pocket expenses incurred on your behalf.

Airline "Rez" Agents

Sometimes it's simpler and more direct to book flights, hotels, and ground services with the airline; if you're lucky, you'll find an airline reservations agent who will be everything that a good travel agent can be. The "rez" agent provides essentially the same services, with the exception that he or she will sell you tickets only on the airline he or she represents, or on a connecting airline (interline service). If you have no other choice of airline, or know that you want to use a specific airline, you usually can get a lot of precise information, clear-cut professional advice, and instant bookings via the airline's computer network.

Most of the airline reservations agents I've dealt with have been well informed about hotels and able to give me all the information I needed to know. If it's a good airline, the reservations agent will usually have carefully compiled source books and a lot of information at his fingertips (as opposed to many travel agents, who are inundated daily with a confusing array of literature from all the airlines and travel companies, and have to wade through piles of imprecise brochures to locate the latest information). The major disadvantage of dealing with an airline rep over the phone is the interminable wait for service.

Whether you go to a travel agent or an airline representative, it will take some time and effort to locate an adviser you can trust. Keep trying. What a good travel adviser can give you in terms of advice, careful bookings, and saved time is often worth the price of the trip. The best bet is probably a large, international travel company with the sophistication and know-how to deal with all your needs. Stay away from the cut-rate agencies (the ones with the ads for 10-day trips to Puerto Rico for $199), since they're usually more interested in selling vacation packages than in serving the specific needs of the business traveler.

SCHEDULE PLANNING CHECKLIST

- Plot your destination cities in geographic sequence.
- Know the scheduled durations of your flights.
- Find out the approximate time to and from the airport at each stop.
- Prepare a list of appointments in each city.
- Find the location of each appointment on a city map.
- Estimate the time needed for each call.
- Factor in time for the bare necessities, plus time for you.
- Find a travel adviser conveniently located to your office, meticulous and trustworthy, and with computerized booking capabilities. Also make sure you have personal rapport with the agent.
- Give your travel agent enough time to make careful bookings.

2

Making Sense Out of Air Fares

First of all, don't expect to make sense out of air fares. Nobody can make sense out of air fares—least of all the airlines. The current confusion regarding air fares is the result of years of unbending regulation by the CAB (Civil Aeronautics Board), followed by a sudden deregulation a few years ago that has provoked the present chaos. Added to deregulation is the unsettling factor of jet fuel costs, which mostly go up, and which now absorb a massive percentage of the airlines' erstwhile profits. The result is a confusing seesaw between bargain promotional fares offered in competitive panic and alarming rate hikes that all of a sudden make the most ordinary runs seem nearly inaccessible because of cost.

In the good old days all airline fares were more or less the same. Now, with all the hysteria, you can call the same airline three different times, and request—in identical terms—the air fare to a specific destination, and receive three totally different answers. A friend of mine recently priced a trip between New York and Rome, with an extension to Palermo in Sicily, and received three different prices, varying by as much as $300, all from the same carrier.

Nobody knows what to do about the air fares. A spokesman for Olympic Airways recently told me that Olympic used to prepare flight schedules every two years. Then every year. Then every six months. And now they have to update them almost every month. The travel agents are swamped daily with complex fare changes from dozens of domestic and international carriers, and it's virtually impossible for them to keep current. The only encouraging note is the introduction of computer systems by most of the major airlines. Now you can go into airport and city ticket offices and, if the computer programmer has been on his toes, get an immediate screening of the latest prices, just like the stock exchange.

Basically, air fares go up and down according to convenience. The longer the lead time required for booking and the greater the number of restrictions (deposits, lengths of stay, etc.), the cheaper the air fare will be. The faster you want the ticket and the greater the flexibility you require in terms of trip duration, service, and time of flight, the more you'll have to pay.

There's also a price fluctuation according to season, with the highest prices charged on a given route during the peak, or high, season, the lowest during the off season, and an intermediate rate charged during the shoulder in between. (See the glossary for travel term definitions.) Peak and off season vary by route depending on the volume of traffic: Summer is the peak season from the United States to Europe; winter is the peak from the States to the Caribbean. Another price fluctuation is based on the time of the flight, with discounts provided by some airlines on selected routes when you fly between 9 or 10 P.M. and 6, 7, or 8 A.M. Price changes also depend on whether you fly during the week or on the weekend.

Cost-Conscious Bookings

Your company may have a UATP (Universal Air Travel Plan) account, a corporate credit card service honored by most domestic and international airlines. Under UATP, your company establishes credit by the payment of a deposit, and then is billed monthly. Corporate travelers are issued individual credit cards.

Your company may also have a corporate discount arrangement with one of the major airlines. If so, take advantage of it for savings of 20 to 30 percent on regular First Class, Business Class, and Coach fares. To qualify for the full discount, you may have to book directly with an airline, not through a travel agent, and you'll probably need an identification number and a company card. Ask your corporate travel supervisor or the airline rep about what procedure you will have to follow.

On international flights, be sure to book any add-on segments on local carriers before you leave home. If you wait until you're at the destination to book the side trips locally, you might end up paying twice as much and you won't qualify for a corporate discount.

With all the new fares competing for your travel dollar, you may be able to get a larger savings on a discounted fare than you could with a corporate discount. Before buying your plane ticket, shop around for the most economical applicable air fare. Remember, the airlines are no longer noncompetitive and there may be a dozen or so possible fares that will get you where you want to go. On a flight between New York and Boston, for example, American Express reported that there were 38 different air fares that would all get you there.

For the business traveler, the traditional choices of air fare are **First Class** and **Coach** (called **Economy** on international flights). However, in the last few years, many major airlines have introduced a three-class system, with First Class staying basically the same, a **Business Class** (given various trade names) with better-than-Coach service for full-fare-paying Coach passengers (free drinks and roomier seats, if you're lucky), and a third class more or less like the old Coach class for passengers flying on promotional fares. In some cases, as on Air France's inter-European routes, First Class has been eliminated altogether in favor of an expanded Business Class.

The new Business Class service is an attempt by the airlines to woo the full-fare-paying business traveler, who accounts for about 50 percent of all airline passengers and an even higher percentage of airline revenues. Sometimes called ''Executive Class'' (''Clipper Class'' on Pan Am, ''Ambassador Class'' on TWA). Business Class usually provides seating for the full-fare passenger in a separate compartment directly behind the First Class area. The Business Class passenger can usually expect to receive almost the same kind of thoughtful attention as the First Class passenger, with a higher proportion of flight attendants to passengers, more elaborate meals, and a greater meal selection than in Coach Class. Free headsets, drinks, sleeping masks, and slippers are often offered, and sometimes there are separate check-in counters and waiting lounges in the airports. Air France's Business Class service, for example, offers full-fare Economy passengers a separate compartment, plus free cocktails, French Champagne and wine, imported cheeses, cordials, and in-flight movies on selected international flights. (For more on business traveler services provided by international airlines, turn to page 000.)

Most First Class, Business Class, and Coach (international Economy) fares permit you to make free stopovers within a specified area (the ''maximum allowable mileage''), between your departure and arrival points. For example, if you're flying from New York to Rome, you can make a stopover in Madrid for a few nights before picking up your New York-Rome flight again. This type of privilege is definitely worth investigating if you're planning a weekend detour. You can claim all permissible stopovers allowed, even if it means switching to other airlines to follow a zigzag route.

Promotional Fares

If your schedule is flexible, you may qualify for one of the promotional fares, all of which have some restrictions regarding advance booking and payment and minimum-maximum stay requirements. There are some penalties for rescheduling or cancellation—usually a loss of 10 or 15 percent of the fare. Two of the most popular promotional fares are **Excursion** fares, with a minimum-maximum stay limit ranging from 7–14 days to 22–45 days, and **APEX** (Advance Purchase Excursion) fares. APEX fares require advance booking and purchase, usually 21 days prior to departure, plus a minimum-maximum stay requirement that varies by destination: 7 to 180 days in the U.K.; 7 to 60 days in Spain and Italy; 16 to 45 days in Japan.

Another popular type of promotional fare is the domestic **Super Saver,** which offers 30 to 40 percent discounts in exchange for a 30-day advance booking and a 7-to-50-day minimum-maximum stay requirement. Note that fare changes may occur without warning on all fares in this category.

Night Coach Super Saver fares offer about a 50 percent discount with the same restrictions as for daytime Super Saver fares, and, of course, a night flight.

Budget fares are even cheaper than Super Savers and usually require an advance purchase of 21 days, but provide you with no flight assignment or confirmation until seven days before the week in which you request a flight.

Standby fares provide a substantial savings over standard air fares, but leave you hanging in suspense at the ticket counter while the plane is loading elsewhere. Occasionally, Standby is a necessity in business travel if you urgently need to get on a particular flight that is theoretically booked. A cancellation or no-show may save you at the eleventh hour as a seat opens up. Standby is also a terrific value nowadays on long-haul international flights. Travelers to the U.K. and continental Europe have discovered that it's worth it to take a chance on an off day rather than pay nearly double for a standard Economy seat.

Weekend excursion fares involving Saturday and Sunday travel are also available. Also look into booking a ''joint fare'' when you have to travel on more than one airline to reach your destination. One travel representative claims that this can sometimes be less expensive than the cost of a Super Saver plus a separate connecting flight.

FARE PROTECTOR INSURANCE

One precaution sometimes worth making on advance purchase flights is insurance that will cover the amount of your payment if you should have to cancel for medical reasons (a note from your doctor or other proof of illness is required). The policy is called ''fare protector'' or ''trip cancellation'' insurance. Many travel agents offer it.

If you don't take the insurance and have to cancel your advance purchase flight, your only recourse is to cajole the airlines into refunding your money on humanitarian grounds—something they have recently been permitted to do by the CAB. Sometimes it works, sometimes it doesn't. Not too long ago, I stupidly lost over $300 on an advance purchase ticket to Portugal because of a sudden change of business plans. The airline didn't feel sympathetic and my travel agent wasn't interested in helping because he didn't want to lose his commission. I wished then that I had bought fare protector insurance. A note from my doctor could have been arranged.

Other Ways to Go

Depending on the nature of your itinerary, you may also find it worthwhile to look into an air fare tied to a ground package (hotel, rental car, or other feature) at an all-inclusive price. If you will have a free weekend, investigate the **Fly/Drive**, **Fly/Cruise**, and **Fly/Rail** programs offered by most airlines. Or ask your travel agent to check a nonaffinity charter. There might just be an available seat at a huge savings.

AIR FARE CODES

Following is a list of the most common classes of flight service, their code letters (which appear on your ticket and on the schedules), and a short definition of each. Please note that jet and propeller (prop) service have different sets of codes. You'll run into prop flights most often on short hauls between small cities, and in the boondocks on puddle-jumping routes.

Code Letters

F	**A**	**First Class.** The best seats in the house. Fully refundable tickets. No minimum-maximum stay or advance booking requirements.
Y	**T**	**Coach** (domestic)/**Economy** (international). Full-

		fare service a category below First Class, with seating behind the First Class compartment. Fares fluctuate by peak and off season. All other fare conditions are the same as First Class. Also known as "Business Class."
S	**A**	**Jet Custom Class/Prop One Class Standard Service.** Usually equal to domestic Coach fares. No First Class compartment on the plane. Propeller One Class Standard Service is usually found on commuter airlines.
R		**Supersonic Transport (SST).** The Concorde.
K	**C**	**Jet Thrift/Supercoach.** Economy in the United States. A category below domestic Coach service, sometimes with no flight service (meals, drinks, etc.). On jets, this is sometimes called "Business Coach" (not to be confused with "Business Class").
U		**No-Reservation Service** (Shuttle).
V		**Standard/Coach Off-Peak.**

Night Flights

The "n" suffix (Fn, Yn, Sn, Kn,) means night flights, those departing after 9 or 10 P.M. and arriving before 6, 7, or 8 A.M. Service is usually the same as on daytime flights, but you can save approximately 20 percent by flying in the wee hours. (This isn't always the greatest idea for women traveling on their own, especially if you'll arrive very late in a city you're not familiar with.) Fn (Night First Class) fares are usually equal to Y (Coach) fares—you sit in First Class but get Coach class service.

Alphabet Soup

Just to confuse the issue, here are some of the fare codes for the newer promotional fares:

YE6	Super Saver.
YWE6	Weekend Super Saver.
YXE6	Midweek Super Saver.
YE46	Various names: a promotional fare usually requiring seven days' advance booking, a minimum stay until the first Sunday after booking (so you can go to church in the new destination), and a maximum stay of 30 days.

YWE46	Weekend version of YE46.
YXE46	Midweek version of YE46. (When the YE46 version flies, if not on weekends or weekdays, we do not know.)
SWE6	Same as YWE6 or YXE6, but on Standard class flight.
YHAP	International APEX, peak season.
YLAP	International APEX, low season.

Isn't that outrageous? Here's a line from the *Official Airline Guide—Worldwide Edition* that may help clear things up:

> For normal fares (YL-YH), the date of commencement on the transatlantic sector determines the fare level applicable to the one way. If round trip travel is during more than one period (i.e., YL outbound and YH inbound) then the fare will be the sum of the two one-way fares (YL + YH).

Come to think of it, forget what we said about understanding air fares. Forget about air fares. Let your travel agent and the airlines worry about the air fares. Just be sure the plane takes you where you want to go, and charge it on your credit card.

A WORD ABOUT FIRST CLASS

First Class is great if you can afford it. Most companies have established policies regarding their employees' flying habits, so be sure to check before you book.

First Class is the most expensive way to fly commercially, except on the Concorde, which is in a class by itself. First Class service usually costs anywhere from 30 to 50 percent more than standard Coach. There are virtually no restrictions except that you be rich. Individual First Class tickets are usually valid for one year, have no minimum or maximum stay requirement, and provide you with unlimited stopover privileges within the maximum allowable mileage. Your ticket will be honored by other airlines belonging to the NATA (National Air Transport Association) and IATA (International Air Transport Association), which together include just about every airline you'd ever want to consider flying.

What do you get in First Class? A special check-in counter and usually a special lounge to wait in, or the use of the airline's frequent-flyer club. A new feature on some airlines is the inclusion of reclining seats as a standard feature of First Class service. Pan Am, for one, provides ''sleeperettes'' for First Class passengers on all 747, 747 SP and L1011 aircraft. The flight attendants are more than attentive to your needs and you can have all you want to drink on the house. The food is not always first rate, but at least they usually make the effort to serve something festive like Châteaubriand or beef Wellington. In any case, it's five stars above the fare served in the back of the plane, and some of the meals are surprisingly delicious.

You also get peace and quiet. Very seldom are there howling babies, rambunctious teenagers, or other biologically disruptive types. An exception to this occurs when the airline overbooks the back section, then crowds the excess passengers up into First Class.

In pragmatic terms, First Class isn't worth the extra 30 percent or more above Coach or the more than double some of the promotional fares. After all, you sit in a seat for a few hours, breathe the same stale, dry air as everyone else, and join the crowd afterward around the baggage carousel. But there's another way to look at it, and whenever I have the choice of being pragmatic or pampered, I never have any problem making my choice.

It isn't the free champagne. That's kind of hokey. And the caviar is usually a bit stale. For me, flying First Class is worth it for two simpler reasons: (1) You get to sit in peace in a wide, comfortable chair without having your neighbor's spare tire rolling over the armrest onto your elbow; and (2) there's usually a little perfume and hand cream in the lavatory.

I always try to fly First Class on long trips, especially when I have a pressing schedule. On a short flight (three hours or less), it's usually not worth it. But on an eight- or ten-hour journey when your physical resources are severely taxed by the length of the flight itself, First Class can make a difference.

NOTE: If your company doesn't permit First Class ticketing, try to get permission to fly First Class in a pinch when Coach is completely booked. One way to do it is to book yourself on First Class and wait on Standby for Coach, then hold the First Class ticket until Coach opens up. On some flights, if you fly after 9 P.M. domestically, your daytime full-fare Coach ticket will be upgraded automatically to First Class at no extra cost. Be sure you have permission to fly First Class in this circumstance.

THE CONCORDE

Recent rumors about the curtailment of the Concorde to restricted routes have left me saddened to think I might never reach that level of disposable income to afford to experience a supersonic flight. It's almost like the ads for Cadillac cars in the old days when one could afford the fuel to get them out of the driveway. As the ads had it, you grew into your Cadillac patrimony with the passage of time and the ineluctable flowering of your bank account. I've always hoped the same thing would happen to me regarding the Concorde. All I ask for is a lower rate of inflation and a few more years.

I want to fly on an SST (supersonic transport) just for the experience. The planes take off almost straight up into the sky like surrealistic birds, their delta wings swept back over the narrow fuselage. At an altitude of about 50,000 feet, the planes achieve a speed of 660 miles per hour, the speed of sound, then pass with a sharp snap through the sound barrier, leaving a fearsome boom in their wake. At Mach 2, double the speed of sound, the Concordes reach a cruising speed of 1,300 miles per hour, or about as fast as a rifle bullet. From that altitude, the clouds seem minuscule and the views are vast—the light in the atmosphere is a purplish black, and you're so high you can detect the curvature of the earth.

Everyone I know who has flown the Concorde has told me they hope never to have to fly a normal jet again. They arrived at their destination alive, fresh, feet unswollen and skin unwithered, brain operating, or at least able to carry them through the first day of business without fatigue or muddleheadedness. You can fly the Concorde via Air France on the following routes: Paris-New York, Paris-Washington, and Paris-Rio, with a new route between New York and Mexico City about to open up. The British Concorde flies the London-New York and London-Washington routes. From New York to London or Paris the flying time is about three and a half hours.

Passengers on the Concorde are not aware of the speed of the plane, only of the smooth, almost effortless quality of the flight. The cabin seats only 100 passengers, hence you are guaranteed attentive service. The seats on the Concorde have specially designed headrests that curve around on both sides, almost like blinders, to grant you a modicum of privacy. Elaborate six-course meals, concocted for the plane by noted chefs, are served rather hurriedly on Limoges china and are accompanied by *brut* champagne and *grand cru* wines.

All transatlantic flights on the Concorde take place during the day, which helps eliminate fatigue and the disorientation caused by jet lag. The planes arrive at off hours when the crowds at customs are the thinnest, further adding to the speed and efficiency of the trip. Passengers book tickets through special Concorde representatives, check in at separate counters at the airport, and wait in exclusive Concorde departure lounges. The cost is 115 to 120 percent more than First Class service. If you can afford it, do it. Let the rest of us eat cake.

AIR FARE CHECKLIST

- Shop around the maze of air fares for the best bargain, or have your travel adviser do it for you.
- Look for Business Class or Executive Class services for full-fare-paying Coach passengers.
- Get fare protector insurance for prepaid flights.
- Check Fly/Drive and other packages.
- Learn company policy on flying First Class. Get permission to fly First Class in a pinch when Coach is booked.
- Fly the Concorde with delight, not guilt.

3

Ticketing Made Easy

Some airlines offer corporate business-traveler services that permit you to write out your own ticket as you dash to the airport. On American Airlines, this service is called ''Express Ticketing.'' On Eastern, it's known as ''Flite-Checks.''

Even if you never write out your own ticket, you still ought to know how to read one. The success of your trip depends on the accuracy of your ticket—the flight number, departure time, airport, destination, and passenger status. Always check your ticket, even when an airline rep or travel agent has completed if for you, especially if it is a multi-destination ticket, or if your itinerary involves travel to destinations the agent may not be familiar with. You also need to check the ticket to see if it's confirmed (OK), OPEN (which means you have paid for but not yet booked a segment of the flight), or merely requested (RQ), a critical difference that may get you a seat on the plane or get you bumped.

Reconfirmation

Once you've booked your ticket, don't ever forget the importance of reconfirming your flight. Many airlines request reconfirmation at least 48 hours before the flight, although most overseas airlines will erase you from the list if you fail to reconfirm 72 hours before. Be sure you know the airline's local requirement. Rules may vary from country to country and region to region.

The Civil Aeronautics Board recommends that you reconfirm 72 hours before international flights and 24 hours before flights from the

Sample Ticket

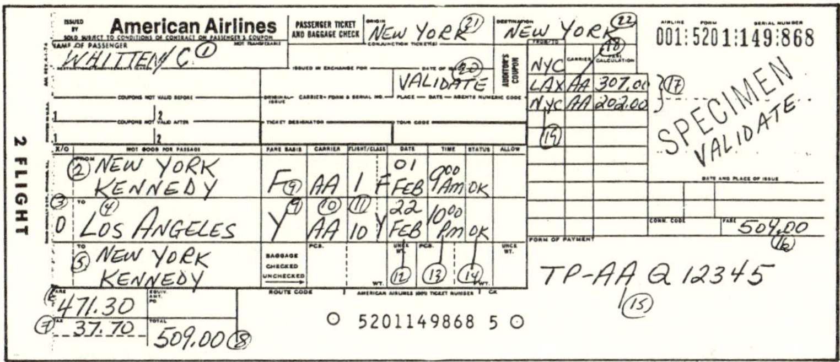

Decoding the Codes:

1. Passenger's name
2. Departure city, airport
3. Number of stops
4. First destination
5. Final destination, airport
6. Correct fare
7. Eight percent Federal transportation tax (Tax schedule to Hawaii differs from that on the mainland.)
8. Total fare
9. Class codes
10. Carrier
11. Flight number, class
12. Departure dates
13. Departure times
14. Flight status
15. Billing number
16. Total amount due
17. Itemized fares
18. Carrier
19. City codes
20. Ticket-issuer validation
21. Origin
22. Final destination

United States to Canada or Mexico. (A quick check with a few of the leading domestic airlines suggests that 48 hours' advance notice is recommended for domestic flights.) The CAB also suggests that you receive *written* reconfirmation from the airline rep or travel agent. If you reconfirm by phone, note the name of the agent, the time and date of the call, and the airline's own confirmation number.

On multi-destination itineraries, you'll need to confirm each segment of your ongoing flights. This should be done for the next set of flights as soon as you reach each destination, and it's especially important in faraway places where schedule changes may have occurred that your travel agent didn't know about. Just remember that without a confirmed ticket and reconfirmation, the often overbooked airlines have a legitimate excuse to even out their load—at your expense.

With some of the smaller regional airlines, especially in places like the Australian outback or the Grenadines, it's often impossible to confirm a flight before you get there. On these flights, your ticket will read RQ (requested). As soon as you arrive in the area, have your ticket confirmed and your status changed to OK in writing. The chances are you won't have a problem getting on the flight, but you might inadvertently hit a crowded season and end up waiting for the next flight, which leaves the following week.

Special Meals

The time you reconfirm your ticket is also the time to request a special meal. Virtually every airline offers passengers a choice of meals for restricted diets (low cholesterol, low sodium, low calorie, low carbohydrate, diabetic, vegetarian, and kosher). Some airlines also offer full-fare-paying business travelers a selection of meals on most flights. Full-fare-paying passengers on American Airlines usually have a choice of cannelloni, seafood platter, crab Louis, fresh fruit salad, the ''Great American Hamburger,'' or other special dishes from the ''American Traveler Menu,'' in lieu of the standard airline meal. All special meals must be requested from 24 to 48 hours in advance.

Advance Seat Assignment

When you reconfirm your ticket, also remember to request an advance seat assignment—again, from 48 to 24 hours before flight time. Many major airlines, armed with new computers and eager to solicit the high-yield business traveler, can now provide you with a seat assignment up to 330 days before the flight. On round-trip or multi-leg journeys, many airlines can also provide you with a seat assignment and boarding pass for the entire trip when you check in the first time. TWA, which initiated the service, calls it ''Round Trip Check-In.'' Your boarding pass for the first flight gets you aboard—and in the same seat—for each subsequent leg of the journey.

When you reconfirm your flight and request an advance seat assignment, tell the airline rep or travel agent where you prefer to sit: window or aisle, smoking or nonsmoking, forward or aft, or by the bulkhead. Be sure to specify that you're a full-fare-paying Business Class passenger if the airline has a special Business Class seating area. If not, note that in Coach the bulkhead seats and the seats beside the emergency exits have the most leg room. Engine noise is most noticeable in the back of the plane; the seats nearest the galley and the lavatories are not the greatest for peace and quiet. If you're troubled by air sickness, you'll find the seats directly over the wings the most stable.

Each type of aircraft has its own seating configuration, and there are additional variations from airline to airline. Following are typical seating arrangements of four common types of aircraft.

SEATING CONFIGURATIONS

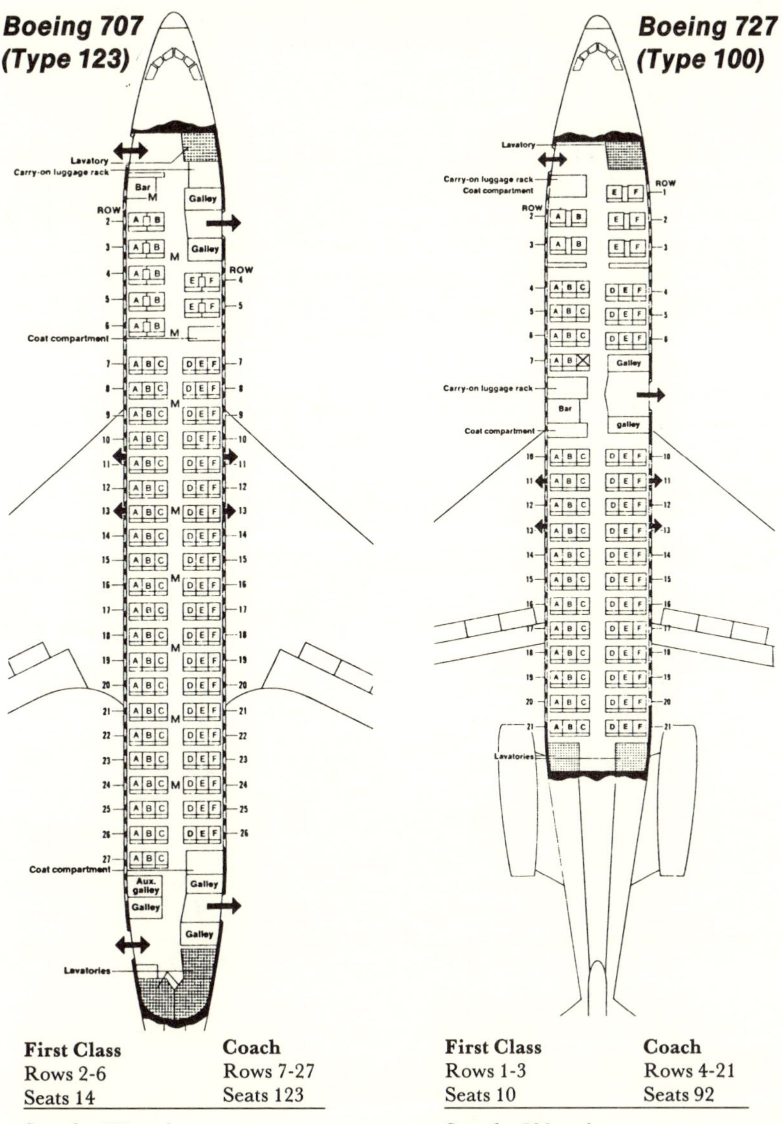

First Class	**Coach**	**First Class**	**Coach**
Rows 2-6	Rows 7-27	Rows 1-3	Rows 4-21
Seats 14	Seats 123	Seats 10	Seats 92

Speed—595 mph
Range—3,970 statute miles
Length of Plane—145 ft. 1 in.
Wingspan—130 ft. 10 in.

Speed—590 mph
Range—2,130 statute miles
Length of Plane—133 ft. 2 in.
Wingspan—108 ft.

Boeing 747

McDonnell Douglas DC-10

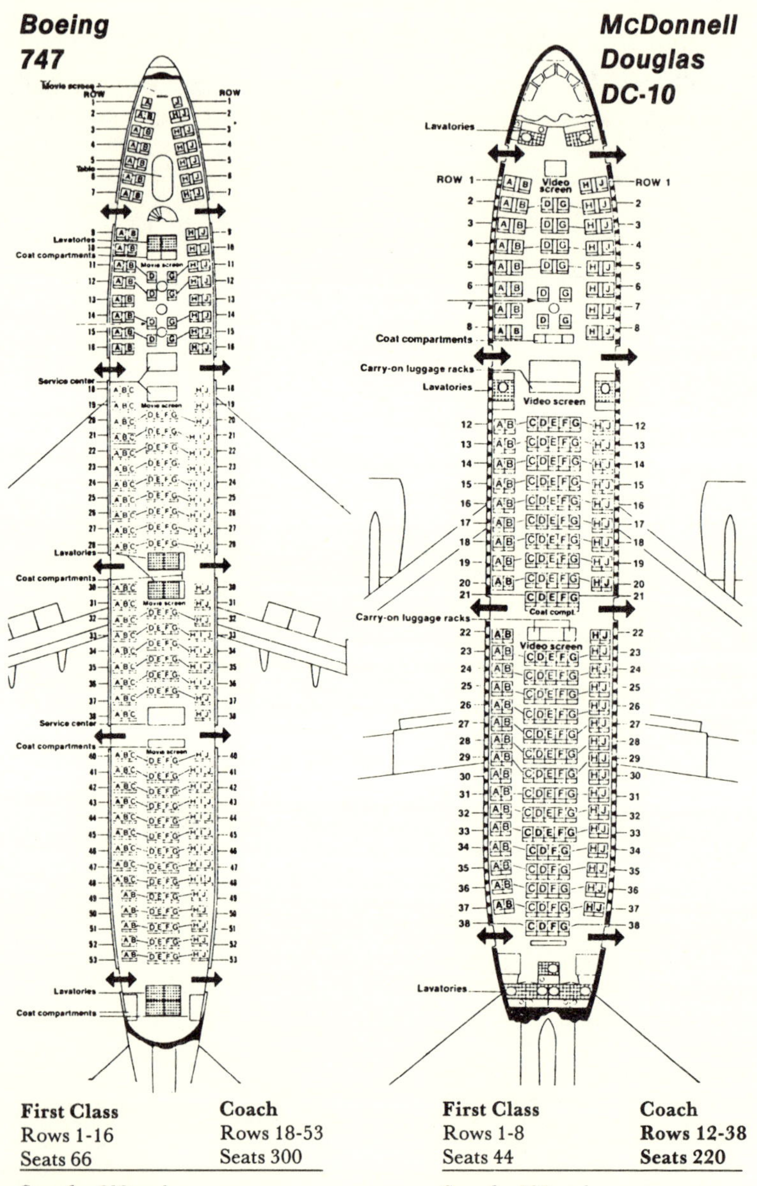

First Class	Coach
Rows 1-16	Rows 18-53
Seats 66	Seats 300

Speed—600 mph
Range—5,850 statute miles
Length of Plane—231 ft. 10 in.
Wingspan—195 ft. 8 in.

First Class	Coach
Rows 1-8	**Rows 12-38**
Seats 44	**Seats 220**

Speed—595 mph
Range—3,930 statute miles
Length of Plane—182 ft. 3.8 in.
Wingspan—155 ft. 4 in.

Selecting Your Clubs

Chrisjean Whitten, a long-time member of several airline clubs, logically recommends that you join the clubs of the airlines that fly to the destinations you most frequently visit and offer the best services. She has found Pan Am Clipper Clubs in South America, for example, an orderly and welcome refuge from the activity of the airport proper. In general, she thinks the airline clubs are especially useful places for women traveling on their own. They're clean. They're comfortable. They're good places to leave your hand luggage or catch up on your paper work when your plane is delayed. And they're usually filled with attractive people who are there for the same reason you are—business travel. (If your company won't reimburse you for airline club membership fees, notes Chrisjean, you can deduct the expense from your income taxes.)

One of technology's recent contributions to the ascent of man is the introduction of automatic airline-ticket dispensers, available in selected airports. If you happen to know the flight you want, you merely stick your credit card into a slot in the face of the machine, punch a few buttons, and zip! Out pops a prewritten ticket and a boarding pass. Not all airlines have automatic ticket dispensers, nor do many airports. But if this type of space-age service tickles your fancy, by all means give your favorite airline a call and find out what kind of automatic service they offer.

THE OAG

The *Official Airline Guides (North America Edition* and *Worldwide Edition)* are each the size of the Manhattan telephone directory and contain more information on national and international air schedules and fares than you'd ever want to confront in a lifetime. Fortunately, they are almost exclusively the domain of the travel agent.

However, the *OAG* does publish a series of *Pocket Flight Guides* that are indispensible to the serious business traveler. These paperback books are portable distillations of the larger compendiums.

The *North America OAG Pocket Flight Guide* is the *vade mecum* of domestic travelers, as is the *Europe and Middle East OAG Pocket Flight Guide* for international travelers. Each edition is eight inches high, four inches wide, and from 200 to 300 pages long, with flight information on arcane destinations like Mandan, North Dakota, as well as on the predictable cities such as Miami and Milan. The *Pocket Flight Guides* are updated every month and are sold by 12-month subscription; the cost of each edition, at press time, is $37, plus mailing charges.

You need the *OAG Pocket Flight Guides*. For subscription information, write to:

OAG Pocket Flight Guide
2000 Clearwater Drive
Oak Brook, Illinois 60521

or call toll tree:

Within the U.S., except Illinois, Hawaii and Alaska   (800) 323-3537
From Illinois   (800) 942-1888

There is no toll-free number for residents of Hawaii, Alaska, Canada, or U.S. Possessions.

OAG Sample

The inside front pages of the *OAG Pocket Flight Guides* contain all the code information you'll need to read the schedules, including time zone, city codes, days of the week, food service, class of service, and so forth. Here's a sample:

Code		Code	
LAS	Las Vegas	**F/Y**	First Class/Coach
ATL	Atlanta	**72S**	Boeing 747 (200)
PDT	Pacific Daylight Time	**L10**	Lockheed L1011
EDT	Eastern Daylight Time	**D8S**	DC8
X6	Daily except Saturday	**B**	Breakfast
8:00a	8:00 a.m.	**SL**	Snack/Lunch
12:22p	12:22 p.m.	**L**	Lunch
DL233	Delta Airlines Flight 233	**S**	Number of stops

In plain language, if you want to catch the 10:15 A.M. flight from Atlanta, Georgia, to Las Vegas, Nevada, you will take Delta's Flight 1155, arrive at 12:22 P.M. Pacific Daylight Time, sit in either First Class or Coach, fly in an L1011, be served a snack/lunch, and make one stop. You can fly any day of the week.

Instant Info

Familiarity with the *OAG Pocket Flight Guides* will permit you to make quick travel decisions on your own without having to contact a travel agent or the airline representative. For example, if you finish your appointments a few hours early, you can simply check the *OAG* for the next flight out and head for the airport. Conversely, if a business contact would like you to stay over a few extra hours, you can check the *OAG* to be sure you can catch a later flight or get out the following day.

The *OAG* is also a must for planning quick weekend escapes. Once you know how to use it, you just reach into your briefcase and pull out the schedules to find the next flight to the beach or the nearest ski resort. You'll also need the *OAG* to know what buttons to push to extract the correct ticket from those new ticketing machines.

THE AIRLINE CLUBS

As part of your advance planning before a business trip, you should consider the advantages of joining an airline traveler's club. Many business travelers find it definitely worthwhile to spend between $30 and $100 a year for membership in Pan Am's Clipper Club, American's Admirals Club, TWA's Ambassadors Club, or one of the other clubs operated by most U.S. and some foreign airlines. Once a member, you can enjoy the club's facilities every time you're in the airport, no matter what class of service you're flying. Many airlines also permit you to use club facilities in the airport even when you're flying on another airline.

What You Get: A Sampling

At Pan Am's Clipper Club, which has 31 lounges in the United States and abroad, you get to wait for your flight in the comfortable private lounge, with free cocktails, coffee or tea, and the use of the telephone for local calls. Flights are announced in the lounge, and if you ask, the receptionist, host, or hostess will usually alert you to your flight when it is called. Membership comes in three sizes: one-year, three-year, and lifetime, with special discounts for members 60 years old or more. Your spouse receives free membership privileges, and you can cash checks up to $100 with your membership card and proper identification outside the lounge from the ticket agent.

TWA's Ambassadors Clubs have 18 domestic and six international facilities. Club members may drop their luggage with a Skycap, then proceed directly to the Ambassador Club lounge to check in and pick up boarding passes for both the outgoing and return flights. Free coffee, tea, and fruit juice (mornings only) are provided, and in most places, there are phones for free local calls. At about half the Ambassadors Club's U.S. facilities, conference rooms are available; these should be booked as far in advance as possible.

Other U.S. airline clubs offer similar airport facilities in the U.S. and abroad. Prices range from $35 to $95 a year. If you're interested in joining one, pick up a club application at the airline's airport or city sales office, or write to:

American Airlines Admirals Club
P.O. Box 61616
Dallas/Ft. Worth, Texas 75261

Braniff International Council
P.O. Box 61747
Dallas/Ft. Worth, Texas 75261

Continental Airlines Presidents Club
Los Angeles International Airport
Los Angeles, California 90009

Eastern Airlines Ionosphere Club
International Airport
Miami, Florida 33148

Northwest Orient Airlines Top Flight Club
Minneapolis/St. Paul International Airport
St. Paul, Minnesota 55111

Pan American Airways Clipper Club
P.O. Box 2782
Boston, Massachusetts 02208

TWA Ambassadors Club
P.O. Box 20287
Kansas City, Missouri 64195

United Airlines Red Carpet Club
P.O. Box 2247
Boston, Massachusetts 02107

Western Airlines Horizon Club
P.O. Box 92005
World Way Postal Center
Los Angeles, California 90009

Some non-U.S. airlines also provide airport club facilities, some free of charge, others for a fee. For more information, see Chapter 12.

SPECIAL SERVICES FOR BUSINESS TRAVELERS

Separate from the airline clubs, many national and international airlines offer business travelers a special ''frequent traveler'' association, as introduced by Pan Am in 1973. These associations are usually by invitation only, or by specific request, with your eligibility determined by how much you travel an airline in the course of a year. Some businesses holding corporate travel accounts with an airline receive membership for all their executives who travel. Otherwise, membership usually depends on your individual track record.

American Airlines calls its promotion "AA Advantage." Northwest Orient Airlines calls its program "VIP Travel Plan." And Western Airlines names its promotion "VIB," for Very Important Business Club. More originally, there's Air France—"Service Plus"; JAL—"Global Club"; Iberia Airlines—"Club Fiesta-Iberia"; KLM—"Courtesy Cardholders"; Pan American—"FT" or "Frequent Traveler"; and SAS—"Royal Viking Courtesy Card."

Frequent traveler services vary by airline, but generally, participants receive special membership cards, with their seating preferences and other travel data recorded on a computer profile. They also receive baggage tags identifying them as frequent travelers, private booking numbers to call for reservations, First Class lounge and check-in privileges, protected reservations (against bumping), advance seat assignments, preferential baggage handling, pins, plaques for million-milers (some with little gilt eaglets you attach for every 25,000 miles you fly), quarterly or semiannual newsletters. Other courtesies are sometimes extended.

If you fly a national or international airline with any regularity, the chances are the airline has already identified you and invited you to become a member of its frequent traveler program. If you have not been solicited and think you're eligible, contact the airline's public relations or protocol director, or ask an airline sales rep whom to contact. The requirements aren't always stiff. On Pan Am, for example, Frequent Traveler membership is available to anyone who applies, with no restrictions as to annual numbers of Pan Am flights or accumulated mileage. FT privileges are extended to Clipper Club members as well.

Also, a number of airlines have instigated special incentive programs for frequent travelers. Various prizes and discounts are given to passengers according to the number of miles they travel on one carrier in a year. Recently, American Airlines awarded a New York businessman with a free round-trip First Class ticket after he chalked up 50,000 miles on American—all in a single six-week period. Even if you travel as few as 12,000 miles, an airline may have a prize for you. Next time you fly, ask your airline sales representative if the airline has a similar incentive program.

A NOTE TO AVIOPHOBES

Some of my most intrepid traveling friends are complete ninnies when it comes to climbing on a plane. One, a fabulous adventurer in his early 40s who has floated down the Amazon on a raft, driven an old Fiat from Capri to Thailand, and captained his 80-foot schooner from Turkey to Pago Pago, is so terrified of flying that he makes an absurd spectacle of himself every time he flies. In the departure lounge he sneaks into the men's room and downs a lethal array of potions, any one of which would knock out a dinosaur. Then, with hands clenched and a glassy stare, he sits immobile until boarding time. Once in his airplane seat, he immediately covers his eyes with a plaid sleeping mask and stuffs wax sleeping plugs in his ears. A minute later he topples over in a stupor. His snoring has been known to disrupt the entire First Class.

Unfortunately, on a business trip you can't express your aviophobia quite so indulgently. The chances are you've got to be on your toes, or at least mobile, by the time you disembark. That rules out overdoses of drugs or excessive alcohol, that other mainstay of the aviophobe. (An aviophobic Greek friend of mine once got so loaded on a flight from Athens to London that he arrived three days late after an inexplicable detour to Amsterdam.)

If you're an aviophobe, rest assured that you're not alone. Over 25 million Americans suffer from the same symptoms: bloodless lips, sweaty palms, myopic stares, palpitating hearts, and extremities that don't stop shaking. According to a well-known pop psychologist, the fear of flying is symptomatic of a lack of trust invariably resulting from certain infantile experiences. If you're not in charge, the theory goes, who's going to get the plane back down on the ground? Certainly not the pilot.

Yet, somehow, almost all of you manage to survive your airborne excursions. Surely you've read the statistics about safety of plane travel. But did you know that flying a plane is about 25 times safer than driving your car? Or that on the average some 650,000 passengers board 2,500 airplanes and fly 600 miles every day in the United States alone, with a 99.999 percent chance of making it to their destinations?

"So what?" you're undoubtedly saying. "What has that got to do with the fact that I have to fly to Akron in the morning?"

You're right. Aviophobia is not a joke. Have you tried hypnosis? Psychiatry? Yoga? Biofeedback? Transcendental meditation? Another job that doesn't require you to travel on a plane?

Education and relaxation are the keys to overcoming aviophobia. Familiarize yourself with the overwhelmingly favorable statistics regarding flight safety. And drive out to the nearest airport to observe the mechanical ease with which the planes land and take off.

Back at home, practice a deep-breathing exercise. Sit erect in a comfortable chair with your legs uncrossed and your hands resting at your sides, or lie flat on the floor with your feet flopping at ease to the sides and your hands by your hips with the palms turned up. Close your eyes. Inhale deeply through your nostrils, pulling the air down into your lungs as far as you can, expanding your diaphragm so the air will sink down even further. Hold the air down for a slow count of four, then slowly exhale from the bottom of your diaphragm up, letting all the air out through your mouth. As you exhale, try to concentrate on all the muscular tension in your body. Try to let that tension flow out with your breath as your chest cavity sinks back to its normal position.

Repeat the deep breaths three or four times, each time expanding your diaphragm a little bit more, and each time releasing more and more tension. If you do this simple exercise correctly, you will feel remarkably more relaxed in a very short time. Practice it at home so you can do it again in your plane seat to help you overcome the tension caused by aviophobia.

If yours is an especially acute case of aviophobia, you may want to solicit the help of a course or clinic designed to treat aviophobia, or phobias in general, which are conducted in many U.S. hospitals.

Or you can contact Captain ''Slim'' Cummings, a former airline pilot who, for years, conducted a series of Pan Am seminars for aviophobes. Now Captain Cummings operates his own business—mostly for executives and corporations—called **Freedom from Fear of Flying, Inc.** At corporate invitation, or when general interest indicates, Cummings brings his seminar program to a city and conducts three or four meetings during one week. The course includes various forms of logical and psychological persuasion, a tour of an airport, and a ''graduation flight.'' If you can't wait until he gets to your city, mail him a check for $25 and he'll send you his helpful booklet and a cassette tape designed to soothe the beasts of aviophobia every time you have to board a plane. According to Slim Cummings, it really works. You can reach him at:

Freedom from Fear of Flying, Inc.
2021 Country Club Prado
Coral Gables, Florida 33134
Telephone (305) 261-7042

Despite her millions of miles of air travel, Chrisjean Whitten remains a confirmed aviophobe. Her advice is simple: Ignore it. Sit on the aisle. Keep your eyes glued to the olive in your vodka martini, and, at all costs, avoid looking out the window. If you should get stuck near the window, she suggests, ask the stewardess for three pillows. Put one under your head, one across your eyes, and one on the top of your crown (in case of a crash). Pretend to sleep. Meditate on how much your mother loves you. And ignore the snide comments from your seatmates.

From the opposite point of view, I love to fly. I find the power of the jets on takeoff exhilarating and the views from on high an unending surprise—the edge of night as you fly into the dawn, the patterns of landscapes, the architecture of the clouds. I always remind myself that flying is a privilege of the twentieth century. In another time and place, someone like me would never have gotten more than 50 miles from home and never more than a few feet off the ground.

Ticketing Checklist

- Subscribe to *OAG Pocket Flight Guide* and learn to use it.
- Join airline club(s).
- Study air ticket diagram and codes.
- Reconfirm all flights.
- Book advance assignment.
- Order special meals in advance.
- Use airport ticket dispenser for quick ticketing.
- Find and make use of special airline services for business travelers.
- Contact Captain ''Slim'' Cummings for advice on how to overcome aviophobia.

4

Hotels: Your Home Away from Home

Your hotel is not only your home away from home. It is also your office away from home. It provides you with a bed to sleep in, a place to bathe, a closet for your clothes, a desk to put your papers on, a telephone to connect you with room service and the external world, curtains to draw against the stark unfamiliarity of the cement wall outside, an air conditioner whose monotone hum will drown out the squeals of laughter from the next room, a Gideon Bible (I once memorized most of the Book of Ecclesiastes in Gila Bend, Arizona, while waiting for a replacement part for my car), a television to lull your hard-working brain into a soporific limbo, and, if you're lucky, a genuine oil painting on the wall that you can squint at and pretend is a photo of your latest love. Your hotel may also have a closed-circuit television system that features blue movies, usually male-oriented but sometimes useful for distracting lonely business travelers from those business travel blues.

When Is a Hotel Not a Hotel?

When it's a motel or a resort. To distinguish among them, a **hotel** is usually located in a city or in a downtown or residential area, near restaurants, shops, entertainment centers, or other amenities. Services usually include a doorman to open the door of your taxi, porters to carry your bags up to your room, valet service, cleaning and laundry, coffee shop, restaurant, cocktail lounge and/or room service, news-stands and shops (in the larger hotels). There may also be special services for business travelers, such as secretarial assistance, translators at international destinations, a telex machine, meeting rooms, audio-visual equipment, and convention facilities.

Motels: By definition, a motel caters primarily to the automobile traveler and is typically located on or near a major highway, near an airport, or, sometimes, in suburban and downtown areas. Some motels, or city motor hotels, provide almost the same services as a regular hotel. But other motels offer weary travelers little more than a decent bed, a bath, and a place to park their cars—at a bargain rate. Unlike hotels, many motels take the registration number of your car and ask you to pay for the room when you check in—a reasonable precaution as they have no way of knowing when you'll leave, or of preventing you from making a fast getaway. Since the majority of motels are located outside city limits where real estate comes cheaper than in town, they frequently offer attractive swimming pools, free of charge, to their guests—useful if you'll be in your car a lot and need some real exercise to keep you finely tuned.

Resorts: The term ''resort'' usually refers to a hotel-vacation complex with the emphasis on relaxation, sports, and good times. By necessity, resorts are almost always located in a vacation area near the mountains, on a lake, or by the sea. Typically, they provide little in the way of services for business travelers, but a lot in the way of golf, tennis, swimming, riding, or just wide open spaces.

That's not all bad. If you'll be working in an area near a resort complex, why not stay at the resort and enjoy the fatigue-breaking pleasure of nine holes of golf before sunset, a swim in the sea before your morning coffee, or a fast tennis lesson during your lunch break? Many resorts also have gyms, saunas, whirlpools, and other health-club facilities—just the thing to perk you up after a hard day of business calls. If it works logically for your trip, staying in a resort is not cheating! The benefit to your health and spirits will serve your employer by your improved efficiency and effectiveness (not to mention longer lifespan), just as much as it will add to your own pleasure.

CHOOSING A HOTEL

Location Counts

The first thing to consider before selecting your hotel is the location. Get out a map of the city you're going to, mark off the locations of your appointments, and find out which hotels, motels, or resorts seem most convenient to them all. You don't necessarily have to stay in the downtown area if your appointments are all out in the suburbs, and there's an acceptable hotel or motel nearby. In choosing a location, also consider other factors that may influence the quality and success of your trip. The hotel should be near restaurants if you've got business entertaining to do, or shops, movies, theaters, and museums if you'll have some free time. The safety of the area is another critical consideration—you don't want to find yourself a prisoner on the edge of Porno Row or the DMZ, with no taxis available and no place to go.

Facilities

Next, consider the hotel's facilities. Will you be renting a car? If so, does the hotel have a garage, parking lot, or a nearby parking area? Free? At a discounted rate? Does it have a coffee shop? Restaurants? A telex machine, if you have to send or receive messages? Does it have direct-dial phones in the rooms so you won't have to wait for the operator to finish telling the desk clerk about her weekend date before placing your urgent Monday morning telephone calls?

Does the hotel have 24-hour room service, if you'll be getting in late without having had your dinner, or if you'll have to leave in the morning before the coffee shop opens? Does it have a laundry? Dry cleaning? A valet service? A hairdresser? A health club or sports facilities? Meeting rooms or secretarial aid? An airport limousine (or courtesy car)? An in-house travel agent? A concierge who will book you a good table for one in your favorite restaurant?

Reputation

The game of 20 questions continues. What is the reputation of the hotel or motel? Modern and efficient? International? A little threadbare but filled with a charm and class that the gilt-chandeliered chain hotels can't come close to emulating? Is it a convention hotel filled with roaming waves of florid, sports-jacketed men wearing spangled red fezzes and polyethylene name tags? What kind of people go there? This is important. Don't be afraid to acknowledge your preferences. Passing in and out of hotels constitutes two-thirds of your social life while on the road and you might as well spend it among people whose style and manners you enjoy.

Cost/Classification

Last but not least, how much can you afford to pay for a hotel room and still stay within your expense allowance? Can you afford a deluxe suite in the best hotel in town? Or a mean little single located above the nightclub and next to the elevator? Does the hotel give corporate discounts? And does it accept your kind of credit cards?

There is no standard classification for hotels, either national or international. Classifications vary by guidebook, advertisement, promoter, country, hotel chain, or, sometimes, even by reservations agent. Usually, you can get the gist of the idea by the nomenclature used. "Deluxe" and "luxury" hotels are the fanciest, with private baths in every room, the largest number of lackeys, in-house services, and crystal light fixtures. "First class" in some places means luxury or deluxe but in other places it means just plain ordinary. In Europe and other parts of the world, first class hotel rooms may not all have private bathroom facilities.

"Second class," "tourist," and "economy" are terms most usually encountered abroad in more realistic countries not as given to hyperbole as we are. Hotels in this category may be modest indeed, perhaps with no private baths, elevator, or other modern amenities.

Stars and other symbols are also given to indicate hotel classification, sometimes on the basis of price alone, other times on the basis of service or facilities. Hotels with five stars are at the top of the heap; lesser lodgings get fewer illuminations.

ACCOMMODATIONS

A room is not just a room in a hotel. You have a choice. You can get a double room, a single room, a twin, a suite, a junior suite, a room with a balcony or a view, or a room with no windows. Here's the difference:

Single room: A hotel room leased to one person, containing a single, double, or queen-sized bed. In many of the newer hotels, a single is merely a double room rented to one person at a rate that is at least two-thirds as much as the rate for two people.

Double room: A room rented to two guests that is equipped either with one large bed for two people, or two double or queen-sized beds, each usually large enough to sleep two people.

Twin rooms: A room that contains two twin-sized beds, leased to two persons at a double room rate.

Suite: Ordinarily a group of rooms consisting of one or two bedrooms and baths adjoining a living room or lounge. Junior suites often have a vestibule or a comfortable sitting area with a couch and coffee table within a large bedroom.

Hotel rooms also vary in price according to their location within each hotel. Rooms on the highest floors away from the lobby and the noise of the street almost always command a higher price than rooms on the lower floors. Similarly, rooms with balconies or verandas (sometimes called ''lanais'' in resort hotels) usually cost more than rooms without balconies or views. Rooms situated in inconvenient locations, such as near the elevator, beside the cleaning closet, or directly across from the service station, should cost less, but do not always do so.

In motels, rooms may fluctuate by price according to whether they're in the main building or out along the parking lot with private entrances and easy access to your car. In resorts, prices vary greatly according to the spaciousness of the room, the view, and the nearby facilities. Cottages, for example, with patios and private swimming pools, or rooms that open directly onto the beach can cost twice as much as rooms in the back overlooking the staff parking lot.

When you make your hotel reservation, you can't always specify where you want your room to be located, but you can try. You can partially determine what type of room you'll get by explicitly indicating the price category you want. Let the hotel know that you want the most expensive category of room, the least, or one at a moderate rate.

MEAL PLANS

As a business traveler, you will probably want to take a hotel meal plan that includes breakfast only or no meals. But you have other choices, some of which provide economical alternatives if you will be in one place for a lengthy period and won't want to bother eating out every day. Several times on long research/writing assignments, I've been holed up in a hotel for several weeks and have found it easiest to have most of my meals in the hotel. The choices:

AP	**American Plan:** includes three full meals
CP	**Continental Plan:** includes a continental breakfast of coffee or tea, rolls or toast, butter, jam, and sometimes fresh fruit or juice. In Scandinavia and the Netherlands, you also may be served slices of cheese or cold meats.
DP	**Demi-pension:** see MAP, below.
EP	**European Plan:** includes no meals
MAP	**Modified American Plan:** includes breakfast, plus lunch or dinner, often from a fixed menu

Note that many APs and MAPs do not always give you a full choice of dishes from the regular à la carte menu. This is not always the case, but in some parts of the world—especially those inundated with groups of tourists—the tourist menu for MAP and AP guests offers noticeably inferior wines and food and is an insult to any self-respecting, paying visitor. This is less likely in established international hotels. But be alert in smaller local establishments and in busy tourist destinations.

Sources of Information

How do you find out about specific hotel facilities, locations, prices, and meal plans? Most guidebooks have precious little information about specific hotel facilities, especially for the business traveler. Your best sources are those mysterious notebooks your travel agent or airline rep keeps hidden below his or her desk. These books usually have a page or half a page of description per hotel, including the location in relation to downtown and the distance from the airport. Some have photographs.

If you have access to one, you can also consult the OHRG (*Official Hotel and Resort Guide*), an OAG-size telephone-directory-style newsprint compendium that would make Johann Gutenberg regret he had ever invented movable type. The OHRG is updated from time to time and is sold by subscription, with occasional supplements issued during the year. If you're interested, write to the OHRG, P.O. Box 5800, Cherry Hill, New Jersey 08034. Also try the HIT (*Hotel and Travel Index*) (aren't these acronyms absurd?), another hotel laundry list published quarterly and sold by subscription for $60 a year. If you want to subscribe, write to HIT, P.O. Box 5820, Cherry Hill, New Jersey 08034.

For national and international hotel chains, consult the yellow pages of your local telephone directory under "Hotels and Motels—Reservations." Or, once in a hotel, ask to see the copy of the *Red Book*, the official directory of the American Hotel and Motel Association.

Your best bet for hotel information, given the fact that none of these publications is designed for the consumer, is to ask your company travel manager, travel agent, or airline rep to find out what you need to know. Or you can call the hotel's reservations number yourself. Check the Directory, at the back of this book, for some useful toll-free telephone numbers.

BEST BETS FOR BUSINESS TRAVELERS

Business travel usually places a lot of demands on you; to compensate, you should make life a bit sweeter for yourself by selecting the best hotels your expense allowance will afford. It's my opinion that you should always aim as high as possible, even if it means taking a less expensive room in the best hotel in town, as opposed to a top room in a so-so establishment. Your justification is simply and correctly that it pays to do everything you can to make your difficult job a little easier and more enjoyable when you're on the road.

In some places, you don't really have much of a choice of hotel categories. A few years ago, I made a marathon business trip down one side of South America and back up the other, a journey that lasted for almost two months. Since it was my first time in the area, I resisted staying at name hotels like Sheraton and Inter-Continental—I felt they might be too slick, efficient, and plastic to impart a real sense of the continent. But by the time I'd gotten to my third or fourth country, I welcomed hotels with American-style service and efficiency. The trip was so demanding on my time and physical resources that I needed plenty of hot water and instant (well, almost) room service, taxis that could be summoned by men in green coats with golden epaulets, fast elevators, and resident photocopiers. I needed to be pampered. And, since in most parts of South America there isn't much of a choice between humble and opulent, I went opulent. Without guilt.

Business Traveler Services

By general consensus, business travelers need comfort, convenience, and efficiency above all else, even at the expense of local color and charm. This fact has not been lost on the hotel chains, many of which owe from 60 to 80 percent of their revenues to frequent travelers. To win this lucrative segment of the market, many hotel chains have developed business-traveler services and amenities similar to those offered by the airlines. Secretarial and translating assistance, photocopying and telex machines, and airport courtesy cars we have already mentioned. Most hotel chains also offer toll-free reservations numbers to call for instant bookings, and a ''guaranteed reservations'' system that secures your room even if you arrive late at night, provided you charge the room on a major credit card and agree to pay for it even if you have to cancel at the last moment.

In addition to these services, most major hotel chains have developed special clubs for frequent travelers, with membership extended to employees of corporations holding corporate accounts doing volume bookings with the chain, or, in some cases, to individuals. Individual membership requirements vary from a minimum number of nights in the hotel per month or year to no prerequisites at all. Among those that offer the best services are:

Hilton International: Few hotel chains have been as alert to the needs of the business traveler as Hilton International, which has established a worldwide reservations network that provides instant bookings and confirmations at Hilton hotels around the globe. Like other hotel chains, Hilton will accept guaranteed reservations when you book the room on a credit card.

For corporate business travelers, Hilton offers EBS (Executive Business Service), through which it will provide you with interpreters, translators, audio-visual equipment, and other assistance. To qualify, your company must guarantee a certain number of room-nights a year on an international, regional, or local basis.

Domestically, Hilton offers business travelers a preregistration and fast check-out service, called "Quick Check." Participants are issued special cards and identification numbers that enable the hotel to write out the registration forms before the guest's arrival, and permit automatic billing to the client's account. To qualify, either the corporation or the individual must stay in a domestic Hilton inn or hotel a minimum of 10 times a year. In some of its big-city hotels, Hilton has also set aside a tower or floor especially for business travelers, with commodious rooms, an open bar where you may prepare drinks for yourself and sign a chit on the honor system, and a concierge assigned to care for your needs.

Inter-Continental: Business-traveler service here is called the "Six Continents Club," which provides members with preregistration and fast check-out services similar to those described for Hilton. Members can also expect to be given preferential bookings and upgraded rooms, when available, plus a courtesy gift in the room (usually a basket of fruit, fresh flowers, or a bottle of wine), and assistance in booking advance reservations in other Inter-Continental hotels. Six Continents Club members are supposedly given preferred seat selection in hotel restaurants, plus check-cashing privileges up to $100. To qualify, you need to stay at an Inter-Continental hotel out of the United States four or more times a year.

Confirmed reservation service at Inter-Continental is called "Positive Reservations." If the hotel is unable to provide you with the room you reserved, they agree to put you up for a night free of charge at a nearby hotel of the same category, plus provide you with transportation to the hotel and back, and permit you to make a free telephone call to your home or office to tell them of your change of plans. (Most hotel chains now offer a similar service.)

Ramada Inns: If you're traveling in the United States, cannot afford a suite, and are obliged to conduct business meetings in your hotel room, consider Ramada Inns. At some Ramada Inns you can take advantage of their "Pacesetter II" service for business travelers. You can request a room or suite equipped with a bed that slips away into the wall (or a separate sleeping area), leaving you with an unambiguous office space.

Ramada does not require use of a major credit card to confirm a reservation, and some business discounts are available.

Hyatt Hotels: Hyatt offers frequent travelers a service called "Regency Club," through which business guests may rent special suites on a private floor equipped with its own concierge. The cost runs between $5 and $30 over the standard room rate, depending on what city you are in. Special amenities include: rapid check-out services, some secretarial assistance, message forwarding, paging services, and even free continental breakfast, cordials, and hors d'oeuvres.

Sheraton Inns: "Sheraton Executive Traveler" (SET) service is only available to corporate travelers whose companies guarantee the use of 150 rooms per year. If your company qualifies, it receives a guaranteed corporate room rate for one year, upgraded rooms, and extended holds on room reservations after 6 P.M.

Rodeway Inns: Best of all in terms of hotel amenities for business travelers is Rodeway's "Executive Choice Deluxe" rooms, available at some 40 Rodeway establishments. If you can get one, you'll find a private steambath or whirlpool included in your accommodations. What could be nicer?

HOTELS AND THE WOMAN BUSINESS TRAVELER

Now that women constitute some 30 percent of all business traveler bookings in hotels, many hotel chains are getting excited about soliciting this market. Opinions seem to differ regarding what services to provide. Sheraton, Hyatt, and Marriott are in the vanguard of those who intend to do nothing, on the premise that women don't want to be treated differently from their male counterparts. In the other camp, Best Western International, Ramada, and Howard Johnson are making such changes as redecorating rooms in feminine fashion, and providing full-length mirrors, skirt hangers, and shower caps.

This may be just my opinion, but it seems that somebody is missing the point. On one hand, the problem women business travelers regularly face is being ignored, while on the other hand, the old vanity clichés are being offered as substitutes for actual improvement. It would seem that the welcome extended to a woman business traveler, a concern for her comfort and safety, and the respect accorded her by the hotel staff should rate far above shower caps and pink bedspreads. Skirt hangers and shower caps *should* be provided—they should have been standard 50 years ago. What is needed is a change of attitude. Women business travelers are actually people.

All is not lost. According to *The New York Times*, Best Western International has instructed its staff not to call women guests ''Honey'' anymore.

The elegant Coleman Hotels—the Fairfax in Washington, the Tremont and Whitehall in Chicago, and the Navarro in New York (currently being renovated)—deserve special mention here for the studious effort they are making to understand and satisfy the needs of women business travelers. Security and comfort top the list: single-entrance lobbies, frequent but discreet security patrols, a special unpacking service (upon request), full-length mirrors and scales in the bathrooms, hair driers and other appliances (available from the concierge), and secretarial assistance are some of the amenities Coleman Hotels offer.

Most important is the apparent sensitivity of the Coleman management to the attitudinal aspects of the hotel experience. The desk clerks are trained to greet women guests with special courtesy, and to give out room numbers to the bellhops with discretion—rather than broadcasting them for all to hear. Preferential seating in hotel bars and restaurants is provided, and bartenders are instructed not to honor ''send that lady a drink'' requests. Little things like can add up to a totally positive experience, and, in my opinion, make the intimately run, elegantly smaller hotels a valuable alternative to the impersonal large hotel chains.

BOOKING TACTICS

No matter what hotel chain or category of hotel you select, the first rule is to book ahead. This is especially important in populous cities with too few hotel rooms, which, at the time of writing, seems to be most of the world. Booking ahead, by the way, means as much as a month in advance when possible (which, unfortunately, it usually isn't).

If you run into an NA (not available) situation with a hotel when booking through a small travel agency or on your own, try again by booking through a large outfit like American Express, which may have blocked scores of rooms in the hotel in a prior wholesale deal. Or try through your airline, especially in cases where the airline owns the hotel chain. It, too, may have a group of preblocked rooms.

When you book your hotel, be sure to indicate the type of room you want (single, double, junior suite), the meal plan you prefer, your arrival and departure dates, and your estimated time of arrival. Also request that the hotel limousine or courtesy car pick you up at the airport. If you make the reservation on your own, the hotel may request a deposit. Don't object: This prepayment helps secure the room. If there's no time to send a check by mail, have the hotel bill you for the deposit on your credit card.

Securing a Room

The next trick, once you've selected your hotel and booked a room, is making sure the room will be waiting for you when you arrive. Hotels rely on the same insidious overbooking techniques as the airlines, and it's not uncommon for people with reservations and paid deposits to get thrown out on their ears when they try to check in.

Unfortunately, you can't count on telephone acceptance of your reservation, even when it's made directly to the hotel's booking agent or toll-free telephone number. And you can't count on the payment of a deposit to secure the room, because you can't be sure the hotel has actually received it in sufficient time. This happened to me in Jamaica recently. The charming San Souci Hotel in Ocho Rios had never heard of me or received my deposit when I showed up at the door, even though I had made my reservation and paid my deposit to the airline representative three weeks in advance.

What to do? First of all, avail yourself of any and all guaranteed reservation services offered by the hotel. Second, insist on getting a written record of your confirmation—either a copy of the hotel's confirmation form, or, barring that, the hotel's own confirmation number—from the booking agent or hotel rep. All reputable hotels will offer this assistance. Western International Hotels, for instance, will provide you with a written confirmation of your reservation upon request, and, if you arrive by the time stated, will have the room waiting for you.

If you pay a deposit in advance, you'll also need to know how and when the deposits were sent. This information should be provided for you in detail by the agent or airline rep doing the booking. If you have time, you can write ahead to the hotel yourself and include a deposit. It seems an old-fashioned way to operate, but it usually works, which is more than you can say for a lot of computers.

Late Arrivals/Confirmed Reservations

If your plane is getting in around 6 P.M. or later, you must inform the hotel, Otherwise, they'll bump you at the stroke of 6 (or 4 P.M. in resort destinations). If you're going to be late, you should make a confirmed reservation by authorizing the hotel to charge you for the full amount of the room on your credit card whether or not you show up. When you make a confirmed reservation, the hotel is obliged to hold the room for you until check-out time the following day, or put you up, free of charge, in an equivalent room at a nearby hotel.

Corporate Discounts

If your company qualifies for a corporate discount with a hotel chain, you should make the booking yourself to get the full benefit of the discount. Example: If you're eligible for a 20 percent discount and you book through a travel agent, the travel agent's commission is deducted from the discount first, and you get only the percentage that remains. If you book on your own, with no commission withheld, you and your company realize the full benefit.

Usually the best corporate discounts are given by the large hotel chains—some provide savings of up to 50 percent on standard room rates.

HOTEL CHECKLIST

Choose a hotel, motel, or resort on the basis of:
- Proximity to business calls
- Nearby amenities
- Safety of area
- Garage/parking lot
- Coffee shop/restaurants
- Meal plans (AP/CP/EP/MAP)
- Types of room (single/double/twin/suite)
- Telex facilities
- Direct-dial phones in room
- 24-hour room service
- Laundry/dry cleaning/valet
- Gym/tennis courts/sauna/pool/masseuse
- Airport limousine service
- In-house travel agent
- Reputation
- Clientele
- Corporate discounts
- Cost
- Credit cards

Look for hotels with the best business-traveler services:
- Quick check-in and check-out
- Guaranteed reservations

- Business traveler clubs
- Special amenities for business travelers

Be sure to:
- Book as far in advance as possible.
- Make confirmed (positive, assured) reservations, especially for late arrivals.
- Get a copy of booking form and/or booking number from your travel agent or booking agent.
- Get full corporate discount.

5

Business Travel by Automobile

On many occasions, business travel commitments require you to drive, either in a rental car or in your own. You may have to go a hundred miles across back roads to a small town where a key client is mysteriously located. You may have a lot of traveling to do in and around your sprawling destination city. Or you may have to cover a three- or four-state area by car with a trunkload of business samples.

CHOOSING THE RIGHT CAR

Whether you're renting a car or buying one, there are many things to consider when making your selection. If you're used to a small car with a stick shift, choose this type for business purposes. If you rent a high-powered behemoth, you'll feel as if you were floating across buttered tarmac while sitting on your living room couch. Conversely, if you're used to driving a big American car, you'll probably feel vulnerable in a small stick-shift type. For travel outside the United States, you may have to adapt: large cars with automatic transmissions are not generally available for rent in most other countries.

For superhighways and long-distance cruising at high speeds, you'll be safer and more comfortable in a large car than in a subcompact. But for itineraries that include narrow roads and a lot of back-country driving, a smaller car with a stick shift is preferable.

You may also need air conditioning to survive in comfort, especially in the southwestern United States. Once again, air conditioning is not generally available in rental cars outside the U.S.

BOOKING RENTAL CARS

Renting a car is often a necessary and integral part of planning a business trip, and you should know how the system operates.

If you'll need a car at your destination, reserve one in advance when you book your plane ticket or hotel. Have your airline rep or travel agent book it for you, or, if your company has a corporate account with one of the car rental firms, reserve the car yourself through the company's toll-free number to realize the full benefit of the discount.

Corporate discounts vary from 5 to 40 percent off the standard rates, with the average about 20 percent. Some companies also include free collision insurance with the discount. If you're eligible, be sure the clerk who takes your reservation incorporates the discount and free insurance into your rate. Sometimes these get overlooked.

Rental cars are graded by size and cost into categories such as luxury (or deluxe), full-sized, intermediate, compact, or economy (sometimes referred to as subcompact). If you have a preference for a specific kind of car, book with a company that offers what you want. Hertz rents all manner of Ford cars; Avis rents GM models plus some Japanese makes.

Rental cars are offered in a variety of billing plans that can affect the final cost dramatically. A friend of mine recently rented a Japanese subcompact from Avis in New York for a one-day, 200-mile trip and ended up paying an outrageous $139. Concurrently, Chrisjean Whitten rented a larger Hertz car in Florida for two weeks and paid just over $200, total.

Shop around. Be sure you get the most advantageous rate in terms of the duration of the rental, the type of car, and the distances you'll be traveling. In some circumstances, an all-inclusive rate (with mileage included) is cheaper than a lower rate with an extra fee charged per mile. Some car rental firms are now eliminating the mileage charges altogether; the savings can add up to as much as 33 percent. Hertz was the first to do this on a nationwide basis and others have begun to follow.

When you book a rental car, know in advance the type or category of car you want, the year of the model, whether or not it has air conditioning, and, if you can find out, the average number of miles the car gets to a gallon of gasoline. You won't want to plow half of your per diem cash allowance into the gullet of a gas guzzler.

As you undoubtedly know, to rent a car, you'll need a major credit card—or a credit account with the car renting agency—in lieu of a cash deposit of about $300.

Rental Car Clubs

If you have frequent need of a rental car, you'll probably find it worthwhile to join one of the car rental companies' fast-booking clubs and get one of their credit cards (usually accomplished on the same application). When you apply for membership, you fill out a form stating all the necessary data about your car preferences, driver's license number, and credit card number. Your profile is kept in a computer and is pulled out automatically when you rent a car.

As a member of the **Hertz #1 Club**, for example, you get fast reservations by calling a special toll-free number. You give the agent your #1 Club account number, your flight number (where applicable), and you tell him when and where you'll need the car. That's it. Your reservation will be confirmed on the spot over the phone, and the rental agreement will be filled out and waiting for you at the Hertz counter. Your driver's license and a major credit card are required.

Hertz #1 Club membership also provides you with an instant ''Express Car Return'' system when you bring back the car. All you do is fill in the mileage on the rental agreement and drop it and the car keys into a special Express Car Return box. Your completed statement and bill will be mailed to you the same day. Anyone who applies and passes a credit check is eligible for #1 Club membership. Most other leading car rental firms offer similar services.

In addition to the #1 Club, Hertz also has a ''Five Star Card'' for VIPs. Membership requirements are more stringent and members are given the same speedy service as #1 Club members, plus $50 check cashing privileges. Avis, National, and other car rental companies offer similar—if less complete—services.

Alternatives to #1

Many of the lesser-known rental companies offer perfectly good cars and service at lower rates than the leading companies. There's no reason you shouldn't use one if the company has a reputation for reliability, which you can check with your travel agent or the AAA (see below). Just be sure that the car rental pickup point at your destination is in the arrival terminal of the airport, not three miles out at the edge of the service runway behind the TWA hangar. And be sure the company includes such civilities as adequate service, a full tank of gas at pickup, and convenient drop-off locations.

Before booking, check your itinerary carefully to see if you really need a rental car. If your business calls are confined to the downtown area and not scattered hither and yon throughout the industrial suburbs, you may do better by local taxi. Also consider the geographic layout of your destination city. In Houston, Miami, and Los Angeles, you'd be stranded without a car. But in New York and Tokyo, you'd probably find one a liability.

Fly/Drive Programs

Before renting a car, investigate the possibility of a Fly/Drive program in which you get an all-inclusive price for plane fare, rental car, and hotels, with surcharges levied according to the hotels you select. If it's applicable, this type of package might save you a bundle on a multi-destination business trip, and would provide you with great flexibility for a weekend excursion. Car rental rates are much lower in a Fly/Drive package than they are in a straight, nondiscounted rental. The hotels available in a Fly/Drive program are usually listed in a booklet given to you at the time of purchase, with literally dozens of chain hotels (Holiday Inn and the like) to choose from in a five- or six-state area.

Booking Limousines

My basic philosophy while on the road is to conserve my own resources, whenever possible, by letting someone else do the work. Why not rent a limousine with a driver, or at the very least, a taxi, instead of bothering to rent a car and getting nervous in traffic jams yourself?

If you can't afford your own private limousine, you can afford the airport limo that will deliver you to your hotel. Some airline tickets can be purchased with ground transfers included in the prices. Ask your travel agent if this can be arranged.

If you're traveling fancy and want to lease a private limousine, do it before you go. Limousines aren't always as outrageously expensive as you think, especially when you'd otherwise spend a fortune on taxis making a difficult round of calls. I rented a limousine (it was really a taxi, but the driver had a fancy hat) in the Canary Islands a few years ago when I was writing a guidebook and needed to travel all over Gran Canaria Island on a one-day fact-finding trip. In terms of my time and professional efficiency, it was economical to pay a driver to take me. Had I gone on my own, trying to drive, find my way, stop and observe, and make copious notes, it would have taken two or three trips, and would have been more expensive.

I once rented a limousine in London when traveling with a photographer, his assistant, and huge cases of equipment after a transatlantic shooting aboard the *S.S. France.* We were traveling from the hotel to the airport and had too many suitcases and gear for the three of us to fit into a taxicab. The limousine cost only a few dollars more than two taxis would have cost; besides, we had the fun of traveling in a dark green Daimler with a liveried chauffeur who addressed me as ''Madam'' and provided us with a fur lap rug.

BUSINESS TRAVEL IN YOUR OWN CAR

If you must use your automobile for business travel, the burden of making the car trip-worthy rests on you. That means being responsible for keeping your car in tiptop shape, with regular checkups and first-class maintenance. Read your owner's manual—if your car is secondhand and doesn't have a manual, write to the manufacturer, giving the make and year, and ask for one. Most manuals provide a servicing checklist that should be followed religiously.

Buy good tires (steel-belted radials are a worthwhile investment), and be sure they—and your spare tire—are in perfect condition. Have the oil checked before the start of a long trip. Fill the gas tank. And, if you plan to load the car down with heavy samples, adjust the air pressure in your tires. Keep the windshield clean. Sometimes, commercial car-wash stations leave a waxy deposit on the glass; you can get it clean with an ordinary glass cleaner and paper towels.

For winter driving, equip your car with all the needed gear: chains, ice scraper, and even a small shovel and a bag of rock salt if you'll be driving through really frigid areas. If you're insecure about driving in heavy snow or on icy surfaces, take the trouble to have someone teach you a few techniques.

You will probably want a car with a radio, and perhaps a tape deck to play your favorite music on long journeys. I have a friend who plays her French lessons on tape, practicing her pronunciation as she traverses the Midwest.

Also worth considering (in the U.S.) are CB radios, which have become commonplace in the last few years. They're useful to call for help if you should break down in the middle of nowhere.

Road Wisdom

Since I do not know a spare tire from a cam shaft, I am not one to offer keen advice on how to change a tire in three minutes flat or lift the car hood and check the oil convincingly. My solutions to car problems are to: (1) abandon the vehicle wherever it collapses; (2) stand beside it on the edge of the road (with fresh lipstick and my hair combed), looking helpless; or (3) get hold of the nearest tow truck and damn the expense.

However, despite my automotive ignorance, even I have proved resourceful in places where no assistance was available. Once, on a research trip, I was driving a Volkswagen in the rugged mountains of Lesotho (then Basutoland), a small independent kingdom and former British protectorate in southern Africa. I was on a narrow dirt road in the middle of nowhere when suddenly the accelerator cable snapped and the car rolled to a stop. After staring blankly at the engine for a while, an ingenious traveling companion and I stuck a pebble under the little lever in the back that revved up the engine and kept it racing, straining madly against the brakes. When I put the car in first gear, I had to hang on to the emergency brake to keep the car from roaring off into the bush as we raised a cloud of dust and took off down a treacherous incline. The car was racing so fast I had to drive with my foot pressed hard on the brake, and I barely managed to stop when we unexpectedly rounded a bend in a cloud of dust and rolled up in front of a barricade, face to face with two startled customs officials. To stop the car, I had to turn off the ignition, and it took us an hour to find another pebble that would fit under the lever and get the car charged up again. We finally did get out of the wilds and onto a paved road in the Orange Free State. But we also managed to burn out the brake linings and had to spend three nights on an isolated farm watching an Afrikaner farmer chopping up rocks in a sheep field, while we waited for the car to be repaired.

In any case, if you want to learn more about the inner workings of your car, take a course at your nearest state college, or make a point of asking your mechanic to explain things when they go wrong. You can pick up guides to car care at most bookstores. Bit by bit the engine will start to become comprehensible, or so they say.

You can also purchase one of the automobile maintenance guides, some of which are written especially for women (although why women should see a machine differently from men beats me). Two of the most popular books: *What Every Woman Should Know about Her Car* by Dorothy Jackson and *Basic Car Care* by A. M. Pettis.

KEEPING TRACK: MAPS AND EXPENSE ACCOUNTS

Whether you drive your own or a rental car, you'll need to know in advance where you're going and you'll need to have a system to keep track of all your automobile-related expenses.

As far as maps are concerned, most people who drive in the U.S. for business keep a copy of the *Rand McNally Road Atlas* at their beck and call (also see the information on services provided by the AAA, opposite). Plot your journey on the map in advance, checking the distances and the types of roads you'll be traveling on. Don't build an itinerary that will require 18 hours of straight driving. It can be done, especially with the aid of caffeine or pep pills, but it's not recommended. Endurance limits vary by individual; a maximum daily average would be about 10 hours of driving.

When you plan a driving trip, allow time for frequent road stops, at least once every two or three hours. You need to move your legs to get the circulation going, and you need to rest a bit from the strain and monotony of driving. Stops like these may cost you a little in time, but you gain a lot in long-term endurance. When you stop, don't just sit at the counter of a roadside diner and drink coffee. Walk around. Bend over. Do some jumping jacks. Put on your sneakers and run in circles. Do absolutely anything that will wake your body up and activate your reflexes.

Also plan ahead how you will keep your travel expense records. If you rent a car, your expenses will include the rental fee, mileage, and insurance fees, plus gas, tolls, and parking. Get and keep receipts for everything, even tolls (these can be obtained upon request from specifically marked booths on all bridges and toll highways). And don't forget to include taxi or bus expenses to and from the car rental office. Keep track of your expenses in a small notebook or in your daily planner. Do your homework at rest stops, or in the evening at your hotel. But do it. You'll be amazed at how the quarters and dimes and gasoline expenses add up.

If you use your own car for business travel, your business-related costs are reimbursable either by your employer (depending on what kind of arrangement you have), or they're deductible as business expenses from your income taxes. Your employer may reimburse you for some car expenses, but not all. In that case, be sure to claim the balance on your itemized tax deductions.

In addition to gas, tolls, and parking, you may claim as legitimate business expenses a portion of your auto maintenance and servicing fees, the cost of new tires, radios, CB units, and tapes (if you can demonstrate that they have a business-related function). You may also deduct the depreciation on your car, which is usually set at a fixed percentage rate based on the cost, age, and category of the automobile. For explicit laws regarding legitimate deductions for business travel by automobile, ask your own accountant, your company accountant, or tax adviser from the Internal Revenue Service.

AAA: THE BEST DEAL IN TOWN

The Automobile Association of America is an exceptionally good value for anyone who owns a car and/or does a lot of automobile travel for business purposes. It's especially recommended for women who will be traveling on their own. Each regional chapter of the Association is an autonomous entity affiliated with other Associations across the country, with a total of almost 900 AAA offices in both the United States and Canada.

Membership fees vary by area, ranging from $22 to $48 a year.

What you get with AAA membership:
- Emergency road service, 24 hours a day, 365 days a year, with more than 17,000 service stations under contract in the U.S. and Canada to call.
- Emergency towing—free of charge—to the nearest AAA-contracted service station.
- Expert trip-planning advice and worldwide travel services, including hotel, airline, vacation, cruise, and rental-car bookings.
- Personalized ''triptiks'' (detailed strip maps with mile-by-mile information), compiled especially for you by the AAA and tailored to your itinerary.
- Personal accident, baggage, marine, and European car insurance is available on request for an additional fee.
- AAA Traveler's Checks (in association with Thomas Cook), free of charge.
- Up to 30 percent discount on Avis and Hertz rental cars (in most areas) with certain qualifications.
- AAA road maps, available at no extra charge, with some city maps available—take note!
- Free domestic and Caribbean tour books. Be sure to check the useful AAA domestic *Citibooks*.
- Affiliation with automobile clubs in about 17 foreign countries, including Canada and Mexico.
- Exclusive discounts in certain locations.
- Assistance in obtaining tickets to special sporting or theatrical events.
- Forms from the Department of Motor Vehicles (for drivers' licenses, automobile registration, etc.).
- Free notary service at many AAA offices.
- Help in arranging auto financing at preferential interest rates at some offices.
- Bail bond protection insurance, in case you get locked up in the

pokey for doing 80 in a 40-mile-an-hour zone through Tuscaloosa, Alabama.
* Passport photo service at less-than-commercial rates.

The AAA is also the only place in the United States where you may obtain an International Driving Permit (see Part 2, ''Travel Planning: For the World'').

For the nearest AAA, check your local phone directory or contact the AAA Administrative Headquarters at 8111 Gatehouse Road, Falls Church, Virginia 22042, telephone (703) 222-6332.

NOTE: American Express has introduced something called the Driver Security plan to its cardholders. For a fee of $16 a year, the plan provides some of the features of AAA membership, such as an amount deductible on any road tow, Rand McNally Trip Plans and maps, guaranteed arrest bonds, insurance, and other features.

DRIVING ON YOUR OWN

Since most modern women never question their right and ability to drive anywhere in the United States and other parts of the world, I really don't believe it necessary to advise you here not to pick up hitchhikers or let yourself run out of gas. Surely you know how to handle your car and yourself on the road to your own and the law's satisfaction. You know when to maintain anonymity, when to keep your doors locked, and how to avoid playing highway games with attentive machos (ignore them). (If you don't know these things, and must drive for business purposes, enroll in a driver education program for a refresher course.)

There are times and places, however, when driving—and arriving—on your own can impose a feeling of uneasiness. I remember once driving alone from Málaga, Spain, to Portugal on a research/writing assignment. It's a long drive. You go up over the Sierra de Málaga and across the plains of the Guadalquivir River to Seville, then northwest on a beautiful but twisting road that runs through stands of birch trees and olive groves bordered with low stone walls that harbor some of Spain's most famous fighting bulls. On an extremely narrow stretch of macadam just over the Portuguese border, the right front tire of my small rented Seat blew out just as I was trying to pass a fume-spouting truck. I barely managed to get the car under control and over to the side of the road without causing an accident. The truck crew kindly stopped to change my tire. They were burly, uneducated men, but being Portuguese, were imbued with a special courtesy one finds everywhere in that country. The men refused my offer of payment and waved me on my way. I was grateful, relieved, as I was alone in an isolated area.

When I had been on the road for about 11 hours, I finally decided to give up for the night in the old Portuguese town of Beja in the Lower Alentejo. I checked into the hotel and rushed down to the dining room just before it closed, still dusty and rumpled from the long drive. I ordered my dinner from the waiter, speaking to him in Portuguese, and sat back to relax over a glass of wine.

Sitting near me were two British couples, obviously upper class and with a suggestion of decadence about them, a type that seems particularly drawn to Portugal. Evidently, they didn't think I understood English and they began speaking about me.

"Isn't it a pity," said one of the women, eyeing me spitefully and suggesting from the finality of her intonation that she thought I was a prostitute. I didn't say a word. I calmly looked back at them and listened. "Where do you suppose she came from?" the other woman asked. "Pretty piece, that," answered one of the men jokingly. "Wonder what that's fetching for the night?"

I flushed with anger and was about to stand up and throw my *caldo verde* in their faces when it suddenly occurred to me that I was responding with that feminine reflex that makes us automatically feel guilty when we are caught alone, without "belonging" to another person, or having a clear purpose, in a public circumstance. What did it matter what they thought of me? I was doing nothing illegal, merely minding my own business.

I didn't throw my soup, but instead watched the couples calmly, almost amused. When they got up to leave the dining room, staring at me with rude curiosity as they passed my table, I smiled directly at them and said simply, in English, "Good night."

AUTOMOBILE/RENTAL CAR CHECKLIST

- Choose the best car for the type of travel you must do.
- Shop around for the best rental-car rates.
- Reserve a rental car in advance.
- Check Fly/Drive for savings.
- Be sure to get full corporate discounts.
- Join a rental-car club for quick pickup, return, and billing.
- Keep your own car serviced and ready to go (get an owner's manual with a servicing checklist).
- Get good maps of your route and destination cities.
- Plan for careful accounting of auto-related expenses.
- Join the AAA.

6

Money Mileage

Managing your money on the road is just as important as managing your time. Never be without sufficient funds when you're away from home. You'll have to do some careful calculations in advance to plan a budget that will cover all your expenses, foreseen and unforeseen.

Credit Cards

The first rule, of which you are undoubtedly aware, is not to carry a lot of cash. If you lose it or are robbed, there's no compensation. Plan to pay for the bulk of your business-travel expenses (hotel, rental car, meals, and flights) with credit cards or traveler's checks, or a combination of the two.

If you plan to pay with a credit card, check to see that the hotel you're staying in accepts the card you intend to use. Some hotels are persnickety on the subject, and you might find the cashier staring at you blankly as Chrisjean did not long ago in Bermuda when she pulled out her American Express card. Rental cars and meals in established restaurants can almost always be covered by credit cards—again, check in advance to be sure the card you carry is acceptable. You might also consider getting an oil company credit card if you'll be doing a lot of driving, and a credit card for the telephone.

Paying for business expenses with credit cards saves you the trouble of carrying a lot of cash, and it also provides an automatic record of your expenses. As a safety precaution, always keep a record of your credit card numbers and expiration dates in a separate place from where you keep the cards. Also keep the emergency numbers to call should your cards be lost or stolen. Reporting a loss promptly before the cards can be used will save you any liability for unauthorized charges. (See also Chapter 14, ''International Money Matters.'')

Traveler's Checks

Traveler's checks are another safe and convenient way to carry money when you travel, and, once again, the check numbers should be carried separately from the checks themselves. Keep a record of the checks you spend on the form provided. If you should lose your checks, report the loss at once to the issuing company and you should receive an immediate replacement. Buy traveler's checks in the denominations you'll need: tens and twenties for small items, fifties and one hundreds for more expensive purchases and entertaining.

The leading traveler's checks in the United States are issued by American Express, Bank of America, Citicorp, and Thomas Cook. You can obtain free traveler's checks through Thomas Cook, Barclay's Bank, and Deak-Perera, as well as special AAA traveler's checks issued to members in conjunction with Thomas Cook. The others charge a 1 percent commission, paid at the time of purchase.

If you're traveling internationally, it's to your advantage to buy the currency of your destination country, or traveler's checks in that currency, before leaving home. Foreign currency traveler's checks and cash may be purchased from most leading banks; your bank may not have the moneys you need on hand, so give them several days' notice.)

When you return from a trip and have traveler's checks left over, cash them in immediately and put the money in a bank where at least it will earn interest. There's no reason to hold the checks for your next trip—traveler's check companies have grown rich on the interest-free ''float'' of money from checks not yet cashed in.

Cash

In addition to traveler's checks and credit cards, you'll obviously need a certain amount of cash to pay for tips, taxis, cups of coffee, tolls, and so on. Keep $50 to $100 in cash with you all the time, with plenty of coins and small bills for tips. When you're in an airport or checking into a hotel, keep some change handy in your pocket for tipping—it's easier than having to fish through your handbag when you're loaded down with travel gear.

Personal Checks and Letters of Credit

Always carry your personal checkbook with you when you're on the road. In an emergency, you can usually manage to pay for something or get cash with a personal check, provided you have sufficient identification.

Also, ask your banker about issuing you a letter of credit. This will introduce you as a solvent member in good standing to the bank's correspondents elsewhere and make it easier for you to obtain cash or credit if you should be in need. Some banks provide international identification cards to customers. Morgan Guaranty Trust Company of New York, for example, offers a World Check Card that introduces clients to correspondent or branch banks abroad. With the World Check Card, Morgan customers receive check-cashing privileges for amounts up to $1,000.

EMERGENCY FUNDING

There's nothing dumber than running out of funds on a business trip, and it's usually up to you to plan your expense allowance accurately to be sure you're covered before you go. However, sometimes it's not always possible to anticipate what you'll really need. While I was on a long journey through South America, my employers tightened up on funds despite my warning that the money I was carrying was not sufficient for a two-month trip (back then, I had no credit cards). The result: I ran completely dry after a month and a half on the road and had to hole up in Rio for an extra 10 days while the company wired down additional money. Of course, I couldn't have been stranded in a more delightful spot, and after I'd done all the work I could think of to do, I finally gave up and spent a week on the beach. The delay ended up costing me a missed assignment when I finally got home. And it cost my employers several thousands of extra dollars—I was staying in a deluxe hotel and couldn't move to cheaper lodgings because I didn't have the money to pay the bill.

Some credit card companies, such as American Express, have cardholder dispenser programs through which you can automatically purchase several hundred dollars' worth of traveler's checks from company offices or outside-access machines open 24 hours a day. The checks are billed to you on your credit card. Participation in programs of this type usually requires a special application. Call your credit card company to see what similar programs they offer. (Note that you cannot always get cash through traveler's check dispensers in foreign countries.)

Another way to get emergency funds is by cable or telex from your home. Upon notification, your bank will telex an order for cash payment to a correspondent bank at your destination, a procedure which can be accomplished overnight, or, as happened to me in Rio, it can take a week or more. Air tickets can also be prepaid and transmitted to you in this fashion, through the airline or a national or international travel company.

The main idea, however, is not to get stuck for funds, but to plan your budget carefully and realistically.

BUDGETING FOR REALITY

Calculating travel budgets requires an eagle-eyed assessment of the nature of your trip, the cost of goods and services at your destination, and a detailed per diem analysis of your planned activities. Most travel budgets are calculated on a daily allowance predetermined by your company. Sometimes this is more than adequate; other times it's so out of line that you're hard pressed to do your job and still pay your bills.

As most business travelers pay for the big four (hotels, rental cars, flights, and meals) with credit cards, the important calculation you should make before you leave is how much you'll need to cover your daily cash expenses. Here's a list of what usually gets paid for with what:

Credit Card	**Cash/Traveler's Checks**
Hotel:	Tips
Telephone	Tolls
Special services	Parking
Room service	Gas/Oil
Laundry/cleaning	Taxis/airport limos
Rental car	Airport taxes
Restaurant meals	Overweight charges
Entertainment	Drinks on plane/headsets
	Bar bills
	Business supplies
	Personal (cigarettes, etc.)

Per Diem Budgeting

To arrive at an estimated expenditure per day, you must break down your itinerary on an itemized basis. You don't need to be exact—some days will cost more than others. The important thing is to come up with a realistic average. If you're not renting a car, eliminate the cost of the car itself, plus gas, tolls, and parking from your budget. Then add on an estimate for taxis and other transportation.

Theoretical Daily Expense Budget (* = Card, † = Cash)

Hotel	$ 65*
Breakfast/lunch	$ 15†
Dinner	$ 20*
Rental Car (at weekly rate)	$ 20*
Gas	$ 15†
Tolls/parking	$ 15†
Tips	$ 10†
Telephone	$ 10*
Cleaning	$ 5*
Miscellaneous	$ 15†
Total	**$190**
*Card	$120
†Cash	$ 70

Chrisjean Whitten has found that she needs about $300 a week to pay for her cash expenses, even if she pays for her hotel, rental car, and meals with a credit card. Her per diem allowance has been about $180, which is supposed to include all of her expenses (even those paid for by credit card), with the sole exception of her air fares. As few big city hotels go for as little as $50 a night any more, she found this budget barely workable.

When you're calculating your budget, do some careful homework on the costs of transportation and services at your destination, especially when you're traveling abroad. In countries where the dollar has taken a pounding in recent years, you may need almost twice Chrisjean's allowance. In Paris, good hotel rooms start at $100; in Geneva, a lunch for two goes for $75; and in West Berlin, a three-minute phone call to New York from a hotel is about $40.

If you're looking in guidebooks for price information, be sure the information you're basing your budget on is up to date. A book published in 1981, for example, probably contains editorial material, including prices, written in the first half of 1980 or even late 1979.

The Critical Contingency

Always add a contingency factor to your budget to cover you in case of emergency. Add up your estimated daily expenses and then add

10 to 30 percent to the total, depending on the nature of your trip and your familiarity with the destination. The less you know about a place and the more complex your assignment, the higher the contingency factor should be.

Never neglect to include a contingency. Cheat if you must by burying the additional amount in your various daily expenses to hide it from your employer's eyes. Don't feel dishonest—the contingency factor is your margin of safety in a calamitous world where nothing, especially prices, can be counted on. I used to sneak in a whopping 30 percent contingency on all assignments for one company I worked for. I knew I would need it. And whenever I returned from a trip, I was always applauded for not exceeding my budget.

Cutting Corners

If your per diem allowance is really slim pickings, you'll have to find ways to cut corners on your expenses. Don't cut corners on your hotel, however, at least not in terms of its safe location and general acceptability. Do look for savings in less expensive rooms within the good hotels—one leading hotel in Paris, for example, has a slew of mean little nests up under its mansard roof that go for less than the more spacious lower rooms.

In rental cars, select smaller, gas-efficient models, and also look around for a company that offers lower rates. Weekly rates are often a good value—you may end up paying less than you would on a daily basis even if you only need the car for four or five days.

Air fare savings can be had by wading through the mud puddle of promotional fares, night flights, and standbys to see what savings are possible with your schedule. As far as food is concerned, you can always have a picnic of fruit and yogurt in your hotel room, or order from the appetizer section of the menu. Ask the hotel concierge or bell captain to recommend a good local eatery instead of the usual business-traveler hangouts.

I personally feel that companies that shortchange their business travelers in terms of essentials do an even greater disservice to themselves than they do to their traveling employees. Stinginess generates bad feelings, for one thing—imagine a business traveler breaking his or her back to win business for the company, all the while feeling like a pauper and having to skimp on such necessities as food. Tightfisted companies also impose inconveniences on their travelers, perhaps unwittingly, that cost more in terms of wasted time, inefficiency, deadened spirits, and lost business than they could cost in revenue.

If you feel your travel allowance is short of what you'll actually need out there in the cold cruel world, prepare a careful budget to demonstrate your point and speak to your boss, company travel manager, or someone else who can either make the needed adjustments or give you tips on how to make your budget work. Keep in mind that you're a woman and you will be traveling on your own. That's not to say you're handicapped. It is to say that the facts of life often make it more difficult for a woman to move about on her own than a man, and she should insist on being prudently protected.

TIPS ON TIPPING

Tips can add up to a major cash expenditure when you're traveling, and you should provide for them adequately in your budget.

When you're in transit, plan to pay porters the equivalent of about 50 or 75 cents a bag, slightly more if your luggage is particularly bulky or heavy. For any unusual service or prolonged waiting (such as asking a porter to hold your bags while you put your car in the long-term parking lot), pay double the usual rate. For budgeting purposes, multiply the tips you estimate you'll have to pay times the number of trips you'll make through an airport (coming and going), plus the number of times you'll check in and out of a hotel.

Taxi drivers in the United States ordinarily receive tips ranging from 10 to 20 percent—a median 15 percent ought to do the trick. Taxi drivers abroad do not always expect tips as high as those we generally give in the United States, but I usually tip about 15 percent anyway to avoid shortchanging anyone.

In most restaurants, a tip of 15 percent is the usual, with 20 percent the norm if service is particularly attentive. (If you are treated poorly, tip 10 percent or less, or not at all.) In many countries, a service charge is automatically added to your restaurant, café, or bar bill. When this occurs, it's customary to leave an additional 5 percent of the bill as a tip, or 10 percent if the service has been especially to your liking. When a service charge is automatically levied, it is stated on the menu. If you're not sure, examine your bill to see what's included, or ask the headwaiter.

The maitre d' and sommelier also require tips when they have rendered any service. Tip the maitre d' about $5 as you leave the restaurant (proportionate to your bill, of course—if you had a lunch of shrimp salad and the bill is only $12, tip $1 or $2). The sommelier should receive approximately 10 percent of the cost of the wine; this should be paid to him directly—but discreetly—as soon as he finishes pouring the first round.

Women, as you undoubtedly know, have a bad reputation when it comes to tipping—probably because many of us are new to the business of going out alone or entertaining business associates, and also because most of us have only recently been introduced to the delights of the expense account. For your own purposes, be aware of the fact that money does make the world go around, especially in impersonal situations when you are away from home and unknown to the people who are serving you. A good seat in a restaurant can be had for a folded bill slipped to the maitre d' upon entering the restaurant. Impeccable wine service at dinner can be had by a generous gift to the sommelier. A friendly smile and an extra maraschino cherry can be yours in the hotel bar if the bartender remembers how generously you tipped him the night before. Theater tickets and restaurant reservations are yours with a smile if you introduce yourself to the hotel concierge just after you check in and demonstrate your good will in advance with a $5 or $10 bill.

It's no mystery: good service is the direct result of a well-greased palm, and you shouldn't be offended that this is so. Sometimes women are outraged at the lack of attention they receive in hotels and airports without benefit of tipping, but these are usually not women who work or function economically on their own. Do they think that all those threadbare employees are present to service their needs out of some kind of personal generosity or class obligation or gratitude? Some women—perhaps those who complain about the "servant problem" and project vague fantasies about what surely was not theirs in bygone centuries—seem to think that this is so.

You're not one of them. You work for a living and so do the people you have to tip.

Tip frequently and well, especially when you're in a place you plan to visit often or when you want someone to do something extra for you. Learn to tip with style. Have small bills and change readily available in your pocket or an easy-to-reach corner of your purse for tipping porters, doormen, and bellboys. In restaurants or with a hotel concierge, be especially discreet. Permit the gent to accept the money without forcing him to go through any ego-shattering adjustments. To learn how to tip, watch some of the more polished men when they do it. Have a bill prepared, folded into a small rectangle, ready in your pocket. When you approach the maitre d' or concierge, pull the bill out of your pocket, concealed in your palm, and extend a half-closed hand, almost as if you were going to shake his hand. Transfer the bill to him quickly and firmly, then withdraw your hand, By being discreet, you protect the person receiving the tip from appearing to grovel for it, or from being seen by others accepting the very thing his livelihood depends on. It's a funny business, fraught with psychological subtlety. But learn to do it. It's usually the only way to get the service you require.

KEEPING EXPENSE ACCOUNTS

Keeping track of your business expenses while traveling is especially important, as virtually everything you spend when you're on the road is business related and either reimbursable or tax deductible.

Plan ahead how you will keep your expense records. Credit card receipts, restaurant stubs, and other receipts should be kept in a file folder in your briefcase or travel bag, or stuffed into a secure slot in your date book or wallet for processing later. It's your unreceipted expenses that add up quickly—these you'll have to remember to record.

For my expense records, I always carry a small leather daily agenda with an address book in the back (a fabulous one made by Hermès with quarterly inserts that I received as a present some years ago). In this book, each day is given a full page, with ample space for a day's worth of appointments as well as room for a record of my cash expenses.

Most stationers carry small leather- or plastic-bound notebooks that fit easily inside your handbag or briefcase, and that list typical business expenses on daily sheets. In these, you simply fill in the amounts of each expense and tally the totals, by category, at the end of the day. One of the worst-looking and most functional of these notebooks is an 8-by-10-inch spiral-bound version published by Dome, entitled *Expense Account Diary* that is available at many stationers and notions shops. (If you can't find one, write to Dome Publishing Company, Dome Building, Providence, Rhode Island 02903.) This book, like others published by Dome, is designed to comply with U.S. tax regulations, and it's extremely informative about what you can and cannot legitimately claim as a business expense. Categories of business expenses listed include:

• Breakfast	• Baggage charges
• Lunch	• Entertainment
• Dinner	• Gifts
• Hotel or motel	• Telephone
• Transportation:	• Tolls
Plane	• Postage
Railroad	• Auto expenses:
Taxi or bus	Gas/oil/lubrication
Auto rental	Repairs

Tires/supplies	Depreciation: ___ miles @ ___ ¢
Parking	• Office expenses
Washing	• Trade shows
Insurance	• Miscellaneous

Keep in mind that any expenses for photocopying, secretarial assistance, leasing of conference rooms, trade-show supplies, pens, pads, pencils, local guides, maps, and tips are all legitimate business expenses.

You might also take a look at Dome's *Simplified Weekly Bookkeeping Record*, designed primarily for companies and people who operate their own businesses, but of special value for the detailed alphabetical listings entitled ''Legal Deductions Allowable if You Are Engaged in a Trade, Business, or Profession.'' Some items you may want to include on your corporate expense account or for your own tax records are:

- Driver's license fees
- Passport fees
- Passport photos
- Visa fees
- Inoculations for foreign travel
- Checking account bank charges
- Safe deposit box rental
- Theater tickets if used for business or profession
- Baggage charges

For specific advice on managing your expense accounts, speak to your accountant. Also see Part 5, ''The Business of Doing Business,'' for more information on travel and entertainment expenses.

MONEY MILEAGE CHECKLIST

Funds
- Be sure credit cards are accepted in hotels and restaurants you wish to patronize.
- Get oil company and telephone credit cards.
- Carry all credit card and traveler's check numbers separately.
- Carry emergency telephone numbers to call if checks or cards are lost or stolen.
- Redeem traveler's checks promptly.
- Prepare coins and small bills for tipping.
- Buy foreign currency traveler's checks or cash.

- Take personal checkbook.
- Get letter of credit or identification card from bank.

Budgeting
- Use up-to-date sources when calculating budget.
- Account for inflation and dollar devaluation.
- Estimate itemized per diem budget, divided into cash expenses and credit card expenses.
- Add a contingency factor of 10 to 30 percent of the total.
- Keep an accurate expense record in a daily diary.
- Keep and file all receipts.

7

Insurance Coverage on the Road

There are four basic types of insurance coverage to think about when you're planning a business trip. The first is **health insurance**, which covers you for hospitalization and various medical expenses, just as your regular hospitalization and major medical policies do. The second is **personal accident insurance** (sometimes called ''flight insurance'' or ''travel accident insurance''), which pays you a fixed sum for ''loss of life, sight, or limbs'' while you're on a plane or en route to or from the airport in a motorcoach or limousine. Policies of this type are available covering from $25,000 to about $200,000.

The third kind of insurance covers damage, theft, or loss of your personal belongings at home or when you're traveling, and usually comes under the designation **personal articles floater,** which is purchased separately, or added to, an existing homeowner's policy. The fourth kind of insurance is **excess valuation insurance**, which is purchased from the airline upon your departure at a fixed rate per $100 of coverage, and which covers your baggage for theft, damage, or loss only when it is in the possession of the airline. A similar kind of insurance is called **baggage and personal effects insurance.**

Health Insurance

Most good medical insurance policies cover policyholders whether they're at home or traveling. You may already be adequately covered for hospitalization and major medical expenses—speak to your insurance agent or your company insurance manager about your existing coverage. Blue Cross and Blue Shield, for example, covers policyholders at home and abroad, although the policyholder is usually required to pay the bills locally and to file for reimbursement when he or she gets home. Blue Cross and Blue Shield is also sticky about records and receipts, and they will nitpick if the wording on a claim isn't perfect. Be sure to find out before you go what kind of documentation is required.

For more information on medical coverage when traveling abroad, see Part 2, ''Travel Abroad: Planning for the World.''

Loss of Life . . . etc.

Personal accident insurance (travel accident or flight insurance) can be purchased from many travel agents or at the airport from dispensing machines for a single trip or flight only. Flight insurance covers you while you're on the plane; travel accident insurance covers you when you're on the plane or traveling to or from the airport in a limousine or motorcoach. This kind of insurance does not overlap your normal health insurance, since it does not cover any actual medical expenses incurred when you're traveling. It does pay you or your beneficiary a fixed compensation if one of three events should occur: you die; you lose a hand or foot, or both, or combinations thereof; you lose the vision in one or both eyes.

Some credit card companies offer cardholders automatic travel accident insurance policies when the plane ticket or other travel service is paid for with the credit card. American Express, for example, automatically provides their cardholders with a $75,000 travel accident policy as a privilege of membership. Additional travel insurance is offered to members at a group rate of about $3 for $250,000 worth of coverage.

Insuring Personal Possessions

For adequate protection, your personal possessions usually require itemized insurance coverage, since many general policies have a maximum cutoff point that does not relate to the actual value of the lost goods. This is the case with most homeowner's insurance policies, which restrict the amount recoverable for unitemized goods to as little as $100 per category. If the category is jewelry or furs, the insurance won't begin to cover your actual losses.

If you have a homeowner's insurance policy, check with your insurance agent to find out precisely what you're covered for when you're traveling. You may want to add a personal articles floater to your existing policy. This covers the declared value of your possessions, as individually itemized. It can be added to your existing homeowner's policy, or it can be purchased separately at a reasonable rate. It will cover the declared value of the goods you take with you on the trip, such as your watch, jewelry, expensive clothing, furs, electronic gear, samples, and so forth, against theft, loss, or damage, no matter where you are. Coverage of this type is usually based on the class or category of goods—furs, jewelry, cameras, clothing, etc. If you purchase articles while traveling that belong to an insured category, your new purchase will usually be automatically covered for a grace period of one to three months, without being specifically itemized.

Note that all insurance policies waive responsibility for everything, including you and your belongings, in case of "War . . . radioactive or nuclear contamination . . . vermin . . . or inherent vice . . ." (What, do you suppose, is inherent vice?)

Rates for personal articles floaters vary by the area in which you live and the type of articles insured. Your premium should be somewhere in the neighborhood of $1 to $2 for each $100 of insurance protection purchased. An insurance agent acquaintance of mine recommends that you insure only those valuables that you use constantly (and travel with), such as your watch and a favorite ring, which are most liable to loss or theft. Keep your other goodies at home locked up in a wall safe behind a painting, or in a bank safe-deposit box.

Excess Valuation/Baggage and Personal Effects

To make life easier for yourself, you might forget about the personal articles floater and instead purchase excess valuation insurance or baggage and personal effects insurance on a one-shot basis for each trip. Excess valuation insurance is purchased directly from the airlines at a favorable rate when you check in, and it covers your checked baggage against loss, theft, or damage over and above the airline's declared liability while it is in the possession of the airline. A long list of items, such as your camera and jewelry, is excluded from this coverage. For more information on it, see Part 4, "On the Road."

Baggage and personal effects insurance may be purchased from many travel agents or from dispensing machines at the airport. This insurance covers your baggage and your personal possessions (clothing, cameras, jewelry) for up to $2,000 against loss or damage anywhere in the world. Many items are excluded from this coverage, too: usually cash, securities, and professional papers.

Automobile Insurance

If you plan to rent a car on a business trip in the United States or abroad, be sure your collision and personal-injury insurance will cover you when you're driving a rental car. Protect yourself doubly by purchasing all available insurance offered by the car rental company. Note that some foreign car-rental agencies will not provide you with insurance protection unless you have a valid International Driving Permit (see Chapter 13, "If You Drive").

INSURANCE COVERAGE CHECKLIST

* Check existing medical insurance policy for national and international coverage.
* Find out how to make claims when medical expenses are incurred away from home.
* Buy travel accident insurance from a travel agent or airport dispensing machine; see if you are already covered by a credit-card policy.
* Check homeowner's policy for travel coverage of personal possessions; add personal articles floater.
* Plan to buy excess valuation insurance or baggage and personal effects insurance at the airport.
* Check automobile insurance for coverage abroad.

8

Making Every Trip Memorable

The world is as interesting as you make it. If you arrive in a city (any city, be it the City of Light or Omaha), and keep your nose to the grindstone during the day, then lock yourself in your hotel room with your business papers and a TV at night, your experience will be commensurately stimulating. But if you find out before you go what's of interest in the area, what people eat and the kind of music they play, the famous places to visit, and the famous native sons whose books and poems and plays you can read and whose art you can study, then you'll educate yourself and at the same time have a worthwhile experience.

Even if the things you experience turn out to be a bust, do them, with humor and a sense of adventure, just for the heck of it. I remember once being holed up on Gran Canaria Island working on a travel book, repeatedly reading exotic descriptions of the traditional *gofio* eaten by the indigenous Guanche people, and of the famous Canary Island wrinkled potatoes. *Gofio*, I finally found out, is a god-awful wheat or barley dumpling that tastes like papier-mâché. And wrinkled potatoes are just that—wrinkled potatoes. So what? I'm one of those simpleminded people who gets a kick out of knowing about things like *gofio* and Canary Island wrinkled potatoes, just for the fun of it.

There is a Canary Island wrinkled potato waiting for your discovery in every destination in the world. It might take the form of chitlins and corn pone. Or *Kalamari* and ouzo. Or *ceviche,* the raw fish served throughout the Andes. Or a *torte de guanabana* (a meringue pie made with soursop apples) in Venezuela. Or chitons peeled off the rocks and eaten raw in Bonaire in the Netherlands Antilles. (I was once handed one by a native scuba instructor and I actually ate it. It was disgusting.)

Or your Canary Island wrinkled potato might be something to soothe another of your senses. Like beautiful paintings in the local museum. Or leather-bound books in the local library. Or fabulous country and western or blues or jazz or hard rock or New Wave or Bobby Short or fado or bouzoukia or flamenco, or any of the beautiful and soulful or jarring and pure-energy sounds made by every culture and subculture everywhere.

Plan to visit an Indian reservation in your spare time on your next business trip to a western U.S. city. Read the leading anthropologists of the area before you go. Or plan to go to a ranch and ride a horse. Play golf. Visit a health club. A special institute. A university. An antiques center. A crafts center. An archeological dig. A historical monument. Or a seafood restaurant down by the harbor.

If you know a little about the area you're going to before you go, something about its history and culture and literature and architecture and economics and politics and sports and natural history, you'll have a point of reference or two that will guide you to interesting encounters once you're actually there.

And you'll find people. People who are interested in the world usually manage to find one another as a by-product of shared activities. People who are not interested in the world usually manage to find other people as boring as they are. Or they stay completely to themselves and find nobody at all.

If your passion is business, learn something about the economy of the area. If it's Omaha and your business is grain, read *The Merchants of Grain* by Dan Morgan, and study the world flow of commodities, the history of agriculture, and the domestication of wild foodstuffs. Plan to visit the grain exchange and a wheat farm. Stick your nose inside a grain elevator.

In short, look beyond the confines of your professional functioning. Like most everyone else in this age of specialization, you are probably a specialist of some sort managing some aspect of business that interrelates with a hundred other aspects of the same business, and that keeps you so busy you never have the chance to stick your head outside into the light. It's the allegory of Plato's cave. You're looking at shadows, partial truths etched in the darkness, secluded from the full dimensions and color perceivable in the bright daylight. By all means, stick your head out into the bright sunlight. Find out what makes your job and your company and your business and your competitors and your suppliers and your associates and yourself tick.

There's another thing to do before leaving on a business trip. Find someone who knows someone in the area you're traveling to. There are no contacts better than friends of friends or friends of your family or acquaintances of your great-aunt or old school chums or former associates of the guy whose office is adjacent to yours. Before leaving for a business trip, ask everyone you know whom they know in Omaha. Get the names and addresses and telephone numbers. Have your friends call for you or write letters of introduction. And call the contacts yourself before you leave, explaining who you are and why you are calling. Then extend an invitation for dinner, brunch, breakfast, or a drink after work.

Also contact every organization, club, or association you have any affiliation with to see what they may have cooking at your destination: alumni associations, commercial interest clubs, health clubs, civic organizations, charitable groups, bird watchers, stamp collectors, anything.

If you don't belong to any groups, join some. Use the organization as a point of reference that will guide you to new people and new activities. Even if you just get your country club to line you up with a golf club at your destination, think of what a great weekend or free morning you could have.

The activities and points of reference you look for depend entirely on your personal interests, the possibilities in the area you're going to, and the amount of free time you'll have. Whatever you do to make the experience of business travel a little more rewarding, do it. There's not one reason in the world why you shouldn't take advantage of every opportunity for fun, personal development, and sharing.

BACKGROUND BRIEFING CHECKLIST

- Buy a guidebook to your destination.
- Find out what's of special interest and establish a free-time project.
- Get reading material (local histories, natural phenomena, authors, poets) on the area.
- Contact friends of friends and extend an invitation.
- Look for shared activities through clubs, groups, and societies.
- Plan ahead what free-time activities you will pursue.

Part 2

TRAVEL PLANNING: FOR THE WORLD

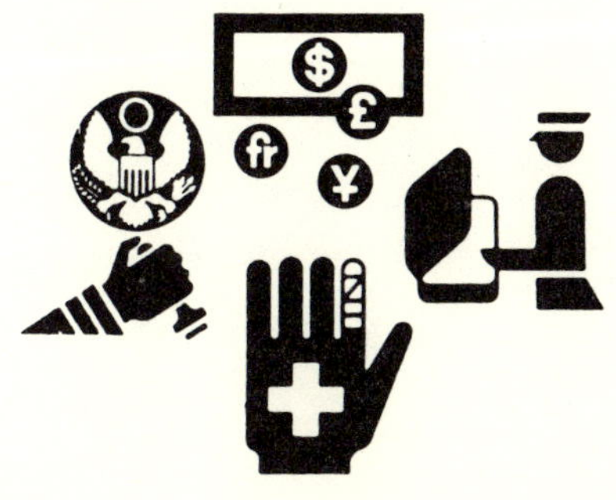

9

Vive la Différence

Packing your briefcase with a language primer and a guidebook to Gothic cathedrals promises more excitement than packing a city map of Des Moines, Iowa, and a report on corn futures. But there's a trade-off. Business travel abroad can present as many problems as blessings, especially when you're in a country you've never traveled to before. Problems like not understanding the language. Or, in countries with nonphonetic alphabets, not even knowing which button to push on elevators when the floors are indicated not in numbers, but in words. Or, after you've just traveled 3,000 miles to make a tenuous business appointment, trying to confirm it over a telephone antedating the Battle of Verdun. Or nearly missing an appointment while waiting for your room-service breakfast, which finally arrives charmingly presented on a silver tray with a pink linen napkin and a fresh rose in a white porcelain vase, an hour and a half after you rang for it.

Vive la différence—provided you do your homework and know what to expect, which, for international travel is even more important than for business travel at home.

COUNTRY BRIEFING

The first thing to do when planning an international business trip is to obtain literature on your destination from a travel agent, airline, or tourist bureau, and buy a good guidebook to the area you're going to.

Try to find a serious guide like one of the *Blue Guide* series, or Nagel's Encyclopedia-Guides, which give real facts and figures, history, and a sense of place, not just a lot of platitudes about charming churches.

A good general reference book to have on hand for travel all over the world is *Pan Am's World Guide*, which, in over 1,000 pages, covers more than 120 countries and is updated periodically. It contains all kinds of information ranging from local business hours and electric current to lively briefings on what to see and do. You can get the *World Guide* from most bookstores, or by writing to the attention of the book's redoubtable editor, Ms. Maureen Hickey, Sales Promotion Department, Pan American World Airways, Pan Am Bldg., New York, New York 10166. Send $8.95, plus $1 for postage and handling.

Be sure the guidebooks you buy include legible maps of your destination cities, or try to buy separate maps at your local bookstore. National airlines and tourist offices are also possible sources of guidebooks and maps, although their publications often are slanted more toward generating business than toward imparting unprejudiced information.

If you find it impossible to get good travel guides, maps, and source material in your local bookstore, contact **The Complete Traveller** or **The Hammond Map & Travel Center** (see Chapter 1, ''Travel Planning like a Pro,'' for addresses and telephone numbers).

Once you've tracked down the guidebooks and maps you need, start learning the basics about each area you'll be traveling to. Find out the name of the international airport. Learn what kind of transportation exists from the airport to the downtown area, how much it costs, and which is the most efficient way to go. Find the location of each of the leading hotels, and select the one most convenient to your business appointments (which, by this time, you've targeted on your map).

Check the weather charts and estimate what the weather will be like when you are there. Remember, the seasons reverse when you cross the equator. It's winter in Buenos Aires, Auckland, and Mbabane, Swaziland, in June, July, and August; summer in December, January, and February. Tropic zones usually vary only by wet and dry season, although high-altitude cities, like those in the Andes, are topcoat cold even near the equator. During tropical rains, which are usually impenetrable downpours, nobody goes out; they wait instead for the rain to stop, which it invariably does in a matter of minutes. If you'll be on a tight business schedule in a tropical area during the rainy season and won't have 20 minutes to wait under a palm tree, be sure to carry a collapsible umbrella.

Most guidebooks will give you some indication of what to wear in each city—whether it's formal or informal, or whether you'll need extremely lightweight clothes or thermal underwear. In all temperate climates with medium to heavy annual rainfall, always be prepared with some kind of portable rain gear.

You'll also need to know the prevailing business hours and siesta times, and prolonged national or religious holidays that may interrupt your business schedule (Carnival in Rio, Semana Santa in Spain, Ramadan in Moslem countries, etc.).

Local customs should also be examined for clues as to etiquette and attitudes toward women traveling on their own. In most European destinations, you can usually expect standards of behavior equivalent to what you'd find in the United States—with some modifications (see the discussion of Latin attitudes in Chapter 23, ''Brief Encounters''). But in other parts of the world, such as the Moslem countries, women are not treated equally. In Saudi Arabia, for example, you should know before you go that women are expected to cover their arms and knees, and they should never smoke in public or in front of business associates unless the host lights up first.

NOTE: For very useful information about proper decorum for women in the Orient, *The Women's Guide to the Orient*, published by Japan Air Lines, contains specific information regarding social etiquette in 11 Oriental destinations. Did you know that pointing with the forefinger is unspeakably rude in Malaysia? Use a closed fist and your thumb instead. Or that in Japan it is considered rude to wear your overcoat into the office of a business associate? (For more information on JAL's excellent publications, see Chapter 12).

Before you go, you should also check your guidebooks, as well as recent periodicals, for information regarding local politics. If the country is run by a fat colonel who took over in a coup, you want to be prepared to see the troops and submachine guns, and to keep your opinions to yourself. You should also find out what's happening currently in that part of the world. If Italy or Argentina are besieged with kidnappings, or if the country is in the midst of a civil war or witnessing a volcanic eruption, you might want to know about it before you go.

COUNTRY BRIEFING CHECKLIST

- Obtain international guidebooks, maps.
- Familiarize yourself with:
  Airport information
  City layout/local transportation
  Climate
  Social structure
  Etiquette/business practices
  Politics

10

International Entry Requirements

Generally, U.S. and Canadian citizens do not need passports to visit the Caribbean or Mexico, but they do usually need tourist cards, which are distributed and filled out on the plane or at the border. They also need some evidence of citizenship or residence upon return—usually a birth certificate or voter registration card is required (if in doubt, take your passport).

Travelers from the United States to Western Europe need valid passports only. Most other countries require shots (yellow fever, smallpox, or cholera), visas, transportation tickets to onward destinations, or other special documents (such as bank statements affirming financial solvency). There are many exceptions to these rules, and as the rules change frequently you'd be wise to check the special entry requirements with the country's embassy or consulate. Examples of typical complications: Brazil requires smallpox and yellow fever inoculations only if you are traveling from an infected area, but requires a yellow fever inoculation certificate if you're headed for the Belém area. Another typical variation: Bulgaria does not require visas of travelers who enter for more than 48 hours and stay for less than two months, provided the travelers have prepaid at least three days' worth of hotels, meals, and other ground services through Balkantourist (the Bulgarian government tourist organization) in the United States, Europe, or at the border. Only travelers entering without prepaid vouchers are required to obtain entry visas.

Many other types of inoculations such as for infectious hepatitis, plague, typhus, typhoid fever, dengue fever, and routine immunizations such as diphtheria, polio, and tetanus are recommended or required in some countries in certain circumstances. The most complete international immunization information I've come across is the *World Immunization Chart* distributed with membership in **IAMAT** (International Association for Medical Assistance to Travellers)—see Chapter 15.

Passports

To obtain a passport, U.S. citizens must apply in person to the Passport Division of the Department of State, or to the U.S. Passport Agency, which has offices located in Boston, Chicago, Detroit, Honolulu, Houston, Los Angeles, Miami, New Orleans, New York, Philadelphia, San Francisco, Seattle, Stamford (Connecticut), and Washington, D.C. (see "Directory of U.S. Government Services," page 302). In other U.S. cities, you may apply to the Clerk of the nearest Federal Court, and at some post offices.

To obtain a passport, you must furnish the following items:

- A previous passport, or a birth certificate (or copy thereof), affixed with a certified registrar's signature and seal. If you do not have such proof of birth, check with the passport office to find out what other documents are acceptable.
- Other proof of identity, such as a driver's license or government identification card of any kind (credit cards, library cards, and social security cards don't count).
- Fourteen dollars ($10 passport fee plus $4 execution fee) in the form of a check (personal, certified, or traveler's), money order, bank draft, or cashier's check. Most passport agencies refuse to accept cash.
- Two prints of the same recent photograph, 2″ × 2″ in size, showing a frontal view of your face (measuring not less than 1″ or more than 1⅜″ from the chin to the top of the hair), printed on nonglossy paper in either black and white or color, and taken not less than six months previously. Vending machine photos and full-length photos are not acceptable. Both photos should be signed in the center of the reverse side.

In certain circumstances, you can apply for your passport by mail to the nearest passport agency and save money in the process, provided:

- Your previous passport is less than eight years old.
- You are able to submit your passport by mail with an application.

- Your previous passport was not issued before your eighteenth birthday.
- You do not wish to include a family member on your passport.
- You are not applying for an official diplomatic, or no-fee passport.

To apply for a passport by mail, send a check or money order for $10 along with your old passport, a filled-out application (Form DSP-82, available from passport agencies and many travel agencies), and two passport photographs signed in the center of the reverse side.

Allow several weeks for your passport to be issued, or as much as several months if you're applying by mail in the busy summer season. If you plan to do a lot of traveling, request a passport containing 48 pages instead of the normal 24. Once issued, the passport is valid for five years.

Tip: When you're getting your passport photos taken, have six or eight extra prints made and keep them in the back of your wallet in case you need them for an international driver's license, visa, or other document.

Tip Number Two: If you're in a big rush to get your passport, try soliciting the aid of a representative of an airline. A few years ago, a very helpful lady at Pan Am got my passport application around the corner from the back office and saved me hours of waiting on the tourist-crowded lines.

Visas

Technically, visas are special permits issued by a government to foreign travelers, giving the travelers permission to enter the country, often under specific circumstances and for a limited period of time. Requirements vary by country—some countries require visas plus onward tickets or bank letters; others ask for documents stating why you have come. For a thorough briefing, obtain a brochure entitled *Visa Requirements of Foreign Countries,* published by the Department of State several times a year, and available for $1 from your nearest passport agency, or from the Superintendent of Documents, U.S. Government Printing Office, Washington, D.C. 20402.

If the country you're planning to visit requires a visa, apply at the nearest consulate of that country, or at the country's embassy in Washington, D.C. Some travel agents are also equipped to help you get visas. Allow plenty of time to obtain a visa, especially if you're requesting one by mail. The national airline or national tourist office of the country may be able to issue visas or expedite your application—be sure to contact them if one is near. Visas are also usually obtainable abroad at the country's consular office or embassy in major capitals or in a neighboring country.

If you're planning to carry a lot of business samples, you may need to obtain a commercial visa that will permit you to bring your samples into the country without paying duty, as well as take them back out again. If you're not bringing in samples and cannot otherwise be identified as a business traveler, it may be easier to apply for a tourist visa and save the complication of answering a lot of confusing questions.

Some visas are issued as separate documents, while others are stamped on a page in your passport, then filled out and signed. You may be required to pay a fee (tax deductible if your trip is for business purposes), and/or produce signed photographs of yourself. Always, you will have to produce your current, valid U.S. passport.

Note to Noncitizens: If you are a U.S. resident, but not a holder of a U.S. passport, you will most probably be required to show a Treasury Sailing Permit (Form 1040C) when you embark from the United States, to prove that you've paid your federal taxes. Treasury Sailing Permits may be obtained from the nearest District Director of Internal Revenue. You'll need to show your Green Card, the passport of your country, tickets for travel, and assorted financial documents. Call the Internal Revenue District Office nearest you to find out what's required in your case.

Inoculations

All officially required inoculations must be recorded on the yellow International Certificates of Vaccination, available from most private physicians, at municipal and U.S. health clinics, and from passport agencies. To be valid, the certificate must be completed with your name, sex, and date of birth. Each inoculation recorded in it must be separately entered, dated, and signed by a doctor, and stamped with the seal or designation of an officially accredited vaccination center (your family doctor may well have this accreditation). Since many vaccinations are not effective for several days after you receive the inoculation—and are not accepted by customs officials until then—be sure to allow sufficient time before your scheduled departure for the shot to "take."

Smallpox: Vaccinations extend for three years after the inoculation and are valid beginning eight days after the date of the first successful primary vaccination, or, on the day of the inoculation if it is a revaccination. Since the World Health Organization announced the virtual eradication of this disease recently, many countries, including the United States, have dropped it from their entry requirements.

Yellow Fever: Vaccinations may be given only at official Yellow Fever Vaccination Centers (see your local phone book under ''U.S. Public Health Service''), and your certificate must be stamped by the center to be validated. Yellow Fever vaccinations are valid for 10 years, beginning 10 days after the date of the vaccination; or from the day of a revaccination.

Cholera: Vaccinations may be given by private physicians or professional medical groups. They are valid for only six months beginning six days after the first injection.

Other immunizations that may be recommended for various international destinations are typhus, typhoid fever, plague, infectious hepatitis, and dengue fever (a mosquito-borne disease, often deadly, endemic to parts of Australia, New South Wales, and Southeast Asia). Routine immunizations against polio, tetanus, and diphtheria are also advisable, especially if you'll be traveling in out-of-the-way places away from medical assistance.

The yellow International Certificates of Vaccination also contain a spot for your ophthalmic information. As a precaution, have your ophthalmologist fill in prescription information for your glasses or contact lenses here.

For further information, request a free booklet entitled *Health Information for the International Traveler* from the Superintendent of Documents, U.S. Government Printing Office, Washington, D.C. 20402.

ENTRY REQUIREMENTS CHECKLIST

- Renew or obtain passport.
- Check visa or other document requirements.
- Obtain Treasury Sailing Permits for noncitizens.
- Obtain necessary immunizations.
- Inform yourself of advisable health precautions for your destination.

11

Coping with Customs

You have two concerns regarding U.S. Customs: (1) how to bring back what you took out of the country without paying duty on it; and (2) how to bring new purchases into the United States and pay only the minimum duty.

Customs also means getting yourself, your belongings, and your business materials into the countries you visit, but this is usually not a problem. Most countries permit you to bring in standard tourist articles such as a camera, radio, or phonograph, a small typewriter, sports gear, and a carton or two of cigarettes, without challenging you or imposing a duty assessment. Your briefcase and papers, a small dictaphone, recorder, or calculator won't be questioned. However, if you're traveling with an unusual number of trade samples—or some very valuable samples—you should take the precaution of bringing a letter written on your company letterhead (plus some copies), addressed ''To Whom It May Concern,'' and stating that the materials you're carrying are not intended for personal purposes or resale. Or you may require a commercial visa or an international permit, sometimes called a *carnet*. Call the trade division of the embassy or consulate of the countries you're going to visit.

Generally, it's the U.S. Customs you've got to prepare for. Before you go, register all your valuables (jewelry, imported cameras, tape recorders, calculators) with the nearest customs district office or customs regional office. Or plan to register your possessions at the office at the international airport before you embark from the United States. At JFK Airport in New York, U.S. Customs does not have agents in all terminals, and you sometimes are required to check your bags, then walk across highways, grassy malls, and dirt construction sites to reach the customs office in another terminal. In any case, plan on allowing sufficient time for this maneuver. There will probably be a line at the customs office and a short to long wait. The customs officer will ask to see everything you plan to declare, so be sure you have the articles with you, not packed in the bags you just checked in. You will be given a certificate of registration and asked to write a description of each article, which the officer will then examine before stamping and signing the certificate. Keep the certificate with your documents and show it to the examining customs agent when you re-enter the United States. Precision in your description of your valuables will make everything clear when you return and save you a bundle of time and money. Note that your certificate is good for an unlimited number of trips outside the United States—take it with you every time you go and are carrying some or all of the articles listed.

When you make purchases abroad, keep all receipts in your handbag or wallet so you can produce them for the U.S. Customs agent upon your return, if requested. (If you plan *not* to declare an item, be sure the receipt for it is not carefully filed among your other receipts.)

DUTY FREE

The duty-free allowance for U.S. residents returning from abroad has been raised to $300 on the premise that the trinkets you used to be able to buy abroad for $100 now cost three times that much. At least. That means that for every international trip of 48 hours or more (provided you have claimed no exemptions within 30 days), you may bring home goods worth $300 (based on fair retail value) without having to pay any import assessment. If you are returning from the U.S. Virgin Islands, American Samoa, or Guam, you may bring in $600 worth of goods duty free, plus four liters (or 135 ounces) of alcoholic beverages, a kindness that has been extended to those islands since they rely primarily on tourism for revenue.

From all other destinations, if you have not exceeded your exemptions and are returning with no more than one quart of alcoholic beverages, 200 cigarettes (one carton), or 100 cigars, you may fill in just the top part of the customs form distributed to you on the aircraft, and make an oral declaration to the customs officer when you return.

If you have spent more than your allowance, you are obliged to record your purchases item by item, giving the cost of each item or its equivalent in dollars. This includes gifts and clothes purchased abroad that you're wearing (for which you will be given about a 25 percent discount). The duty on goods over and above your $300 exemption will be taxed at a flat rate of 10 percent for the first $600. Over $600, duty will be assessed individually according to the particular item, its classification, and value. Whether you plan to give an oral declaration or not, be sure to pack all your declarable purchases in one suitcase. (If you're returning from a $600 duty-free zone, the second $600 worth of goods will be charged at a flat rate of 5 percent.)

Restrictions

Be aware before you go of U.S. Customs restrictions on products made from endangered species of wildlife (tortoiseshell jewelry, crocodile bags and shoes, and some kinds of furs—leopard, cheetah, and others). If you try to import articles made of these materials, they will most likely be confiscated from you at customs, with no compensation. The government also bans meats, vegetables, fruits, and other fresh food products under almost all circumstances. Your jar of Fortnum and Mason marmalade is safe—only the unprocessed delectables are verboten.

Also be aware that virtually everything you take out of the country is liable for duty when you return. That includes foreign-made articles of clothing previously purchased abroad, and imported garments you have bought in the United States. If you're taking your old Burberry raincoat to London and a new St. Laurent suit from the Rive Gauche boutique on Madison Avenue to Paris, be sure to take the sales slip or other proof of purchase with you. I've found that this isn't usually a problem unless the clothes are obviously new and were originally purchased in the destination you've just returned from. Nevertheless, forewarned is forearmed.

Duty Rates

Duty rates vary according to the type of article and where it comes from. The U.S. Treasury makes a big distinction between most favored nations—on whose goods a reasonable rate of duty is charged—and a big list of Communist baddies ranging from Albania to Tannu Tuva in the U.S.S.R.—whose goods are taxed at a rate of up to 110 percent of their value. The U.S. Customs' handly little booklet called *Know Before You Go* (Available free of charge from the U.S. Customs Service, P.O. Box 7118, Washington, D.C. 20044, or your local customs bureau—see Appendix), contains a fascinating list of goods in both categories. Example: Pearls, temporarily or permanently strung with a clasp, will be assessed from 12 percent to 27 percent if they come from a favored nation, but 45 percent to 110 percent if they were bought in a Communist nation.

Truffles, you will happy to know, are duty free.

There's another category of countries called "GSPs," meaning "generalized system of preferences." The GSP list includes goods manufactured or handcrafted in developing nations and admitted to the United States duty free to help the exporting nations improve their balance of payments. It's worthwhile getting a copy of the GSP brochure from the U.S. Customs (same address as above) to find out what items from which countries can be brought in without taxation. There are some potentially good buys: silver from Peru (often of good quality, with some antique pieces available); cut but unset stones (excluding emeralds and diamonds, but not excluding aquamarines, amethysts, and other sparklers) from Brazil; big chunks of amber from Morocco.

A WORD ABOUT DRUGS

You're a dope (pun intended) if you take any illegal powders, pills, grasses, leaves, fungi, sugar cubes, resins, or ampules with you when you go abroad unless they're honestly labeled and prescribed medications. Even with prescription drugs, you can avoid suspicion and time-wasting examinations by taking only what you need for the current trip, and leaving all medications in their original bottles. If the medications contain any narcotic or habit-forming drugs, have your doctor write out a certificate attesting to the legitimacy of their use.

Most countries regard the possession of hard or soft drugs as a serious crime punishable by prison sentence. According to the U.S. Bureau of Consular Affairs, close to 2,000 U.S. citizens have been incarcerated in foreign jails, many of them on drug-related charges. Sentences for drug abuse are worth thinking about: from two to ten years in most countries, a minimum of six years at hard labor plus a fine in some countries, and death in other nations (Turkey, Algeria, and Iran, among them).

CUSTOMS CHECKLIST

- Register valuables with U.S. Customs before you go.
- Obtain duty-free information; plan duty-free purchases.
- Label all medicines.
- Obtain a doctor's certificate for narcotic or habit-forming medicines.
- Eliminate all drug remnants from your suitcases, handbags, and pockets.

12

Services for the International Business Traveler

The U.S. Government, foreign governments, embassies, trade commissions, private firms, and national airlines all provide some measure of service to business travelers, and it would be worth your while to take advantage of what they offer. Find out well in advance of your scheduled departure what guidelines, tips, advice, and services are available regarding sales and investment opportunities in your target countries. There's a lot of information to be gleaned from the experts, and you'll have a head start if you inquire before departure.

THE U.S. DEPARTMENT OF COMMERCE

For starters, the U.S. Department of Commerce maintains a fairly well-run division, the U.S. Commercial Service, which supplies contacts, tips, general information, and hard, cold data on foreign business opportunities. Most large city district officers of the Commerce Department have a U.S. Commercial Service division, with a useful research library and resident experts. It may take four or five phone calls to the Commerce Deartment before you manage to reach the right person. Ask to speak with an international trade specialist. There are about 47 U.S. Department of Commerce District Offices in the United States. Check your telephone directory.

The three principal services that are provided by the Department of Commerce to business travelers are the Agent Distributor Services

(ADS), the World Traders Data Report (WTDR), and the Trade Opportunities Program (TOP).

Agent Distributor Service

The Agent Distributor Service will provide the names and addresses of up to six foreign business contacts interested in your products or services. The Commerce Department needs from 30 to 60 days to get reports of interested agents or distributors from the field (through the U.S. Foreign Service); usually they request a catalogue or brochure that describes the nature of your business and your products. Requests are made by country: the cost of the service is $25 (per country).

World Traders Data Report

If you need a kind of Dun & Bradstreet profile of a foreign corporation, the Commerce Department will give you a World Traders Data Report. This is a study made by the U.S. Foreign Service based on a local company's sales, products, financial status, credit rating, and other factors. If the company has ever been investigated, the report will be on file in the Commerce Department's computers in Washington and can be pulled for you about two weeks after notification. If a new study has to be made, allow up to two months. To request a World Traders Data Report, write to the nearest Commerce Department district office or to the U.S. Department of Commerce, Room 1033, Washington, D.C. 20230. Ask for Form 431. The forms are free; the cost per report is $40 (as of press time).

Trade Opportunities Program

Commerce also operates the Trade Opportunities Program (TOP), which alerts subscribing corporations to the latest business developments and opportunities as reported in the dispatches of the U.S. Foreign Service. Reports, in the form of computer printouts, are made by matching the business specifications of the subscribing company against the data telexed from abroad. The company is charged a small fee for each printout, which is deducted from the subscription fee.

Other Services

In addition to ADS, WTDR, and TOP, the Commerce Department publishes a daily newsletter Monday through Friday, called the *Com-*

merce Business Daily, which lists all bids for U.S. Government contracts (mostly domestic, but with some international bidders). And commerce publishes a mind-boggling array of market reports and surveys on economic and commercial activities around the world. Among its publications: *Foreign Economic Trends* (reports on 100 countries), *Foreign Market Reports* (published monthly), *Overseas Business Reports,* and so on. The State Department also publishes economic and commercial material, some of which is distributed through the Commerce Department. To learn what's published and free of charge, write to the General Publications Division, Office of Media Services, Room 4827A, Department of State, Washington, D.C. 20520, and ask to be put on the mailing list.

Another government agency that is worth finding out about is the **Office of Commercial Affairs,** a division of the State Department, which may be reached at the Bureau of Economic and Business Affairs, Department of State, Washington, D.C. 20520; telephone (202) 632-0669. When planning your trip, you should call or write the office for information regarding what services they offer to international business travelers.

YOUR FRIENDS AT THE U.S. EMBASSY

There are about 250 U.S. Embassies and Consulates scattered around the world, which are supported by U.S. taxpayers' dollars, and, presumably, able and willing to offer you assistance when you're traveling abroad on business. Most embassies and consulates have a commercial attaché—otherwise known as the Economic Officer of the Commercial Section. He or she can advise you regarding local commerce laws, commercial visa and import/export regulations, and maybe even guide you to local contacts or sources of commercial information. Some Foreign Service assistance, such as the World Traders Data Report, is collected and compiled by the embassy or consulate at the destination, and then is made available to the public through the U.S. Department of Commerce.

To find out what types of business information are available from the U.S. Embassy or Consulate, a spokesperson for the State Department recommends that you write directly to the Economic Officer at your destination. State the nature of your business and the types of information or assistance you're seeking. For the names and addresses of key U.S. personnel, write to the Superintendent of Documents, U.S. Government Printing Office, Washington, D.C. 20402, and ask them to send you a brochure entitled **"Key Officers of Foreign Service Posts"** ($1.50 at press time). This booklet identifies the major players at all U.S. Embassies and Consulates, and it will permit you to contact the appropriate officer by name—a shrewd bit of diplomacy when you're asking for favors.

In addition to commercial information, U.S. Embassies and Consulates are equipped to handle many crises that befall U.S. travelers. If you're robbed and left penniless, for example, the embassy will almost always advance you sufficient funds to get back home. But they will place a mean-looking stamp in your passport that restricts its further use until the loan has been repaid in full.

Or, if you should get locked up in the pokey in some tragicomedy of misunderstanding, call the U.S. Embassy or Consulate immediately. Ask for legal assistance. The embassy may or may not be able to spring you, but they will confirm that your rights are being respected. In cases of minor infractions, they will usually help straighten out the snafu. (For additional comments on foreign imprisonment turn back to Chapter 11 and read the section entitled ''A Word about Drugs.'')

Other traveler services provided by the U.S. Foreign Service include:

- Lost passport replacement—good for 90 days
- Notary services (for a nominal fee)
- Absentee voting supervision
- Research libraries and information sources (also found at U.S. Information Service libraries)
- Warning and assistance in cases of civil disturbance.

Don't expect the U.S. Foreign Service to help you arrange transportation or accommodations, hold your mail, or cash personal checks. For a list of U.S. Embassies and Consulates in the major cities around the world, see the Appendix.

INTER-AMERICAN CHAMBERS OF COMMERCE

The American Chamber of Commerce, the many international branches of the Chamber of Commerce, and national trade organizations are other potentially helpful sources of trade information for international business travelers. Many countries operate chambers of commerce within the United States, with offices in Washington, D.C., New York, and other areas important to trade or with large immigrant populations. Check in your phone book for listings under the name of the country you plan to visit.

If you can't find the organization you're looking for in your local phone book, get in touch with the embassy of your destination country in Washington, D.C., its consulate nearest you, or its representative at the United Nations in New York. The embassy may be able to provide you with the same types of information and services offered by the Department of Commerce. It can't hurt to place a long-distance call. Ask to speak to the economic officer or the commercial attaché.

Also contact the U.S. Department of Commerce directly to see what international business services or information they offer. Write or call:

Bureau of International Commerce
U.S. Department of Commerce
Washington, D.C. 20230
Telephone (202) 377-5341

Other valuable sources of international trade information—sometimes provided for a fee—are:

World Trade Information Center
Department 1AB
One World Trade Center
New York, New York 10048
Telephone (212) 466-3063

Market Research Clearinghouse
500 Fifth Avenue
New York, New York 10036
Telephone (212) 354-2424

Common Market Information
Director of European Community
2100 M. Street, N.W.
Washington, D.C. 20037
Telephone (202) 872-8350

ASSISTANCE FROM THE INTERNATIONAL AIRLINES

Many airlines are keenly interested in soliciting the business of the frequent traveler, especially in these days of low-profit promotional fares. Some of the national airlines of foreign countries are well in advance of U.S. carriers in their awareness of the needs of the international business traveler, and in the services they provide.

No airline seems to have done quite as much as **Japan Air Lines,** which provides extensive service to business travelers, as well as some of the best guidebooks around.

JAL offers Global Club membership to passengers who have made ten transoceanic flights with JAL, and it permits Global Club members to use its First Class Sakura Lounges. The airline also provides a

Business Class service called Tachibana Cabin for Executive Class on most 747 flights, a section behind First Class reserved for executives who want peace and quiet.

In Tokyo, JAL provides business passengers with extensive office facilities in the Executive Service Lounge in the Imperial Hotel. Available free of charge are telephones for local calls, typewriters, calculators, and a bilingual staff to help you make contact with business people in your field. Photocopying service is available for a nominal fee, and moderately priced secretarial and translation services can be arranged on three days' notice.

JAL (as well as Pan Am and Northwest Orient) will arrange to print business cards for you in English/Japanese or English/Chinese for about $5 per one hundred cards—allow two full weeks for this service. If you're in a rush, request 24-hour service at the JAL Executive Service Lounge in Tokyo. (This service is not available outside Japan.)

JAL will help you arrange business contacts with Japanese companies through JETRO (Japan External Trade Organization). They will also provide you with background briefings and analyses of Japanese companies, the Japanese economy, and various industries, pulling the reports from a well-stocked computer data bank. If you're carrying heavy samples, JAL will arrange to pick up your cases from you upon arrival and transport them to one of five major cities in Japan, and then pick them up again and return them (for a reasonable fee). JAL Executive Hotel Service will provide you with a guaranteed room in a top hotel at a favorable rate (in most cities), plus provide you with a 6 P.M. check-out time on your last day. For this service, JAL must have 24-hours' notice.

The JAL guidebooks are written by knowledgeable, witty, English-speaking insiders and can be ordered by mail from Japan Air Lines Literature Distribution Center, P.O. Box 618, Old Chelsea Station, New York, New York 10011. (With typical Japanese efficiency, my order of books arrived within a week after I mailed in my request.) Among the best for women business travelers: the very useful *Executive's Guide to the Orient, Business in Japan, Woman's Guide to the Orient, Business Guide to the People's Republic of China,* and the amusing *VIP's Confidential Guide to Tokyo.* This last book and the *Businessman's after Hours Guide to Japan* both include sections on "the pleasure principle"—for the most part exclusive of pleasure for women—but so what. The rest is interesting and useful.

Air France defines its business traveler services in three categories: the Concorde, which U.S. National Press Manager Peter Steward describes as a "super executive jet" (see Chapter 2); First Class—called "Première;" and Business Class—known as "Classe Affaires."

In addition to a special check-in counter at the airport, seat reservations at the time of booking, special boarding of the aircraft, and a separate seating compartment, Classe Affaires service provides passengers with: "preferential access" to accommodations and business facilities at Meridien Hotels (owned by Air France and located in Paris, New York, Houston, Boston, and some 35 international destinations). This service—available only when you book the hotel through Air France—can be of considerable value, especially in overcrowded cities like Cairo, where hotel rooms are extremely hard to get. On middle-distance routes (mostly in Europe), Air France has introduced something called "New European Service," an upgraded and expanded Business Class service in place of First Class.

In addition to its Business Class facilities, Air France has a frequent-travelers' club called "Service Plus." Membership is established at the local Air France office, presumably on the basis of how many times a year you fly Air France. With Service Plus membership, you receive a membership card that entitles you to preferential treatment at the airport and in the air, with access to special check-in counters and lounge, plus a guaranteed seat on your flight. Service Plus exists as a recognizable entity in all of Air France's 150 worldwide destinations from the City of Light to the South Pacific.

Last but not least, Air France has recently published a most helpful booklet entitled *Business Traveler's Guide*. It contains business tips and useful addresses of all sorts, including U.S. banks and brokerage houses, mostly in Paris. If you want one, write to Air France, Dept. NYC P.B., 1350 Avenue of the Americas, New York, New York 10019.

British Airways has a Business Class service called "Super Club," which operates only on transatlantic routes. Special seating in a Super Club cabin is provided (with just six seats across on 747 aircraft). Seat reservations are guaranteed, and drinks and headsets are provided free of charge.

In addition, BA operates a frequent-travelers' club called "Executive Cardholders," which used to be free but, at press time, is about to require payment for membership. Cardholders get to check in at the First Class ticket counter, have the use of 56 lounges worldwide (with free drinks provided), and they can cash personal checks for up to $50 in local currency. A two-for-one discount is also offered, in which a cardholder and spouse can share a room for the single room rate—this service is available in selected hotels worldwide.

Business travelers on BA may also take advantage of Worldwide Business Centres, a company that provides a wide range of services to full-fare-paying BA passengers, some free, some on a pay-as-you-use basis. The centers exist in 13 international destinations. You may have your mail, telephone messages, and telexes sent there free of charge. You may rent an office, hire a secretary, and have your name listed in the building directory or the local telephone directory (for a reasonable fee), and you may take advantage of copying, messenger, courier, and other services. To apply for Executive Cardholder membership, or to inquire about the Centres, apply at your nearest BA ticket office, or at the BA counter at the airport.

Lufthansa German Airlines has given careful consideration to the needs of international business travelers and has prepared a predictably thorough set of travelers' aids and services. In addition to hotel and rental-car reservations, Lufthansa will also reserve a conference room for you or arrange translation or secretarial service at cost in many of their 107 destinations worldwide (make the request at least five days in advance). If you need bilingual business cards, Lufthansa will print them for you for a nominal fee—request the cards when you make your reservation, then pick them up when you arrive at your destination. The airline will also hold mail for Business and First Class travelers in its local offices around the world: request a set of "Executive Traveler Mail Pick-up" labels when you reserve your seat.

Useful Lufthansa publications include the *Lufthansa City Guide* series, the handy little *Business Guide to Getting Around Overseas,* and a massive compendium entitled *Trade Fairs and Exhibitions,* which is published annually and contains information on what appears to be every important trade fair in the world. Lufthansa also publishes a wonderful booklet called *Fitness in the Chair,* which is discussed in Chapter 22.

For business travelers wishing to learn more about businesses abroad, Lufthansa packages a series of tours called "Profitours," which permit participants to study "the operations and procedures of industries and professions" in Germany, France, Belgium, Italy, and England. Travelers to conventions and congresses in Germany are also given complete assistance ranging from itinerary planning to post-convention tours.

Well done, Lufthansa. For information on business traveler services and publications, contact your travel agent or the local Lufthansa ticket office.

Other Special Airline Services: A Summary

Alia, Royal Jordanian Airlines: Write Alia, Middle East Travel Information Service, P.O. Drawer A, Carle Place, New York 11514, for a helpful "Travel Pak" (no charge), which includes useful tips on how to negotiate the mysterious shifting sands of the Middle East.

El Al: On the airline's "King Solomon" service, a limousine will pick you up at the plane at the Ben-Gurion Airport in Tel Aviv and whisk you across the tarmac to the immigration counter—free for all full-fare-paying business travelers.

SAS Scandinavian Airlines: Write to SAS Marketing, 138-02 Queens Boulevard, Jamaica, New York 11435, and ask to be put on the mailing list for the quarterly *Report for Business Executives,* which is all about the economies of Scandinavia and business opportunities there. NOTE: For all airline services, be aware that business traveler services are apt to change at the whim of the latest V.P. of Marketing, and that none of the above services are to be regarded as permanent.

Sleeperettes

Back in the good old days of aviation, travelers got to climb between fresh white sheets for a real night's sleep on long transoceanic flights. The good old days are here again, almost, as the international, long-haul carriers struggle to win First Class and full-fare passengers. A sleeperette, which comes in many configurations and as many names, is a berth or reclining seat that lets you stretch out and really sleep. **Singapore Airlines** was one of the first to start the trend when they provided "Slumberettes" (berths) and "Snoozers" (reclining seats) on their Singapore-London and Sinagpore-San Francisco flights. Since then, many airlines have added this service, among them **JAL** with "Skysleeper" berths on may 747 flights, **Pan Am** and **British Airways** with "Sleeperettes" for all First Class passengers flying on large-bodied aircraft, and **Air France** with "Jet Snoozers," also offered to First Class passengers on most international flights. **Swissair, Qantas,** and **Philippine Airlines** are among the many other carriers that offer snoozer-recliners. Most of the time they're free of charge, although some airlines add a surcharge in the neighborhood of $50 to $100. Book berths and reclining seats in advance, as in most cases their availability is limited.

INTERNATIONAL BUSINESS TRAVELER CHECKLIST

* Contact the U.S. Department of Commerce regarding ADS, WTDR, and TOP.
* Check with international Chambers of Commerce.
* Ask international airlines for guides, business traveler services, and facilities.
* Jot down the telephone number and address of the U.S. Embassies or Consulates located in your foreign destination.

13

If You Drive

If you will need a car when traveling abroad, it's a good idea to get an **International Driving Permit**, available in the United States only from the Automobile Association of America. You'll need a valid U.S. driver's license, two signed passport photos, and $5. Apply at your local AAA in person, or by mail. If you apply in person, you may have the permit on the spot. By mail, allow several weeks.

Most European countries and other countries frequented by American travelers will accept your U.S. driver's license and do not require an International Driving Permit. Some countries where your U.S. license is valid include Belgium, Denmark, Finland, France, Great Britain, the Netherlands, Portugal, Spain, Sweden, and Switzerland. To be on the safe side, however, get a permit if you plan extensive international travel. Greece and Japan are among the nations requiring one. In some countries, you may also need an International Driving Permit to get auto insurance.

If you plan to rent a car, you'll find Avis and Hertz offices almost everywhere, and the English-based Godfrey Davis in most parts of Europe and the Middle East. When in doubt, the AAA will provide you with a list of reputable car rental companies in foreign destinations.

Rental car rates vary from country to country and are often considerably higher than rates in the United States. Check in advance so you can arrange to rent your car in a country where the cost is lowest. You may also have to pay a hefty surcharge (sometimes as much as $75) if you plan to leave the car in anything but a leading tourist destination.

Check in advance with your travel agent, the AAA, Hertz, Avis, or other car rental companies before fixing your itinerary.

When renting a car abroad, be prepared to rent a stick shift, since automatic transmissions are not favored in most parts of the world. And don't have high hopes about air conditioning. With gas (''petrol,'' in Europe) approaching the cost of pure gold, most of the world is too fuel-conscious to afford such a luxury.

When you book a rental car in another country, be sure you take with you the confirmation slip, or at least the leasing firm's own confirmation number, as proof of booking. This is especially important if you'll be traveling during the high season in popular tourist centers. If the company you book with does not have the type of car you requested, they should provide you with another car of a higher, more expensive category, a custom normally honored in the United States as well.

RULES OF THE ROAD

Driving habits in various parts of the world are as idiosyncratic as the national temperaments, and you'll just have to learn to accommodate them. In Britain, Ireland, Cyprus, the present and former British West Indies, Hong Kong, Singapore, Malaysia, and other outposts of what was the British Empire, remember to drive on the left side of the road. This takes some getting used to—you have to work the gears with your left hand instead of your right, and you frequently find yourself sailing self-righteously down the wrong side of the road directly into the oncoming traffic, swearing all the while at the crazy drivers. Also, as a pedestrian, watch your toes in countries where the traffic bears to the left. More than one visitor has been sideswiped by oncoming cars after carefully checking for traffic in the wrong direction.

When it comes to right-left gymnastics, the worst roads I've ever had to deal with were the strip roads in Zimbabwe Rhodesia. They consist of two narrow strips of pavement just a tire's width wide running down a long, dusty, unpaved road. The idea is that you ride down the middle of the road with your right and left wheels balanced on the narrow strip of pavement (a task in itself when your car is small and the wheels barely fit on the inside edges). When you see another car coming (which, fortunately, happens infrequently), you steer your car over to the left so that your right tires are on the left strip of pavement and your left tires are bouncing along in the dirt. The system works reasonably well in principle, but in reality, rain and erosion have washed away the dirt on either side of the narrow strips, sometimes to a depth of 10 or 12 inches. After negotiating those deep gullies at 60 miles an hour while balancing on a tightrope, all other driving situations become academic.

As far as mastering the driving habits of each country, I can only wish you a lot of luck. The worst drivers I've ever seen were in South Africa, Greece, and Portugal. In South Africa, there's a suicidal quality to the driving that I can only relate to the repressed hysteria of that nation's politics. In Portugal, large trucks pass directly into the oncoming lane and don't bother to move over or slow down to avoid running oncoming cars off the road. In Greece, every car and pedestrian you see will unquestionably do the most insane thing you can imagine. If there's a woman with a baby carriage on a narrow cement island in the middle of a six-lane highway, she will invariably push the carriage off the island and start crossing the road just as you bear down on her at 90 kilometers an hour. Or if there is a car parked at the side of the road, the driver will inevitably open the door into your traffic lane just as you approach, horn blaring.

There are two schools of thought on how to handle driving situations like these. One advises you to drive defensively with a capital D, which, in some places, means your best maneuver is to practically drive in reverse. The other school of thought advises you to drive in partial ignorance. In this situation, you pretend you are wearing a pair of blinders, like a horse, thereby eliminating from your responsibility all that's happening beside you or behind. Concentrate instead on the narrow wedge of activity directly in front of you. This, by the way, is the only way to get around a Parisian traffic circle.

International Road Signs

Most of the rest of the world has quite sanely subscribed to a series of pictographic road signs that tell you on the spot—with no translation required—what to expect in terms of driving conditions. Illustrated below are some of the international road signs, which you should become familiar with before taking off on your own. Most of the signs are self-explanatory. As a general rule, square-shaped signs inform, triangular signs warn, and round signs command.

Inform

Tourist
information

Fuel

Telephone

First-aid
station

Warn

Road narrows

Drawbridge

Slippery road

Children

Command

Speed limit

No U-turn

Horn blowing
prohibited

No passing

Driving Tips

As to the driving rules in specific countries, my friend Peter Verstappen, editor of many guidebooks (most recently the excellent *Rand McNally Economy Guide to Europe*, 1979), offers these driving tips:

Petrol: Outside the United States, purchase high-test petrol. The low-octane fuels are often barely a grade above kerosene, and your car engine will knock badly on them or actually konk out.

You will immediately notice that the price of gasoline in virtually every country except Kuwait and Venezuela is markedly higher than in the U.S.—a situation that is rapidly being equalized. It's not just the narrow streets of their medieval cities that have kept the Europeans from indulging in American-size cars—who can afford to drive them when it costs $50 to fill the tank?

Be sure to make a realistic appraisal of the cost of gasoline when you're planning your daily expense budget. Note that the Imperial gallon (in the U.K. and Ireland) is equal of 1.2 U.S. gallons (4.5 liters).

Traffic circles: In Europe, cars within a traffic circle must yield to cars entering the circle, except in Greece, Germany, Sweden, Great Britain, and Ireland, where the cars already in the circle have the right-of-way.

Streetcars: Under no circumstances attempt to pass a stopped streetcar: They're sacrosanct in European cities. When the trolley is in motion, you're free to attempt to get around it. Lots of luck.

Mountain driving: All over the Alps, uphill traffic has priority over downhill traffic. In Switzerland, yellow postal buses have right-of-way over other vehicles.

Parking: France, Denmark, and other countries have Blue Zones in which you are permitted to park for a limited period. Keeping track of your parking time is done on the honor system with the aid of a parking disk, a cardboard clock on which you position the hands to indicate the time of your arrival, and which then gets placed prominently on your windshield. Parking disks may be obtained from your hotel concierge, police and gas stations, post offices, and banks.

Spot fines: In many European countries, police may fine you on the spot for minor traffic violations (including jaywalking). Be prepared to pay as much as $60 or $80 if you get caught refusing to yield right-of-way, or committing some other traffic infraction.

Triangular warning signs: Many countries oblige drivers to carry triangular warning signs with reflector lights, which should be placed 50 or 100 feet behind a stopped car on the side of the road. If you're renting a car, be sure the car is equipped with one—you should find it in the trunk.

CB radios: These are forbidden or very carefully controlled in most countries outside the United States—if you were planning on bringing yours to speak with the European truck drivers, forget it.

For a more specific rundown on the rules of the road in various international destinations, inquire at the AAA for information and brochures. One more note: If you're one of those people rudely addicted to blowing his or her horn at every opportunity, be aware of the fact that the use of horns is forbidden in most European cities.

INTERNATIONAL DRIVING CHECKLIST

- Get International Driving Permit from AAA.
- Get destination road maps in advance.
- Rental car reservations:
  Get confirmation slip.
  Comparison shop for best rate.
  Check for drop-off surcharge.
- Familiarize yourself with international rules of the road.

14

International Money Matters

Traveler's Checks in the Local Currency

When you're planning a trip to one of the leading currency countries, you will probably find it to your advantage to purchase traveler's checks in the currency of that country before leaving the U.S.A. These will be issued by foreign travel companies, such as Thomas Cook, or by foreign banks, such as Barclays, and are available through branches of the foreign banks in the United States, or from American Express, Deak-Perera, Thomas Cook, or some U.S. banks. The most readily available foreign currency traveler's checks are German marks, Swiss francs, French francs, Canadian dollars, British pounds, and Japanese yen. Deak-Perera, the international foreign exchange company, issues traveler's checks in most major foreign currencies, with no commission charge. Deak-Perera also permits you to pay for your traveler's checks with a cash advance drawn on your Visa or Master Card account. (To find out what foreign-exchange companies operate in your city, look in the yellow pages under ''Foreign Money Brokers and Dealers.'')

There are several advantages to purchasing traveler's checks in the destination currency before you leave. First of all, you gain a considerable advantage in terms of a competitive exchange rate when you buy a foreign currency in the U.S. Second, it's more convenient to have local currency on hand when you arrive at your destination, instead of being obliged to go to the currency exchange at the airport, with the crowds and burden of your baggage added to the confusion.

Upon arrival, you should have some local change and small bills in your pocket with which to tip porters (should you be lucky enough to find them), and pay for a taxi, limo, or bus into town. Before you leave, purchase a Tip-Pack with $20 worth of change from Manfra, Tordella & Brookes (1 World Trade Center, Suite 3331, New York, New York 10048), or ask your bank to obtain coins in your destination currency.

CURRENCY REGULATIONS

Some nations restrict the amount of their own currency you can bring into the country upon arrival. This is because they don't want their own currency back, or, in some cases, taken out of the country, since it weakens their balance of payments. In these countries, you are usually required to make a currency declaration when you arrive at customs control. Included in your declared amount must be the local-currency traveler's checks you're bringing in.

Rules and regulations change radically all the time. You may want to study the chart below, which lists some countries that currently impose restrictions.

Country	Monetary Unit	Allowed In	Allowed Out
Austria	schilling	*	15,500
Brazil	cruzeiro	*	115,500
Finland	mark	*	3,000
France	franc	*	200 (unless more was declared on entry)
Greece	drachma	1,500	1,500
Hungary	forint	400	*
Italy	lira	200,000	200,000
Japan	yen	*	3,000,000
Norway	krone	1,000	1,000
Phillipines	peso	1,500	1,500
Portugal	escudo	5,000	5,000
Singapore	Singapore dollar	*	500
Spain	peseta	10,000	100,000 (business) 40,000 (tourist)

*Unrestricted

Country	Monetary Unit	Allowed In	Allowed Out
Sweden	krone	6,000	6,000
Turkey	lira	100	100
Yugoslavia	dinar	1,000	1,000

Keep in mind that many countries expect you to keep track of the traveler's checks you cash (whether in dollars or the local currency). You are sometimes requested to show your bank receipts on your way out at customs.

Also remember when leaving a country that some currencies—those that do not float on the international money market—cannot be redeemed for other currencies once you're out of that country. This is true of Brazilian cruzeiros and Jamaican dollars, for example, and for many other currencies as well. If you're using American dollar traveler's checks in the destination, cash no more than the amount you'll actually need while you're there, plus enough to pay the airport departure tax, if there is one.

EXCHANGE RATES

Currency exchange rates fluctuate so wildly that we don't attempt to give a currency conversion chart here, since it will undoubtedly be out of date by publication time. Ask your bank to provide you with a currency conversion chart. Or request one from the foreign-exchange company that supplies you with traveler's checks or small bills for tipping. Local currency rates are usually listed daily in big-city newspapers and in financial magazines.

The trick in establishing the value of a currency in relation to the U.S. dollar is to simplify the arithmetic so you can make calculations quickly in your head. There are different ways of going about this. For instance, if $1 (U.S.) is worth 57 drachmas, then one drachma is worth $.017. That gives a handy measure. If something costs 1,000 drachmas, you just multiply by .017 and move the decimal point over two digits—the item is worth $17.

The easiest way to get around this kind of mental gymnastics is to invest in one of those fabulous new little pocket calculators that cost less and less each year and will convert drachmas to dollars in a flash. Casio makes a great little machine called Melody 80 that not only will convert your money, but also has a digital clock, a calendar, and an alarm, and will wake you up to the strains of Mozart.

THE ADVANTAGE OF USING CREDIT CARDS

Often, there's a real advantage in paying for overseas purchases with your credit cards. You don't have to bother with currency conversions on the spot. And you don't have to pay the bill until you receive it at home two or three months later. You pay according to what the dollar was worth on the date of the purchase.

The leading credit card companies don't always give you the benefit of the doubt when it comes to currency rates. It's not unheard of for them to hold your bill until a more favorable rate comes up.

One way to cover yourself on this is to be sure the person from whom you make a purchase in a foreign destination writes clearly on your credit card slip the official exchange rate on the day of purchase. Armed with that, you'll have some basis for argument should the credit card company claim a more favorable rate of exchange.

EMERGENCY FUNDS

If you lose your traveler's checks or credit cards when abroad, or have them stolen, what do you do? First of all, you notify the issuing companies of the loss so they can immediately put out an alert to stop payment or acceptance of credit on your checks and cards.

Calling five or six credit card companies to alert them to a loss or theft is a bit difficult from some distant corner of the globe. Many credit card companies, as well as private concerns, offer a registering system that costs anywhere from $6 to $20 a year. American Express, for example, provides a service to cardholders that lets them pick up a new American Express card at almost any American Express office, usually within one business day. American Express also offers a **Credit Card Registration Service.** For $9 a year, your cards are registered on a central computer. In case of theft or loss, you simply make one phone call, free of charge, from anywhere in the world, and the registering service will be responsible for alerting the individual card companies.

Many of the traveler's check and credit card companies promise to advance you money either in cash or traveler's checks if you should find yourself in a pinch when away from home. Again, American Express permits cardholders to cash personal checks for up to $1,000 ($200 in cash, subject to availability, and the balance in traveler's checks). A good thing to know about—and a good reason to carry your personal checkbook.

If you should lose your traveler's checks when abroad, the idea is that you go into a branch of the issuing company and receive replacements on the spot. Be sure you know before you go how you can get in touch with the issuing company abroad, where their offices are located, and what to do if you'll be traveling in an area where the company does not have affiliates.

INTERNATIONAL MONEY MATTERS CHECKLIST

- Buy local currency traveler's checks.
- Buy local currency and coins for tips and taxis.
- Get latest currency conversion tables.
- Declare all currency as required.
- Keep all currency exchange receipts.
- Buy a pocket calculator.
- Record official exchange rate on every credit card transaction.
- Keep lists of credit card and traveler's check numbers; join a card registration service.
- Know locations of offices of traveler's check companies in case you need replacements.
- Know what away-from-home financial services your credit card company offers.

15

Health Care International

"The fact that we survive at all," states a vascular surgeon acquaintance, "is remarkable given the number of things that can go wrong with the human body. Add to that," he continues, "the violent disruptions of natural patterns, and the sudden exposure to armies of foreign microorganisms when we travel, and you will rightfully respect the strength of our physical resilience."

Human bodies weren't designed to change climates, environments, diets, drinking water, and sleep patterns radically, in a matter of hours, as they do when we cross oceans and continents in jet planes. Yet somehow we manage to survive with an amazing lack of physical malfunctioning. It's not always accidental. The healthy traveler is usually the cautious traveler.

THE TURISTAS

The most common traveler ailment is an upset stomach accompanied by diarrhea, which can affect travelers simply because of the change in water and food. It's not just Yanks from the antiseptic United States who experience it abroad; many foreign visitors suffer the same symptoms when they travel here.

The *turistas,* also known as Montezuma's Revenge and other fitting names, is usually caused by a large family of common bacteria known as *Escherichia coli* (or *E. coli*), some of which dwell in all healthy intestines. When you change environment, your system is forced to adapt to the intrusion of unfamiliar *E. coli* strains that produce certain toxins your body is not equipped to handle.

Fortunately, there now seems to be some success in the effort toward preventing and curing the disruption of *turistas*. On the drug front, skip Kaopectate and other drugstore remedies; they are useless for this type of siege. Lomotil, a prescription anti-diarrhea drug, can offer relief, and should be carried as a preventative, although it may do more damage than good if you've got something more serious than an *E. coli* upset (see ''Los Microbes,'' below).

A fairly new treatment on the market, available only by doctor's prescription, is an antibiotic known by the trade name Vibramycin. Taken once a day for the duration of a trip, Vibramycin has evidently proved effective in protecting people from *E. coli* upsets. It is not recommended for use for over three or four weeks, nor for children or pregnant women. (NOTE: If you basically prefer to avoid drugs, as I do, the problem with dosing yourself up with antibiotics, even therapeutically, is the undesirable effect on other aspects of your system, and the strengthening of your immunity to antibiotics in general. Ask your doctor for guidelines.)

Perhaps the best curatives for *turistas* are the non-pharmacological ones—the natural substances that replenish the fluids and chemicals your body loses through dehydration during diarrhea. Fruit juice, fortified with honey and a shake or two of salt or tea with honey, are the traditional remedies. Some doctors advise that you prepack a mixture of glucoses and salts (four parts fructose or sugar, one part salt, and one part baking soda). Mix the powders, then pack and seal them in plastic bags. If you get sick on the road, mix a teaspoon of the powder in a cup of water and drink it slowly. The only problem here is getting all the powder through customs without being arrested for carrying cocaine.

LOS MICROBES

Not all stomach upsets experienced by international travelers are as simple as the *turistas,* and you should know before you go what to watch out for.

Most countries that harbor endemic infectious diseases require you to have inoculations before arrival, which we have already discussed elsewhere. However, the inoculations required are not necessarily for the bugs that will get you when you're in a specific area. Most notorious in this category are the amoebas and parasites lying in wait for you in Latin America (some experts claim they're the most virulent in the world), and the minute larvae carried by a snail that breeds in stagnant water in many tropical areas, notably, sub-Saharan Africa. These larvae, which can penetrate your skin, cause the insidious disease known as ''bilharzia'' or schistosomiasis.

None of these disease-carrying organisms should be underestimated, and you should never fail to protect yourself from their disabling attachments. A few years ago, in the Mayan temple complex of Tikal in the Guatemalan Yucatán, I consumed a horrendously bad lunch of some very dead meat of unidentifiable origin, a few fresh vegetables, and a questionably capped soft drink, and came down 24 hours later with some kind of parasitic infection that wiped me out for three or four days. I was traveling on assignment with a photographer and his assistant, a very practical lady who managed to get me some kind of potent over-the-counter drug, and I recovered sufficiently to continue the arduous trip. It wasn't until a month later that I realized how ill I was: I almost drowned when swimming in Rio de Janeiro; a strong undertow pulled me out to sea and I simply didn't have the strength to swim back in. When I got home, hepatitis and intestinal parasites were eventually diagnosed after I had been to a score of doctors. I spent the better part of the next two years recovering from the ravages of those little buggers. My skin used to turn a murky yellow and my eyes got gray by 3 o'clock every afternoon.

The point here is caution. I was not cautious. Before going to South America I had lived in Africa for a long time, had drunk most of the water, had eaten plenty of fresh vegetables and fruits, and never had been sick for a day. I assumed the same immunity applied when I went to South America, and was careless about what I ate and drank. I should never have eaten the fresh vegetables, especially in a remote jungle outpost like Tikal. The meat was out of the question. And I should have examined the suspicious soft drink more carefully.

Precautions and Preventatives

There are several precautions you can take against certain endemic diseases, always under your doctor's supervision. First is an inoculation against infectious hepatitis, which is highly recommended if you're traveling to the semitropics or tropics, especially in Southeast Asia and South America.

Another preventative regularly employed by knowledgeable travelers to tropical areas is a shot of gamma globulin, which helps strengthen the body's immunity to viral infections and other illnesses such as hepatitis. Gamma globulin is one of a class of simple proteins found in plasma and blood serum and it includes most antibodies. The inoculation hurts, but get one anyway. You need to get the gamma globulin shot well ahead of your departure day. Check with your doctor to find out when. If, for instance, you plan to get a yellow fever inoculation too, you will have to take the two shots at least 21 days apart to avoid any conflict.

Water: Unfortunately, for most parasitic infections, there is no preventative except caution. In suspicious areas, you should not drink the tap water under any circumstances. Even if the local water is tolerated by local people, it doesn't mean that your system will be able to fight off resident amoebas, protozoa, and other organisms. The best way to avoid problems with your digestive tract is always to drink bottled water that is sealed when it is brought to your table or hotel room. It's not unheard of for an open bottle of ''mineral water'' to be delivered to you in a restaurant, hastily filled from the kitchen tap just a moment earlier. NOTE: Brush your teeth with bottled water, too. And remember that ice is made from tap water; avoid it in suspicious areas.

If bottled water is unavailable, boil your own drinking water for at least 10 minutes. Use one of those little heating coils. Otherwise use Halazone water purification tablets; drop a few in a bottle of water and allow it to stand for at least 30 minutes.

Milk: Milk and milk products also have to carefully monitored, since in many parts of the world milk is not pasteurized, or is not properly refrigerated before it reaches your table. Milk products to avoid in questionable areas include fresh milk, butter, cream, whipped cream, cheese, and yogurt. Ask for powdered or canned milk instead, and for margarine, if it is available. To find out where you should be most on guard for infected milk products, bad water, and other contaminants, send for the IAMAT World Climate Charts (see page 127).

Fruits and Vegetables: Fresh fruits and ground-growing vegetables are other sources of bacteria and parasites. In many parts of the tropics, vegetables and fruits are fertilized with night soil and are ridden with larvae, parasites, amoebas, and other creatures all waiting to wreak havoc with your stomach.

In questionable areas, avoid raw vegetables altogether, and peel fresh fruits completely before eating them. To be on the safe side, avoid all fruits with gouges or broken skins.

Mayonnaise: Beware of any and all foods mixed with mayonnaise, especially when you're traveling in hot climates. Mayo-drenched chicken and seafood salads are notorious breeders of destructive bacteria and can cause food poisoning. Open buffets, where the food is improperly chilled, are the worst offenders. Stick to the cold cuts and vinaigrette salads.

As far as bilharzia goes, you can avoid it merely by staying out of all stagnant or slow-moving fresh water, including puddles, in areas where it is endemic. If you should be on a business trip to Nairobi and steal a weekend on safari in the bush, don't give in to the temptation to swim in the lovely cool pool at the foot of the waterfall—even that might be harboring the bilharzia-carrying snails.

Like many tropical parasitic diseases, bilharzia is slow to get started, but is completely debilitating for years once it begins to flourish. If you travel in any tropical areas (Africa, Southeast Asia, Central or South America) and come home feeling unusually tired, go immediately to the nearest clinic that specializes in tropical medicine and get yourself thoroughly tested. Many people (including myself) can tell horror stories about spending weeks and thousands of dollars looking for help from regular doctors who often are not equipped to diagnose exotic tropical diseases. Tropical disease centers are rare in many parts of the country; if you think you need one, get on a plane and find the best medical help you can get.

MEDICAL ASSISTANCE WHEN ABROAD

After bugs and bacteria, just about the only health problems that can affect you when abroad are the same kinds of accidents and illness you might experience at home. The only difference is that when traveling in foreign countries you are often at the mercy of doctors whose languages you don't understand, or in hospitals or clinics of unknown reputation and cost.

One way to fix this is to join **IAMAT (International Association for Medical Assistance to Travellers).** This organization is a must for every serious international traveler. IAMAT will provide you with a membership card and a directory listing IAMAT centers and their telephone numbers in some 300 destinations around the globe. You may call for help 24 hours a day, 365 days a year. Almost all of the participating doctors studied in the West and all speak English, and they are familiar with Western medical standards and practices. This is extremely important. An example: Some aspirin substitutes commonly prescribed as painkillers throughout southern Europe are harmless to local people, but cause serious destruction of white blood cells among people of Anglo-Saxon extraction. The offending agent is aminopyrine. It's just one of the many potential problems IAMAT doctors are alert to.

Upon request for membership, IAMAT will send you a World Immunization Chart, which lists in detail all you need to know about health requirements and precautions in 200 countries and dependencies from Afghanistan to Zimbabwe Rhodesia.

Rates for IAMAT's participating doctors are fixed internationally at the equivalent of $15 for an office visit, $20 for a house call (your hotel), and $25 for night calls or calls on Sundays and holidays (at press time). When was the last time you paid a doctor $15 for an office visit? And can you remember the last time a doctor made a house call?

IAMAT is a nonprofit organization and it operates solely on tax-free contributions, which are requested after they have sent you a membership card, the World Immunization Chart, and the IAMAT Directory. For a contribution of $15 or more, they will send you a set of 24 World Climate Charts, which are the most thorough—and indispensable—guides available to world climates in over 1,400 locations. The charts are arranged by city and by month, and also include information on the safety of local water, milk, and food, the altitude of the city, and recommendations on what to wear. These alone are worth the contribution.

For membership, write to the membership office at:

IAMAT
350 Fifth Avenue
Suite 5620
New York, New York 10001

Intermedic, at 777 Third Avenue, New York, New York 10017, offers a similar program and services for a one-year membership fee of $6 (at press time).

If you don't join Intermedic or IAMAT, you'll find that hotels in most international destinations frequented by business travelers either have a doctor on call, or will be able to recommend a good English-speaking doctor or dentist. Or you can inquire at the American Embassy or Consulate. If you have to be hospitalized, or undergo an emergency operation, try to get yourself to the nearest American hospital (if one should exist). Call the U.S. Embassy or Consulate for the best recommendation, and ask them for assistance if you should be in dire circumstances.

Health Insurance

As we have already discussed, most U.S. health insurance policies offer some protection when you're abroad. In fact, many offer the same schedule of payments as at home. Call your insurance agent, or ask the insurance adviser to your company to inform you of your exact coverage and the reimbursement procedure.

Most hospitals and doctors in the world will require you to pay for medical services in cash, and it's up to you to seek reimbursement from your health insurance company when you return home. Since medical procedures and terminology differ around the globe, you may find your bills questioned on technicalities when you try to press your claim. One example frequently encountered is that in Switzerland, hospitals are often called "clinics," which may not be included in your coverage. The way around this is to be certain that all medical and hospital bills itemize in great detail the services, treatments, and medications you have received. Be sure your receipt specifically lists every service and does not lump them together under a catch-all phrase such as "hospital room." (For more information on health insurance, refer back to Part 1.)

If you have any serious questions about the legitimacy of hospital bills, don't hesitate to call the American Consul. He or she has the authority to challenge excessive charges on your behalf.

Assist-Card International

Recently, some enterprising folks have started **Assist-Card International.** Assist-Card provides you with all manner of assistance when you're traveling abroad, including medical and legal aid, medicines, emergency transportation, assistance in tracking down lost baggage or documents, cash advances, and repatriation of your corporeal remains if you should happen to expire while on the road.

Assist-Card has 24-hour-a-day service with nearly 3,000 multilingual advisers ready to jump to your aid in 56 countries in Western and Eastern Europe (except the U.S.S.R.), Northern and Southern Africa, the Middle East, and Mexico.

Membership in the program can be purchased individually for each trip, with rates assessed according to the length of your stay ($20 for a five-day journey, $120 for a 90-day trip, or $350 for an annual membership). Once you pay the annual fee, you're covered for an impressive array of benefits. All medical services up to $3,500 are covered; a doctor comes to your room, an ambulance takes you to a hospital, and, if necessary, a chartered plane rescues you from a Greek island and jets you to a clinic in Zurich. Emergency medications and dental treatments are also included. In addition, Assist-Card International will lend you a cash advance of up to $1,000, put up bail money of $5,000, and provide you with a lawyer whose legal fees are on the house. If your hotel or a local vendor attempts to cheat you, all you do is call your local Assist-Card office any time, day or night, and someone will help you go over the bill or get your money returned, with apologies. Or, if you should miss your APEX flight due to illness, or other causes, Assist-Card will arrange to fly you back home and pick up the difference. A great value. If you're interested, contact:

Assist-Card International
745 Fifth Avenue
New York, New York 10022
(212) 752-2788
Outside New York, call
toll-free (800) 221-4564

For pessimistic do-it-yourself travelers, plan ahead by buying a copy of *Traveling Healthy: A Complete Guide to Medical Services in 23 Countries* by Sheilah M. Hillman and Dr. Robert S. Hillman (Penguin Books).

INTERNATIONAL HEALTH CARE CHECKLIST

- Buy drug preventatives for the *turistas,* following your doctor's advice.
- Prepare glucose and salt powders.
- Know what diseases are endemic to the areas you're traveling to and find out how to prevent them.
- Get inoculated against infectious hepatitis.
- Get a preventative gamma globulin inoculation.
- Drink only bottled water and other bottled liquids in suspicious areas.
- Buy water-heating coil, adaptable to 110/220 volts.
- Buy Halazone water purification tablets.
- Avoid milk, cheese, cream, butter, yogurt, and mayonnaise in suspicious areas.
- Peel all fresh fruit.
- Avoid fresh vegetables.
- Join Intermedic, or IAMAT (and get a World Immunization Chart and 24 World Climate Charts).
- Join Assist-Card International.

Part 3

TRAVEL PLANNING: PERSONAL

16

Dressing like a Winner

Many books and magazine articles have been written on the subject of packing and dressing for business. Some experts piously advise you to throw aside the look you've developed for yourself over the years in favor of some synthetic, sexless, but American-efficient styles. Convenience fabrics that hang like tablecloths but don't wrinkle, spot, crease, fade, or crush. Suits in fabrics that feel creepy against your skin and are not supposed to bag or stretch, but always get pulled out around the derrière. Day dresses in no-nonsense colors with no-nonsense lines that save you the worry of steaming the wrinkles out in the hotel bathroom, but make you look exactly the way your mother always wanted you to look, which is exactly what you've been trying to avoid since you were 13 years old.

That you don't build a business career by dressing or acting in a vulgar manner goes without saying. Obviously, you've learned to adapt your personal style to the particular demands of your professional environment, or you wouldn't be in your job in the first place. I still maintain, however, that there's no reason you should suppress your own identity, sense of femininity, or freedom to highlight your best features, in obeisance to some dogma handed down by antediluvian ''experts.'' The fact that you're a woman has nothing to do with your mental capacity, talent, and job qualifications. If men are threatened or distracted when dealing with a real live female in the course of doing business, then I suggest, respectfully, it's their problem. Not ours.

DRESS LIKE YOURSELF

I once went on a business trip—one of my first—with a suitcase filled with Banlon dresses, a horrible maroon knit suit, and some downright dowdy walking shoes. I had a terrible time. I didn't feel attractive or confident in my business encounters. In fact, I felt as if I were masquerading as someone else's stereotyped idea of how a boring business traveler was supposed to look.

Since then, I've learned that dressing for business in general and business travel in particular requires you to make an artful compromise between a comfortable, appropriate manner of dressing and the special, very personal way you like to arrange yourself. The basis of this compromise is your own good sense. You know that your travel-packing objective is to have clothes that will look reasonable the minute you pull them out of your suitcase. You also know that your objective in dressing for business is precisely that—to do business. You want to look good and display your style and charm. But even more importantly, you want to draw attention to your intelligence, professional capabilities, maturity, and responsibility—not necessarily to your sexual appurtenances.

Building the Basics

The first rule, when building a business-travel wardrobe, is to select clothes you like. Clothes that make you feel confident and attractive. Clothes that make you look like you. There's no reason to buy a practical little dress if you'd really prefer a French three-piece suit. And there's no reason to buy a dress in a sensible puce-colored knit if you look better in a rich plum silk, as long as you wear clothes that are appropriate for the occasion and part of the country or world you are going to.

Roxane Rauch, a former executive of Fashion Capital of the World, as well as the founder of The Lifestyles People, a lecture bureau representing top fashion and beauty experts, confirms my opinion. Roxane says:

In selecting a wardrobe for business, be sure to look the way *you* like to look. There's no reason you can't be soft and feminine in business if that is your style, just as long as you don't go around in lace-trimmed leopard-skin Spandex and décolletage. Some women simply do not look good in hard-edged, man-tailored clothes. If you're one, stick to your own feminine, but business-like style. Just keep it simple and don't let the look get too fussy.

Roxane is the first to acknowledge that the cost of clothes is getting totally out of hand and that it's necessary for almost everyone to be bargain conscious. This is doubly true today when fashions change so radically every season; the expensive suit you buy now will invariably have the wrong shape and skirt length in six months. The only solution to this demand for constant change and expenditure is to ignore it. Build on your own classic look, adding new accessories and one important piece each season. If you're clever, you'll manage to overcome the outrageous price tags on well-made clothes in this era of throwaway fashions.

Investment Dressing

How do you come up with a wardrobe full of attractive, ready-to-go business travel clothes, all within a reasonable budget?

The answer is what Roxane calls "investment dressing." Plan your wardrobe around the good pieces you own, build on what you have, and plan to get varied and extensive use from each article by making sure your clothes work together.

Before going out to shop, Roxane recommends that you make a thorough inventory of what you've got. Draw sketches of what goes with what and snip off a little piece of fabric from the seam allowance or hem of each article of clothing so you'll know exactly what will match what, when you shop.

Eliminate clothes from your list that are not right for business travel—those too bulky to pack easily, those too dressy or too casual, those that require too much care, and those made of fabrics that will wrinkle at the slightest provocation. Also eliminate the white elephants—jackets, skirts, and pants bought on a whim that go with absolutely nothing in your closet.

A NOTE ON FABRICS

There's really no such thing any more as "travel clothes." Most fabrics travel decently, and the classic styles are appropriate everywhere. The fabrics you select will obviously depend on the climate of your destination—you should determine this in advance as part of your preliminary scheduling.

If the weather is likely to be hot and humid in the cities you're traveling to, select clothes made of cotton, loosely cut silk, and lightweight synthetics that breathe. Printed fabrics are practical in hot climates; they tend to show fewer wrinkles than solid colors.

For temperate climates, lightweight wools, wool-and-linen or wool-

and-silk mixtures, and the heavier-weight synthetics are in order. For very cold climates, dress as you would in a temperate climate and add layers as you need them. Include heavier outerwear and/or lightweight wool underwear when it gets truly bitter.

Most knits are great for travel, and there is a wide variety of styles from which to choose, ranging from two-piece outfits to attractive suits and dresses that easily make the transition from business meeting to cocktails to dinner. Some knits can actually be wadded up in a ball, thrown into the bottom of your suitcase, and still emerge looking like high fashion. With two dresses like this, you could travel for a week with an overnight bag. Be sure to include no-cling slips or half-slips.

Another functional, all-purpose fabric for business travel to temperate climates is a good-quality, lightweight wool gabardine. Gabardine usually holds its shape and looks crisp and tailored all the time. It can be layered up or down, depending on the season, and it is comfortable in all but the hottest climates.

Most natural fibers (cotton, wool, linen, silk) wrinkle after being packed and need some pressing. Hanging a garment in a steam-filled bathroom can solve the problem. This may sound like something out of the *Farmer's Almanac*, but it works. You can also purchase a travel steamer, an electrical appliance about the size of a travel iron, available from many department and hardware stores. This gadget emits a fine steam mist when brushed lightly against your clothes. Or you could take a travel iron.

Almost all clothes made of Banlon, Qiana, polyesters, and other synthetics are good travelers requiring minimum care. So are most mixtures of natural fibers with 35 percent or more of synthetic fibers. A general rule to follow when selecting fabrics that travel is to choose tightly woven fibers that hold their shape and spring back quickly—those with a durable press finish hold up especially well—or meshy knits designed not to wrinkle at all. Be sure to select fabrics that will stand up to the rigors of hotel dry cleaning. This is one area where quality is the best investment.

THINK TONAL: CHOOSE PARTS THAT MIX AND MATCH

Several years ago, Roxane Rauch designed a wardrobe of nine separate pieces that could create 19 different outfits. Her ideas are as fresh today as they were then, and she has generously permitted me to adapt them here.

The key to Roxane's concept is color. By working around a single color theme plus a neutral shade, she found she could combine solids, prints, and textured fabrics. The result: an interrelated wardrobe that not only provides flexibility but also is adaptable for all except the hottest or coldest climates.

There are many medium-toned, subtle, yet rich colors to choose your main color from. Some possibilities: berry red, plum, forest green, rust, and ocher, with neutrals in the beige, gray, brown, navy, and maroon categories. In selecting your basic color, stay away from hues that are either too bold or too obviously of the moment. Example: A violent-purple suit with exaggerated shoulders might look good this fall, but you can be sure the style and color will be passé by next spring. If you want to use unusual high-fashion colors, add them in accessories or in blouses, as accents.

Roxane's System

Let's assume you have three or four wearable pieces of clothing in your closet that are suitable for fall-to-spring weather, and you want to build a business-travel wardrobe around them. Let's assume your basic color is plum. Your neutral could be almost anything—gray would be predictable, dark green would be fabulous—but let's take berry red just to make things more interesting.

In the closet you have: (1) A plum wool gabardine suit with skirt and slacks; (2) A textured plum and off-white turtleneck sweater in a mix of wool and silk; (3) Two good blouses, one an off-white Qiana, the other a berry-red silk; (4) A wool challis dress in a delicate pattern of plum, berry red, and beige; (5) A good pair of jeans (for the weekend).

You decide to purchase: (1) one tailored wool plaid (or tweed or patterned) skirt in plum, berry red, and forest green; (2) a plum, dark green, and beige tweed pants suit, with a coordinated plum and beige sweater vest in a wool and linen mix; and (3) a berry-red and white chevron-patterned blouse.

For accessories, a belt or scarf that repeats a color, pattern, or texture will pull a whole outfit together and give it a touch of class and personal flair. Scarves in particular are worth their weight in gold for the fashion mileage they provide when you're traveling. They look good in square, oblong, or long, skinny shapes, or as large wool shawls, and they're easy to pack.

To your sample wardrobe you should also add: (1) at least one large silk scarf that picks up the colors in your clothes, perhaps with a little white thrown in for freshness; (2) a long wool knit scarf; (3) a leather belt with a substantial gold-toned or brass buckle about one inch wide (or narrower if the loops on your slacks are smaller); (4) ditto, in another accent color; and (5) a travel-sized leather shoulder bag.

For your feet you'll need: (1) a pair of leather pumps with a medium heel and a comfortable cut (your "utility" shoes); (2) a pair of color-coordinated suede slingback or ankle-strap heels with a closed toe and a slightly dressier, more feminine look; and (3) if you're traveling to a cool or cold climate, a pair of leather boots with a medium, stacked heel and a classic cut, in a color that matches your shoulder bag. Be sure the boots are cut wide enough around the calf to accommodate the leg-swelling problems that affect many travelers on jet flights.

Your daytime business clothes can be transformed into outfits appropriate for evening almost completely with accessories. Here are a few things to add to the sample wardrobe, which will help you create a cocktail and dinner look, and even get you to a disco: (1) a stylish suede or gold-studded belt; (2) a suede clutch or foldover bag, soft for easy packing, but not too small—you may want to use it in the daytime (by choosing suede instead of silk or velvet, you can get the same wonderful color and still be able to carry the bag during the day); (3) some good jewelry and/or something exotic to put in your hair or around your neck; (4) perhaps a sexy little camisole in bronze lamé that folds down to practically nothing; and (5) gold clip-on ornaments for suede slingback shoes.

Now comes the fun of taking the pieces of your business travel wardrobe apart and putting them back together to create new and attractive looks. By rearranging the components, you can create a classic impression and a sporty impression, a flexibility I find very important. Keep in mind that you should use these recommendations merely as guidelines to establish your own set of fashion components. If you hate dresses, eliminate this one and add another skirt and blouse. Or if you prefer to wear skirts for business, buy a suit with a skirt instead of one with trousers.

The business-travel wardrobe described here provides more than you'll need for a one-week trip. With the use of the hotel laundry and dry-cleaning facilities, you can get additional mileage out of every garment you bring. Count on hotel cleaning facilities for your clothes—they're available virtually everywhere and generally are as reliable as your cleaner at home.

ALTERNATIVE VIEWPOINTS

Let me provide you with two other points of view for organizing your business-travel wardrobe. First, adopt a theme: a single, solid, strong but neutral color for all your skirts, jackets, trousers, shoes, and bags. For example, you have a great black wool gabardine suit with a skirt and slacks, black leather pumps, black calf boots, and a good-looking black leather travel bag. For color, you add lots of easy-to-pack shirts, sweaters, belts, and scarves in whatever hues you like: a rich turquoise silk blouse and a silk scarf in turquoise and crimson, with a crimson leather belt; a Naples yellow silk blouse with a black, white, and soft gold-colored scarf; a crimson silk shirt with an emerald and peacock-blue silk scarf; an off-white shirt with blue and mauve accessories, etc.

I often plan my travel wardrobe this way because it permits me to use strong colors, which I like, in a new and dramatic way each day, depending on my mood. And even though the additions are colorful, the well-cut sobriety of the black gabardine suit makes the look perfectly tailored for business travel. The addition of a matching black gabardine vest (or a knit one) and a black and white houndstooth or herringbone wool jacket would permit even greater possibilities and, with the three-piece suit, would provide sufficient variety for a one-week business trip.

For the summer, you can plan the same kind of travel wardrobe, using white or beige and black as your basics, mixing and matching, or wearing white-on-white, beige-on-beige, or black-on-black in stylish monochrome. Again, add color with vivid tops and accessories.

Another way to organize your business-travel clothes is to buy everything—suits, sweaters, blouses, separates, and dresses—in one of three harmonizing colors. Example: You put together a wardrobe of black/gray/red, or navy/crimson/mauve, or dark brown/beige/and pale-to-medium blues. Every major piece of clothing you buy is in one of these three basic colors. Select mostly solids, but add a few prints and patterns for variety.

With a three-color system, everything goes with everything; every jacket and skirt and pair of slacks you buy works together to give you tremendous freedom and ease of dressing. Add whites and bolder colors for accents in your blouses and accessories. Buy shoes and bags in the most neutral of your colors.

Several women I know who travel for business organize their wardrobes this way. If they travel frequently, they build a business wardrobe exclusively for travel, adding to it items in their three-color scheme and selecting the most travel-worthy fabrics. So that they don't get bored with their travel clothes, they don't wear them when they're at home. They have them dry-cleaned immediately upon returning from a trip and keep them ready to go in a special corner of their closets.

No matter how you organize your clothes, the important thing to remember is to keep your fashion options open. Permit variety, but remember to think about what style of dress is worn wherever you happen to be going. You don't want to make yourself feel uncomfortable by appearing as though you came from another planet. In general, the dress in the northeastern part of the U.S. and Northern Europe is more conservative with colors more subdued than in the warmer, southern areas, and Spanish-speaking countries tend to be on the conservative side. You can create a casual look with a shirt open at the throat for a business meeting in Los Angeles, Miami, or Atlanta, or a dressed-up, classic look with a gabardine suit and a scarf for a meeting in Dallas, San Francisco, Washington, Madrid, or London. In Rome, Paris, New York, or Tokyo, you'll want to look a bit more à la mode, yet still be comfortable in a style of clothes you ordinarily wear at home. You can do it all by a clever use of separates and accessories, by sticking to the classics, and by bringing them up to date and to life by adding generous dashes of your own fashion personality.

SPECIAL CLOTHING AND ACCESSORIES

Lingerie

Nothing is more personal than your choice of lingerie, so I won't presume to tell you what to pack. For myself, I usually find that the following will suffice for a one-week business trip:

- Two pairs of bikini panties (which get washed out at night)
- Two bras (ditto)
- One teddy
- One half-slip
- Four pairs of panty hose (or three plus two pairs of knee-length stockings to wear with slacks), and maybe a sexy pair of patterned stockings or flashy socks to wear in the evening.

Be sure to keep a good supply of stockings with you at all times. If you're traveling in and around the United States, you can always stop in a drugstore and pick up an extra pair of panty hose. When traveling abroad, you may have more difficulty finding stockings that fit or stockings of the same quality and price as those available at home. One friend of mine, who takes off on marathon five- and six-month business sojourns to the far corners of the world, buys 50 pairs at a time, much to the astonishment of the sales clerks.

At night, I usually sleep in the raw or in a large T-shirt or gauzy cotton Indian top (extra large). For a bathrobe, I take a knee-length patterned kimono that folds down to the size of a scarf and doubles as a beach or pool robe.

American hotel rooms are almost always overheated in winter so a light bathrobe will usually suffice throughout the year. Do take something warmer (a lightweight wool or Viyella robe) if you're traveling in Europe or elsewhere outside the United States during the cold season (or if you will be staying at high altitudes). Other people are not as profligate with their use of heating oil as we are.

If you face the possibility of running into very cold weather—or will be in one of the bone-chilling, damp cities of Europe during the winter—take a lightweight wool undershirt, cut low around the neck so it won't peep out from your open-necked shirts. The best wool undies come from the U.K., Scandinavia, and Switzerland, and are remarkably effective as well as soft and silky to the touch.

Take some sort of slippers (a pair of ballet slippers, soft fold-over scuffies, or a pair of lightweight sandals that will do double duty down to the hotel pool). Hotel-room carpets and bathroom floors are likely places to pick up athlete's foot or other pesky ailments. This can be avoided if you keep your feet covered.

Rain Gear

When dress designer Zandra Rhodes was asked by *W*, a leading fashion publication, what she recommended as a travel tip, she answered: ''Take an umbrella. If you use the kind of coloring and makeup I do, rain is your worst enemy. It's startling enough dry, but wet, it's a disaster.''

Take an umbrella, even if you don't use exotic makeup. In fact, buy a small collapsible one that will fit in your briefcase or carry-on travel bag. Or get one of the new umbrellas fitted with a leather or canvas shoulder strap. In any case, carry an umbrella with you all the time, except when you're traveling in the Kalahari Desert.

For warm weather, especially in tropical climates, where short, heavy showers may interrupt the sun every afternoon, carry an emergency vinyl or plastic rain cape or raincoat that folds into a small package. Not all raincoats of this sort look like oversized garbage bags. In fact, some are made of parachute nylon or tinted vinyl and are actually quite fashionable.

For moderate climates, a standard trench coat is probably your best bet. Choose one roomy enough in the shoulders and armholes to go over a suit jacket. Be sure it's a functional, waterproofed coat, not just a stylish bit of khaki with epaulets. I have a raincoat manufactured in the U.K. with a thin rubber lining bonded to the khaki cloth. It's roomy in the shoulders, belted, simple, but very stylish; at the same time, it keeps me dry.

For cold climates, a raincoat with a zip-out lining is useful; so is a classic khaki trench coat that reverses to a lightweight wool plaid (Burberrys, Aquascutum, and Jaeger make the prototypes). Good quality, dark-colored wool coats, again, roomy through the shoulders and perhaps unfitted, may work even better. The fabric isn't waterproof, but a good wool coat protected by an umbrella is probably cozier and more practical in the deep winter months than any other kind.

Take a rain hat, if you wear one: just be sure it folds. And plan to take some kind of rain boots if you'll be in a city like London where it's apt to pour for days at a time. If there's room in your suitcase, take a pair of rubber or vinyl boots made like an ordinary pair of boots. Or carry a smaller pair that snap over your shoes.

Foot Gear

The shoes you select for a business trip are of the greatest importance. If you hobble around in a pair of 3½-inch heels, trying to look sexy, while carrying heavy sample cases on a long day of business activity, you'll throw your back out of line, you'll look ridiculous, and you'll wish you had done otherwise.

Wear the same kind of shoes for business travel as you wear for business at home; make allowance for the loads you'll have to carry. On a trip of a week or longer, both Chrisjean Whitten and Roxane Rauch usually travel with three pairs of shoes: one "good" pair; one a bit more worn, still acceptable, but treasured for their comfort; and one slightly dressier pair. In colder climates, substitute a pair of classic leather boots with a medium heel for the "good" pair of shoes.

Always have two or three changes of shoes with you. Change shoes frequently; your feet need it. Keep one "utility" pair of shoes with you whenever possible, even on the plane or during the day. You can stash them away, wrapped in a Baggie or a cloth, in a large handbag, travel bag, or your briefcase.

Select a pair of utility shoes that are made of soft leather and that are cut a little wider and longer than ordinary. Choose a medium, comfortable heel in a style that provides you with both the softness and support you'll need for long hours of walking. Your best bet is probably a classic pump, spectator shoe, or walking shoe with a short, stacked heel and a moccasin-like front. Get your shoes tipped with rubber toes and heels to help you keep your grip in hilly cities with slippery sidewalks. (Lisbon's marble-mosaic sidewalks are perilous when wet.)

Roxane Rauch, who insists on being comfortable as well as chic, usually carries a pair of "uglies" in the soft leather bag she uses as a briefcase. When she's out and running around the city, she wears the uglies in great comfort. Then, before an important meeting, she slips on her good shoes while in a taxi, or behind a pillar in the building entrance, and arrives light on her feet and looking good. Her utility shoes also serve the function of saving her good shoes in bad weather.

Roxane recommends that you should never try to break in a new pair of shoes on a business trip; too many sores and blisters can result. Wear roomy shoes or boots when flying, especially on long overseas flights, since your feet and legs may swell as a result of the long hours of inactivity and the reduced atmospheric pressure on the plane. You'll also need wider, roomier shoes when traveling to hot, humid cities, since your feet may swell because of the humidity. Knowledgeable European travelers, for example, order shoes a size wider and longer when planning summer visits to hot, humid New York.

If you expect to run into sloppy, wet weather, treat your shoes and boots with a silicone water repellent, available in spray cans from drugstores, department stores, and shoe-repair shops. Some sprays will make even delicate suedes water resistant.

Sports Gear

Just because you're packing for a business trip doesn't mean you shouldn't take some gear along that will get you involved in exercise and/or sports activities when you're away from home. You can jump rope, do a quick set of exercises or yoga on your hotel room floor. You can swim in the hotel pool, jog, play tennis or squash. Or you can work out in the nearest gym. If you're planning a weekend break while on the road, you'll want to be prepared for some real activity: skiing, golf, sailing, or hiking.

REAL GOLD OR NOT REAL GOLD

To wear real gold or not, that is the question. If you've got it, flaunt it—and insure it. Or chicken out and leave it in your safe-deposit box.

Both Chrisjean Whitten and I feel that if you usually wear good jewelry, you should take it with you on a business trip. Otherwise you'll feel like a stripped-down, poor-cousin version of yourself. Neither she nor I wears costume jewelry and therefore we have two choices—to risk taking our valuables on the road or to go without any.

We risk it—carefully. We don't take more jewelry than we can wear in two sittings: a few rings, two pairs of earrings, a bracelet, a watch, a few gold chain necklaces, plus a strand of pearls. We always carry what we're not wearing buried deep in our handbags, enclosed in an interior zippered compartment, or we check it into the hotel safe-deposit box (just like the blue-haired ladies at The Breakers in Palm Beach, who line up for their diamonds every evening at 6 o'clock).

Good jewelry never gets left behind in your hotel room, not even in a locked suitcase. Suitcase locks are notoriously easy to break. In fact, they're a joke. Good jewelry is also never packed in your baggage when you're en route. Without meaning to point a libelous finger, one suspects that some of the baggage crews in some of the world's busier airports are really kid-gloved pros with a magic touch that can ferret out a piece of gold hidden in your lacy lingerie in a flash. What else can they be doing in the two hours it takes them to get the bags from the plane to the luggage carousel? In any case, make sure all they find with their swift, probing fingers is soft articles of apparel—nothing to alert them to the presence of real gold or other valuables.

If carrying your jewelry with you all the time seems like a burden, then leave it at home, and take only what you ordinarily wear on any given day. Insure those items you use most frequently under a personal articles floater, for which you will have to produce sales receipts, or have each piece of jewelry separately appraised (see Chapter 8, ''Insurance Coverage on the Road'').

About Wedding Rings

Wedding rings—real ones, former ones, and bogus ones—can work as useful preventatives against irksome males. If you don't want to be bothered by roving men when you're traveling, or if you want a ready excuse to save you from casual encounters, keep your wedding ring or a facsimile of one prominently planted on the fourth finger of your left hand (right when you're in Europe).

On the other hand (pun, pun), a wedding ring or a ring that looks like one will turn off men you may actually want to speak to. If you're divorced and still wear your wedding ring out of habit, don't hide behind your old status. Try taking it off to see how you feel.

JUST FOR FUN

Now that you've been so boringly practical in planning your business wardrobe, add something totally impractical, something that will amuse you on the road or make you feel more at home. Gloria Vanderbilt reportedly takes a special scented candle, photographs of family in a folding leather case, and her favorite scarves or pieces of fabric to toss decoratively around the room. (Maybe she has a liveried chauffeur to carry the extra baggage?) Chrisjean Whitten takes a large glass bottle of her favorite perfume—glass because she wouldn't dream of putting French perfume in plastic, and large because she likes to use it abundantly. Roxane Rauch takes a small goose-down pillow covered with a Pratesi pillowcase—she hates the stiff, lumpy pillows often encountered in hotels. I always take my favorite belt, a cadet-blue Boy Scout one with a buckle made of fake rubies surrounding a cartoon picture of a bear swinging a golf club. The picture is covered by that special plastic that makes the bear actually seem to swing the club when the buckle is seen from different angles. Pure theater of the absurd.

Permit yourself at least one totally unnecessary and even foolish extravagance when you're packing for a business trip. A gorgeous blouse that breaks all your wardrobe organization lists and will cost $4 to have ironed once it's unpacked. A gauzy 1930s scarf. Your favorite silver bomber jacket. Your 1950s punk sunglasses. Your very own earphones and classical music tapes. Or a pink satin sleeping mask with some French beeswax earplugs.

Whatever your choice, make sure it makes you feel special on your business trip. Make it something that will remind you of another reality (home, family, friends, fun) and that will help keep your intense involvement in your business affairs in balanced perspective. Nothing is more boring than a business person—man or woman—who can never drop his or her business role for a more relaxed, approachable human persona. By taking something along on your business trips from your other (real?) existence, you help yourself make the transition to normalcy easier.

TRAVEL WARDROBE CHECKLIST

- Analyze the clothes in your closet and organize them by color theme.
- Supplement existing clothes with new purchases to build a mix-and-match system.

- **Packing the Basics:**
  Coat
  Suit
  Skirts
  Slacks
  Dresses
  Blouses
  Sweaters (pullovers/turtlenecks/cardigans)
  Vests

- **Accessories:**
  Belts

Scarves
Evening bag/belt/shoe clip-ons
Travel-sized leather shoulder bag

- **Jewelry:**
One or two sets of good jewelry that have been appraised and insured
(do not pack it in your suitcase)

- **Lingerie:**
Panties
Bra/strapless bra
Teddy
Slip/half-slip
Panty hose
Knee-high stockings/socks
Pajamas/nightgown
Robe
Slippers/sandals
Wool underwear

- **Rain Gear:**
Portable umbrella
Emergency raincoat
Standard raincoat (lined/reversible/unlined)
Rain hat
Rain boots

- **Foot Gear:**
Comfortable walking shoes
Good shoes with medium heel for easy walking
Dressy heels suitable for day and evening
Leather boots
Silicone water-repellent spray for shoes

- **Sports Gear:**
Sneakers
Socks
Bikini
Cap/goggles
Others of your choice

- **For Fun:**
Something personal/familiar/outrageous

17

Packing Strategies

In the days before either Chrisjean or I knew a hoot about doing business, we once drove from Geneva to Sintra, Portugal, to stay at the home of a friend. Most of my things were already in the house in Sintra, but Chrisjean was closing out her house and had a dozen huge suitcases, a dog, and a cat, plus me, to fit into her small Italian sports car.

The day we left, the Pope was visiting Geneva. All roads were blocked, and we spent three hours circumnavigating the city before we finally got on the right road and headed out across the Bourgogne into France. The cat retreated to the back of the car and vomited, and we had to pull over to unload all bags to clean up the mess. Meanwhile, Chrisjean's impish white and black Shih Tzu raced away through a stand of birch trees. Chrisjean loped after him like a vision out of Chekhov's *A Lady and a Dog,* shouting, ''Proustie, darling! Come back. Come back!''

The trip was not off to a good start. When we finally got to Saint Étienne, normally a two-hour drive from Geneva, we decided to stop for the night. I asked Chrisjean which bag was her overnight bag. She had not packed an overnight bag.

It was evident, after we had gotten the 12 suitcases, the cat, and the dog up the stairs to the third floor of the old hotel that Chrisjean did in fact need her 12 suitcases. Cans of cat food were in the bottom of one suitcase underneath half a dozen bikinis. Shoes were packed with the right shoe in a brown leather case and the left one in a canvas satchel. The dog's leash was inexplicably tangled in a plastic bag with hair rollers and toothpaste.

All in all, it took us four days to get to Portugal.

Since then, Chrisjean has become one of the most experienced and proficient business travelers I know, even though she still maintains some of her packing idiosyncrasies—toting a full-sized steam iron to freshen up her Italian silks, or packing her right shoe in one suitcase and her left shoe in another (some things never change), or carrying her perfume by the pint, in glass bottles. But for the most part, she now packs more realistically, with an eye on the airline's baggage rules and a keen appreciation of what it means to be burdened with unnecessary baggage.

Baggage Allowances

Baggage allowances for most domestic and international flights are based on a "piece system." Passengers flying First or Coach Class (Economy on international flights) are allowed to carry two pieces of baggage on board. In addition, passengers are permitted to take a carry-on bag in the plane cabin, if it is small enough to fit under the seat. Checked luggage must not exceed 105 inches in overall measurement (total height, depth, and width of both pieces of luggage).

Restrictions also vary by country and route. Sometimes baggage allowances are dictated by the country of destination, which, for example, may enforce a "weight system." If your bags exceed the baggage allowance, you must pay a flat rate per bag according to the length of your flight. To be on the safe side, check the airline's regulations before you go.

After you've determined how much you're allowed, then you must decide how much baggage you want to take. With the absence of porters in many airports of the world, and the frequency of situations in which you're obliged to maneuver your own bags from the carousel, through customs, and then a mile or two out to the airport taxi stand, it's a good idea, when possible, to bring only what you can carry yourself. That includes a fairly sizable shoulder bag, a suitcase for your left hand, and another for your right.

In situations where you have to transport a lot of trade samples or other heavy materials, include enough time in your schedule to allow a porter to do the lugging for you. Or get a suitcase with small wheels attached, or buy one of those collapsible luggage carriers stewardesses use—a good idea in any case. If you're doing a lot of business travel and frequently carry heavy bags, it's very important that you save the wear and tear on yourself. Use porters, friends, new acquaintances met on the plane, wheelbarrows—anything—rather than tax your own resources.

THE BEST SUITCASE

What kind of luggage should you use? Again, we move into the world of the subjective; it's hard to present any opinion that will suit everyone. Some women travelers I've spoken to prefer the new, almost weightless parachute-fabric nylon bags with canvas or leather supports, while other women prefer standard business bags like Samsonite.

There are a lot of choices.

Before making yours, ask yourself some of the following questions to see which type of suitcase most meets your needs:

- How long are your trips on average?
- How many types of clothing do you need to take?
- What materials do you have to carry with you on the plane, and which do you prefer to check?
- How many appliances or heavy business materials do you need?
- Will you be traveling primarily by plane? By car? Other?
- Do you prefer a hard bag or a soft one? A satchel, duffel bag, foldover, hang-up, or a regular suitcase?
- Where will you store your suitcases at home? Would it be convenient if one bag fit inside another?

No matter what kind of bag you buy, never buy a cheap one. Buying cheap luggage is a false economy. A good bag will last for years, hold its shape and protect your clothes, and never humiliate you by breaking at the hinges or popping its zipper and dumping your undies on the baggage carousel.

Years ago, I bought an expensive canvas and leather bag at Mark Cross in New York. It cost a fortune compared to other similar bags, but I carried that suitcase almost steadily for seven years to some 50 countries on five continents and it's still in my closet raring to go. It isn't beautiful anymore—the canvas is now an almost sooty gray and there are chalk marks and the remnants of stickers everywhere. But the cloth is still intact (though frayed). The leather bindings still hold. And the average cost after years of extravagant use is about $25 a year.

Types of Luggage: Advantages and Disadvantages

First, the soft nylon or canvas bags. The nylon bags, the newest on the market, have the distinct advantage of folding down to a sliver, weighing practically nothing, and being durable, somewhat water-proof, and an easy and inexpensive way to carry your clothes. Usually this type of bag is available in a variety of standard designs, most with rounded edges and a slightly pouchy look. The best kind has leather (rather than canvas) reinforcements and straps, and I have seen some very good-looking imported versions in dark blue nylon with dark leather trimmings at Dinoffer in New York.

There are some very inexpensive types of nylon luggage made of paper-thin parachute fabric similar to the expensive kind, but with canvas bindings and straps. We recommend this type only as an extra to be carried folded up in your suitcase for that unexpected purchase, or to pack with a pair of sneakers and a bathing suit for a weekend (you then check your large bag at the airport or a hotel).

The disadvantage of nylon parachute suitcases is their lack of inner construction that denies you a solid compartment in which to place your clothes. Unless you're traveling with no-wrinkle garments, this might be a problem. I also distrust the water-resistance of this fabric.

Canvas or fabric suitcases with leather straps and reinforcements, like the kind made famous by Mark Cross and Gucci, offer a durable, semiconstructed, moderately light, and good-looking choice of suitcase for women business travelers. This type of bag presumably will with-stand wear and tear, rips and snags, and inundations in rainstorms better than nylon luggage. Good bags of this type have wire or metal reinforcements around the edges to help the bag keep its shape. Cheaper bags, you will discover as the glue starts to dissolve, are often reinforced with strips of cardboard.

Canvas and fabric suitcases are usually available in a practical range of sizes and shapes, from small enough to fit comfortably under an airplane seat, to large enough to hold a month's worth of clothes. Some have inner pockets, some do not. I find that inner compartments in luggage—like those in cosmetics kits—never quite conform to what I'm trying to pack.

Leather suitcases, apart from their good looks and classic elegance, are usually very heavy and rigid in structure. With a softer bag, you can always squeeze in an extra pair of shoes. But with a stiffer suitcase, like a leather or aluminum one, when the limit is reached, it is reached. I have a wonderful old leather suitcase that belonged to my grand-father, still covered with decals from the S.S. *Normandie*. I have tried carrying it on business trips, but find, in an age of lightweight baggage, that it is an elegant but cumbersome anachronism. Mind you, I wouldn't mind having a complete set of silky Italian leather luggage—provided I never had to pick it up myself.

Aluminum and/or fiberglass suitcases (Samsonite is the classic) are favorites of many business travelers for their durable constuction, hard surface, built-in combination locks, and virtual indestructibility. Many have inner suit hangers and metal bands that you wrap your trousers around. The only trouble with suitcases of this kind, for me, is that they are so predictable. I hate waiting for a gray suitcase to pop up on the baggage carousel identical to 50 percent of the other suitcases that come around. Why don't they make them in better colors, like burgundy or forest green? Or stenciled with discreet patterns? Why does functional have to mean boring?

Another kind of luggage to consider is the garment bag, the kind you place over hangers and carry held up at shoulder height so the clothes don't fall off inside. A friend of mine who travels almost constantly for business always carries a small dress bag plus a nylon and leather duffel bag directly onto the plane. She asks the flight attendant to hang up the garment bag (planes always have limited space for this type of luggage), and she stores the duffel bag under her seat. Upon arrival, she makes a fast getaway directly from the plane, with no need to wait for her bags to be unloaded.

Some carry-on bags that do not hang up are skillfully engineered to hold a great deal of stuff and still fit under the airplane seat. I have one such bag, a honey-blond suede extravaganza from T. Anthony in New York, that has two zippered pouches on either side of a large central compartment. I have used this bag for many short business trips, plus several two- or three-week toots to the sun. When I unpack it and pull out extra shoes, jackets, hair dryers, beach shifts, sweaters, and six or seven outfits, I'm always astonished at how much it holds.

The advantage of carry-on bags is that they never get lost. You don't have to wait for them to emerge on the baggage carousel after an hour. You can change reservations and switch planes at a moment's notice; this might be a definite advantage on a frantic, multi-leg business trip. And you never have to get to the plane more than 15 minutes before departure time (if you like living dangerously). However, this is not an advised procedure on crowded flights during peak seasons.

Locks and Labels

No matter what kind of luggage you select, always be sure to lock your bags, both before checking it for a flight and when leaving it in your hotel room. Use a small combination lock if the bag doesn't have one of its own. The idea here is to prevent casual pilferage. If thieves really want to loot you, you can't prevent it. But you can stop a light-fingered hotel employee or airport handler from selecting a small gift from your suitcase.

Labels are just as important as suitcase locks. Always label your bags, outside and inside, with your name, home or office address, and telephone number, clearly printed or typed. Use baggage tags that attach securely, or stickers that adhere firmly to the sides of the suitcase. If possible, also include your forwarding address at the destination and place it prominently on the outside of your bag. Should your luggage end up on a flight to Bangkok instead of Brussels, you'll have a better chance of meeting up with it again if it's labeled.

ORGANIZATION COUNTS: YOUR CLOTHES

Now that you've got the perfect suitcase correctly labeled and ready to go, think about how you're going to organize your wardrobe. Your clothes should be placed logically (matching shoes in the same suitcase) in as few bags as possible. Use two medium-sized bags rather than one large one. But use two large rather than four small ones—you can always manage to carry two large suitcases at a time. Four would be impossible.

Place your least crushable clothes at the bottom of the suitcase: flat scarves, nightclothes, jeans, jogging shorts, or other less important items. Then add your sweaters, and those dresses, blouses, and jackets made of knit, jersey, Banlon, or Qiana fabrics. Fold them carefully and place them across the bag evenly.

Your slacks should come next. Align them carefully along the creases and fold them in half, placing a piece of tissue paper inside the spot where they fold. Place them lengthwise across the longest part of the suitcase. If they overlap, shorten up on the fold and try turning the waistband down along the inside of the suitcase—a crease here will show less than one down around the cuff.

Pack your skirts on top of your slacks, again preparing them with tissue in each fold. Fold narrow skirts in half lengthwise, or in thirds from the waist down toward the hem. Full skirts usually come out best if folded in thirds lengthwise with the flaring sides turned in toward the center. Next, add your jackets or lightweight coats folded shoulder to shoulder in half, or curled inside out with the front and sleeves protected by the lining.

I always pack the lightest, most crushable clothes at the top of the suitcase on the premise that there's less to squash them there than at the bottom. As predictable as it sounds, tissue does keep non-drip-dry fabrics wearable after being packed. I can keep even delicate silk blouses quite fresh by laying a strip of tissue down the center of the back before folding the sleeves, and another sheet wrapped around the front and the back once the blouse is folded. I always put my good blouses in plastic sweater bags—the squared-off kind with a zipper closing that holds five or six blouses. The plastic bag helps keep the fabrics buoyant and unwrinkled, and also protects your clothes from the marauding fingers of customs inspectors.

Another trick that works well for suits, jackets, dresses, skirts, and blouses is to leave the dry-cleaning bags on them when you pack. Fold the clothes as you would normally. The plastic slips around a bit, but little pockets of air are created that keep your clothes from getting crushed. The plastic also protects your clothes from dirt and damage.

After you've placed all your clothes in the suitcase, carefully stuff the empty spaces on the sides and corners with underwear, belts, and shoes. Wrap stockings in plastic bags so they don't snag, and cover shoes so the polish and soles don't touch your clothes. High-heeled shoes take up a lot of room. Turn the sharp heels downward toward the bottom of the suitcase, or inward toward your clothes—never outward where they could cut through the fabric of your suitcase.

When you've got everything in, tighten the straps, then cover the entire contents with a large cotton scarf, a piece of fabric, or a plastic dry-cleaning bag. Tuck the cover along the sides of the suitcase to hold the loose blouses and other clothes on top firmly in place. Close the bag and lock it. Now, pick it up to be sure you can get it off the ground.

A Note about Travel Irons

Both Chrisjean and I think travel irons are indispensable, especially on a trip that includes a lot of one-night stops. Almost no clothes can survive packing and repacking and still come out as fresh and crisp as you'd like, unless your entire wardrobe is made of Banlon. On the road, you have to work a bit at your clothes, just as you would at home. With careful packing, you'll need to just touch up your skirts, slacks, and blouses with an iron; if you carry your own, you won't have to wait for the hotel to do it for you, and you won't have to worry about being stuck with rumpled clothes.

The latest generation of travel irons is quite remarkable. Some are barely larger than a pack of cigarettes and come with a dual 110/220-volt capability. In your hotel room, lay a few towels across a table or desk and use that as your ironing board.

To keep clothes looking fresh, especially black and dark colors susceptible to lint, you'll need one of those masking tape rollers. How many times have you worn a black gabardine suit to a restaurant and gotten up with your lap speckled with white lint from the cotton dinner napkin? For this type of emergency, try to find a purse-size tape roller, or carry a piece of tape in your handbag.

ORGANIZATION COUNTS: COSMETICS

The design of your travel cosmetics system is another of those totally subjective topics, like choice of underwear, that can be decided only by you. Keep the following guidelines in mind:

1. Take only cosmetics you're familiar with—you risk irritations and allergies if you experiment.
2. Take only the amounts you need—you don't need a pint of moisturizer for a five-day trip to Detroit.
3. Miniaturize everything you plan to take.
4. Choose cosmetics suitable to the climate you're traveling to—use lightweight makeup in hot climates, and have some darker foundation in case you have a chance to get a tan.
5. Carry only a minimum supply of heavy or bulky items (such as tampons) that can be purchased easily elsewhere.
6. Never pack your cosmetics with your clothes.

To make your own cosmetics and toiletries packing list, use the following list as a guide, crossing off what doesn't apply and adding your own selections.

The Basics:
- Cleanser
- Soap
- Face scrub
- Face mask
- Treatment creams
- Astringent
- Moisturizer
- Night cream
- Eye/throat cream
- Eye makeup remover
- Hand/body cream
- Baby oil
- Deodorant
- Shampoo
- Conditioner
- Hair setting lotion
- Hair spray
- Hairbrush/comb
- Hair curlers/curling iron
- Hairpins/barrettes/combs
- Hair dryer

- Toothpaste
- Toothbrush
- Dental floss
- Razor/blades
- Nail brush
- Nail polish
- Emery boards
- Small scissors
- Tweezer
- Shower cap
- Q-tips
- Cotton balls
- Pumice stone
- Loofah
- Small magnifying mirror
- Douche bag/lotion

Cosmetics:
- Foundation
- Blusher
- Eye shadows/cream/powder
- Eyeliners

- Mascara
- Lipstick/lip liner
- Compact/powder
- Concealing stick
- Perfume

Medicine Chest:
- Aspirin
- Band-Aids

- Medicines
- Vitamins
- Contraceptives
- Tampons/pads
- Sun screen/oil
- Lomotil/Waspeze/ antihistamines/ Dramamine/Paregoric/ Kaopectate/etc.

Condense/Miniaturize/Simplify

No matter what cosmetics and toiletries you select, plan to condense, miniaturize, and simplify. Buy the smallest tube of toothpaste—if you run out, you can buy more on the road. Take only a small amount of shampoo, if it can be replaced, and throw out all excess packaging. Get rid of the paper that holds your razor cartridges and take only the cartridges you'll need. Cut off a few strands of dental floss and leave the plastic case behind. Buy a pocket-sized container of aspirin, the smallest jar of deodorant, and take only a few Q-tips, not the box.

To get your cosmetics down to size, you'll have to repack most of them. Buy small plastic jars and bottles, or save the small sample bottles distributed by cosmetics companies in their promotional giveaways. If you're not sure the containers are waterproof, test them by filling them with water and turning them upside down in the sink. Leave them for an hour or more—if they don't leak, they're okay.

Most liquid cosmetics can be transferred to smaller bottles with the aid of a small plastic funnel. Night creams, thick hair conditioners, and other creams can be transferred to plastic jars with the aid of a round-tipped knife or spatula. Don't fill the bottles and jars to the top—leave about a quarter of the space empty—as the liquids and creams will expand in the low atmospheric pressure of jet planes.

Electrical appliances, such as hair curlers and curling irons, can be miniaturized, too. Look for travel-sized sets of hair rollers—there are some terrific little sets with five large rollers and 110/220-volt adaptability. Clairol's "Set-a-Way" travel hairsetter is the best I've found. It's conveniently packaged, automatically converts to 110 or 220 volts, and the curling rods heat up in 60 seconds.

Spillproof Packing: Cosmetics Bags

There is no such thing as spillproof packing. You never know when a can of hair spray will spontaneously detonate or a bottle of baby oil will spring a leak. On my last trip to the Caribbean (during which, ironically, I was writing this chapter), I tried to open my cosmetics bag. The zipper was stuck. I forced it, breaking it in the process, and discovered that a bottle of nail polish had cracked open during the flight, gluing the lipstick to the toothpaste and tinting my hairbrush a lovely shade of persimmon. It was bad enough as it was—how much worse if the cosmetics bag had been packed in my suitcase.

The odds are against you when it comes to travel spills, so take every precaution you can. Never pack your cosmetics with your clothing, and always buy a cosmetics case that seals securely and is genuinely waterproof. The outside material can be whatever you choose—fabric, leather, or plastic. But the inside of the bag must be lined with plastic or rubber, and it must close with a zipper or something else just as good.

If you can fit all your toiletries into one medium-sized cosmetics bag that will fit comfortably inside your shoulder travel bag, you have made life easy for yourself. If you can't, plan to separate your toiletries into two groups: (1) those you can't live without and that get carried with you on the plane; and (2) those you can manage without for a few days if your luggage should get lost.

My preference in cosmetic bags is a rectangular plastic pouch sealed with a zipper that is commonly found at five-and-ten stores. A bag like this does not have gold initials embossed in cowhide, but you can throw it out as soon as it gets soiled without undue expense or a sense of wastefulness. Plastic cosmetics bags are also generally less bulky than fabric or leather ones. The rectangular shape wastes the least amount of space.

The size of your cosmetics bag will be determined by the amount and type of cosmetics you have to pack. If you use tons of cosmetics, can't live without any of them, and will be away for a month, you'll probably need three large cases—one for basics, one for extras, and one for refills. You'll also need an extra suitcase.

If you're a really good traveler, you'll learn to get by with one medium-sized cosmetics bag that closes easily because it's not jammed to the hilt, and that doesn't add pounds to your carry-on bag.

If you travel frequently, prepare a cosmetics travel kit and keep it ready in your suitcase. After you return from each trip, make a list of all the toiletries that need replenishing and refill all the jars and bottles. You'll always have everything ready to go.

ODDS AND ENDS

In your cosmetics kit, or near it, plan to take a few extra odds and ends that may make life easier in emergencies.

Eyeglasses: If you wear prescription lenses, take an extra pair of specs along, plus your optometrist's prescription in case you have to get new lenses ground.

Sunglasses: If these are prescription, bring an extra pair, too. Travelers from northern to tropical climates should bring sunglasses with a genuine set of filter lenses, not just two pieces of tinted plastic in a fancy designer frame.

Sewing Kit: Some hotels provide guests with matchbook-style emergency sewing kits that are worth their weight in gold. If you don't have one saved from a prior trip, put together a spool of colorless nylon thread, two needles, four straight pins, a few safety pins of assorted sizes, and a roll of masking tape to hold up drooping hems. Use your manicure scissors for sewing. Take an extra button if you're a pessimist.

Spot Remover: I never seem to get the right spots on the right kinds of fabric to make this stuff work, and I usually eliminate it from my packing list. If I end up with cranberry juice all over the front of my best white silk shirt, I soak the shirt in club soda, or baking soda and water. It's amazing how quickly and thoroughly this works.

Travel Alarm: Never trust hotel wake-up services, even though they're right on target 90 percent of the time. Take along your own miniature travel alarm clock.

Utensils: If you're likely to grab a yogurt and an apple for dinner or want to enjoy a cold beer in your hotel room, bring a combination bottle opener/corkscrew, a small spoon, and a paring knife. You might also try bringing your own fixings for coffee: an immersion heater, a few paper filters, a small plastic funnel, a few ounces of your favorite coffee, and a nonbreakable coffee mug. A friend of mine who owns a well-known restaurant in the San Francisco area claims that having his own café filtre on the road saves his good spirits for the entire trip.

PACKING CHECKLIST

Suitcase
- Buy a good-quality suitcase, the style to be determined by length of trip/amount and type of clothing needed/portability/durability/price/home storage facilities.
- Lock suitcase, carry keys safely.
- Use a small combination lock, if needed.
- Label suitcase inside and out with name, home or office address and telephone number, and address at destination.
- Organize clothes by size and weight.
- Fold clothes carefully, using tissue and plastic dry-cleaning bags.

- Pack heavy items around the sides, or in a separate bag.
- Cover shoes with plastic bags.
- Bring a dual-voltage portable travel iron.
- Buy a masking tape roller.
- Complete a personal cosmetics packing list and keep it for future use.
- Throw out excess packaging.
- Repack cosmetics in small plastic bottles and jars.
- Label all prescription medicines; take only what you need.
- Buy a cosmetics bag with a waterproof lining and a tight closing.
- Prepare a travel cosmetics kit for future use; keep it up to date.

Extras
- Extra eyeglasses, prescription information, and a hard case.
- Sunglasses with filter lenses.
- A sewing kit, travel alarm, utensils.
- A café filtre system if you can't stand hotel coffee.

18

What to Carry with You at All Times

Emergency packing consists of the things you take with you in a shoulder bag, small carry-on suitcase, or briefcase on the plane. Everything of value that you're carrying goes into this bag, plus everything you need in order to survive for the next 24 hours. It contains all your travel documents, funds, those items that are necessary for you to perform your business tasks for several days, and the personal clothing and toiletries essential to your maintenance.

Papers, Funds, and Documents

Always carry all your travel documents and funds with you—never pack them in your suitcase. Included in your emergency bag should be:

- Passport
- U.S. driver's license
- International Driving Permit
- Other identification
- Visas/special permits
- International Certificates of Vaccination
- Customs documents
- Credit cards
- Cash
- Traveler's checks

- Local currency
- Personal checkbook
- Bank identification/letter of credit
- Address and appointment books
- Travel club membership cards
- Hotel and rental-car confirmation slips
- Maps
- Itineraries
- Prescription medicines

Personal Items

All essential cosmetics and toiletries—those you need to get yourself presentable every day—also belong in your emergency travel bag. Try to winnow your toiletries down to the bare essentials so you can carry them all with you, efficiently packed in a single cosmetics case. If you can't, at least carry a small plastic bottle of cleanser, moisturizer, foundation, eyeliner, mascara, blusher, lipstick, deodorant, perfume, and a small toothbrush and tube of toothpaste, plus whatever combs, brushes, dryers, etc. you need daily to do your hair. If your suitcase doesn't show up, you can still pull yourself together after a night in a hotel without looking, feeling, or functioning like a disaster.

If you're traveling with any good jewelry, this also belongs in your emergency carry-on bag. So do your daily medicines; eyeglasses and sunglasses; keys; pencils, paper, and calculator; and a good book.

A famous woman journalist reportedly once lost her suitcase on a state visit to China and was obliged to dress for a formal dinner the evening of her arrival. Her solution: a slinky black hostess gown that was packed in her carry-on bag and passed as an evening gown in the eyes of the Chinese.

A slinky black hostess gown won't work for a business luncheon, but a fresh pair of stockings and a wrinkle-proof blouse will.

A basic rule when you're preparing your emergency travel bag is to pack what you would for an overnight excursion. You probably won't have room for major pieces of clothing, but you can add a few accessories—underwear, scarves, and belts—that won't take much room and will make you feel refurbished. A knit vest would help you adjust to changes in climate, and you might add an extra pair of shoes.

THE PERFECT CARRY-ON BAG

The perfect carry-on bag serves as a combined briefcase, handbag, and overnight bag, and is small enough to be carried over the shoulder or

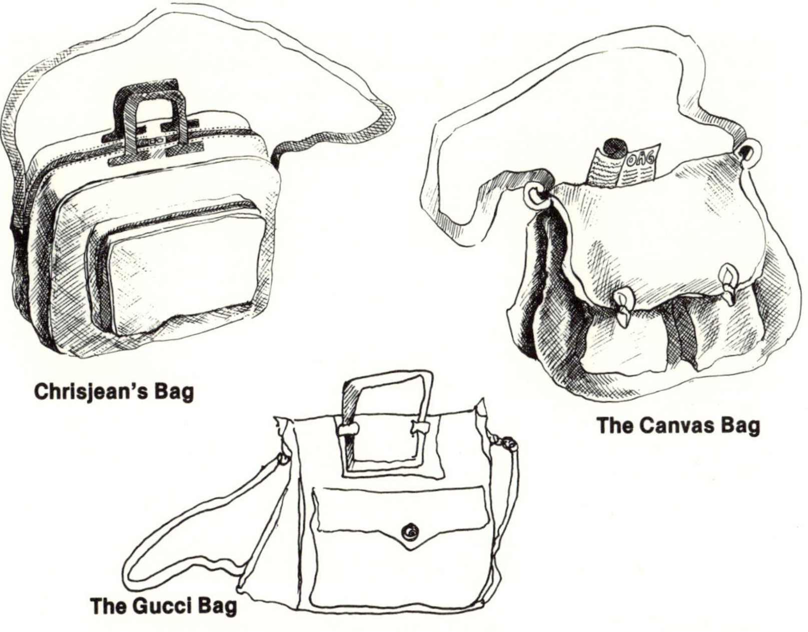

Chrisjean's Bag

The Canvas Bag

The Gucci Bag

easily in one hand. Never choose a bag that's bulky to carry or awkward to pack, and never fill it so full of heavy items that you need two hands to get it off the ground.

The perfect travel bag should have a shoulder strap so you can carry it over your shoulder or across your chest like a schoolbag. It should contain an outside section or pocket that closes with a clasp or zipper for your wallet, travel documents, and other papers. This section saves you the trouble of having to fish to retrieve a pen or passport, and it permits you to separate travel materials efficiently.

Inside the perfect travel bag is a space large enough to hold a medium-sized cosmetics case, an extra pair of stockings, a clean blouse wrapped in plastic, a small jewelry case, and other personal extras, plus appointment books and urgent business papers.

Chrisjean, who carries a lot of business samples on her daily calls, uses a soft Italian leather carry-on bag with two zippered compartments on the sides and one main compartment in the middle. The bag is about one-third the size of a regular carry-on suitcase, and it has a removable leather strap. Chrisjean fills one of the side compartments with business materials, her address and appointment books, plus her personal documents, money, and plane ticket. On the opposite side, she puts her cosmetics, carefully sealed in a waterproof case. And in the middle, she carries emergency extras like a portable hair dryer, stockings, a blouse, a sweater, and an extra pair of shoes.

Another business-traveler friend of mine has invested in a sensational brown suede Gucci bag that is considerably smaller than Chrisjean's, but is perfectly designed for travel. This bag has handles plus a detachable shoulder strap, and an outside pocket that serves as a secure, easy-to-get-into spot for documents. The center section is sufficiently large to hold a modest cosmetics bag and a few personal extras.

A bag this size can be conveniently carried in addition to a briefcase or another carry-on. If this is the type you need, you don't have to go overboard for a Gucci. Use the style as a prototype and shop for a sturdy leather version. There are many similar bags on the market.

I usually carry a canvas camera bag of the sort popularized by Hunting World. This kind of bag has an outside slot on the back for a magazine and your boarding pass, a zippered compartment covered by a flap in the front, and a large center compartment closed by a zipper. Some versions of this type of bag have two pouches in the front closed by a tab, designed for camera lenses but perfect for passport cases, address books, and other travel documents.

About the Cost of Bags

Your travel bags, like your luggage and handbag, say something definite about you, and it's worthwhile to consider with care not only the kind of bag you need, but also the impression you want to create. I have never hesitated to buy the best luggage and handbags I could afford, not only because they look good and give me a sense of pleasure when I carry them, but because they last twice as long as cheaper bags.

In calculating what kind of bag you can afford, you obviously are limited by the amount of cash you can spend. But in terms of assessing the value of what you're getting and its actual cost, you should amortize the cost of the bag over the duration of its usage. If it cost $150 and has a lifespan of four years, the bag has cost you only $37.50 a year, $3.12 a month and 10¢ a day—presumably a bearable expenditure.

Mini-Handbag Supplements

When you're on a business trip, you don't always want to carry your large travel bag, especially when you're going out in the evening or for an hour of shopping during a break in your business schedule.

In addition to my travel bag, I also carry a small, flat rectangular leather or suede purse shaped like an envelope for use when I don't want to lug the bigger bag. I also usually carry a flat, legal-sized leather envelope for my business papers; I often use this in place of a briefcase. Both the small flat envelope and the larger one pack easily. And both fit in my carry-on bag.

EMERGENCY PACKING CHECKLIST

Select a travel bag large enough to carry what's needed, but small enough to be comfortably portable. It should have handles, a removable shoulder strap, and an outside pocket, securely sealed. In it should go:

- Documents
- Cash and checks
- Maps and guides
- Business planner/address book/appointment book
- Business papers
- Calculator
- Pen/pencil/notepad
- Car, home, and luggage keys
- Eyeglasses/contact lenses/sunglasses
- Cosmetics/toiletries
- Jewelry
- Extra stockings
- Scarf/belt/wrinkle-proof blouse
- Flat envelope handbag
- Flat envelope for business papers
- Extra clothing and shoes, if possible
- Prescription medicines
- A good book

19

Packing for Business

Business packing requires the same kind of analytical attention and advance planning as packing your personal belongings. The more carefully you plan, the more efficient your business trip will be.

On the Plane

First decide what business materials you need with you on the plane. These should fit into your carry-on bag or briefcase. You might include the following:

- Appointment book/business agenda
- Address book, complete with all addresses and telephone numbers
- A few business cards/bilingual business cards
- Business proposals, price lists, work notes, briefing sheets, or other essentials needed for your first day's business or your perusal on the plane
- Daily record keeper/expense account forms
- Call reports/office memoranda
- Pen/pencil/notepad
- One business sample, if not too bulky
- Tape recorder/dictating machine

The daily planner, agenda, or appointment book for business travel should be small enough to be easily portable, but large enough to provide adequate space for all the appointments, notes, and expense records. I need a planner that provides at least one full page for each business day, preferably with the hours indicated.

Four Great Organizers

Often it seems that half the time spent doing business is devoted to organizing materials. This seems especially true in the compressed time of a business trip. To make life easier for yourself on the road, design a system before you go that accommodates all the categories of materials your work generates.

File your materials on the road just as you would in the office by placing papers of a certain type together, separated from other categories.

If you have loose sheets of paper, place them by category in plain manila file folders, or in see-through plastic folders bound on three sides. With the plastic folders, you can see at a glance what papers are inside, and the binding on three sides will hold the papers together.

Other folders, a bit more glamorous and interesting to present, are the lacquer-bright and tweed-patterned ones available in some of the chic paper boutiques. Folders like these usually have elastic that stretches around the corners to hold them closed, or they have ties on three sides, and they are reasonably priced.

An accordion file folder might prove to be a perfect second type of organizer, provided it's small enough to fit easily into your carry-on luggage. Once again, use a plain manila folder available from your stationer, or buy a fancier one in patterned papers or fabric. Label the divisions of the folder according to the contents of the papers inside, and try to find space for all your on-the-road papers in one file. Some categories that might apply:

- Proposals
- Price lists
- Order forms/contracts
- Leave-behind materials
- Follow-up letters
- Call reports
- Expense account forms
- Sales reports
- Letters/correspondence
- Office stationery

If you have a lot of papers to organize, you may find that the best solution is to carry a third kind of organizer—an ordinary briefcase.

Organize your papers in separate folders and place them in the bottom of the briefcase, or buy a briefcase with a built-in accordion file large enough to accommodate your materials. A number of great-looking briefcases on the market are scaled down for women, some squared off and with handles in the classic manner, and others more like large envelopes with foldover flaps, to be carried under the arm.

A fourth great organizer is your office, if you manage things correctly. It's up to you to organize your business on the home front so you'll have complete back-up force when you're on the road. Take the time to brief your associates and subordinates, and be sure the appropriate person will be there to fill in reports, file materials, place orders, send out follow-up letters, make appointments, and perform other tasks for you while you're out of town. Establish fixed times and means of communication with your staff—by telephone or telex or mail—and be sure everyone understands the system before you go.

Your Sample Kit

Business travel often requires you to carry samples of one sort or another, plus bulky selling materials. If you have a large presentation kit in a heavy ring binder that converts to a desk-top easel, 300-page sample books, and leave-behind kits, don't carry them. Pack your heavy business materials separately in a sturdy suitcase or sample kit and send it ahead to your hotel or to a business contact at your destination. If you're traveling internationally, have your sample cases airfreighted ahead a day or two before your arrival and held at the airport customs for you to pick up.

Unless you have just a few folders, your business materials should always be packed separately from your clothing. Books, papers, printed products, and heavy samples do not keep your clothes fresh looking and they can actually stain and tear your garments.

If you do not carry a separate bag, pack materials flat on the bottom of your suitcase and cover them with a large cotton square, or use a dry-cleaning bag to provide separation and protection for your clothes. Also keep cosmetics away from your business materials. A report smeared with cleansing cream will not impress a prospective client.

There's a limit to how much dirty work you can do when it comes to the real world of moving goods. Be aware, in advance, that you cannot perform important, income-producing tasks for your company while lugging 100-pound sample cases and sweating like a stevedore. With regard for your health, poise, and job efficiency, make it a rule never to pick up heavy business cases. Use porters, taxicab drivers, baggage carts, curbside check-in facilities, and bellhops whenever possible. Pay for services and assistance when you need them.

By avoiding excessively heavy bags, you are just demonstrating professional and medical good sense. There's no reason you should jeopardize your physical well-being out of job enthusiasm and earnestness. You are not being paid to hurt yourself.

THE CONVENTION NIGHTMARE

I know many women who are often responsible for having expensive, multi-ton display booths shipped to faraway destinations and assembled there by local crews. Inevitably, the screws that join the Plexiglas panels of the display always get lost in transit, and, as the local screws do not conform to American sizes, no replacements are available. The booth remains on the floor of the convention hall collecting dust as the day and hour of the opening approach. Finally, local workmen are called in to weld the panels together, thus making disassembly impossible and rendering the expensive display useless for the future. Or, as a last alternative, a frantic executive makes a hurried international flight, First Class, to deliver a substitute set of screws.

If you are the unlucky person responsible for such an endeavor, be sure you know where to find the screws. Even if somebody else is responsible for getting the booth out of storage—or shipped to Munich from Bolivia, where it was last used—be sure *you* know precisely how the damn thing works and where all the components can be found.

If the conference is well organized, a freight company with strong-armed men will collect and set up the various displays. You will most likely be asked to make an appointment with the freight company in advance, as the men will have many demands on their time. If no assistance is forthcoming from the show's organizers, you will have to know how to assemble the display booth yourself. Before leaving your home office, be armed with the designer's plans and check to see that all the needed parts are intact. Allow sufficient time to hire someone at your destination to assemble the display unit for you. You are responsible for getting the job done, not necessarily for doing it yourself.

BUSINESS PACKING CHECKLIST

- Pack business essentials in your carry-on bag.
- Organize business materials by category in folders, accordion files, or in your briefcase.
- When possible, pack business materials separately from clothing.
- Ship heavy samples ahead to destination.
- Plan alternatives to lugging heavy samples yourself.
- Know how convention displays work and how they are assembled.

20

Keeping the Home Fires Burning

You're not just a cog in the mechanized wheels of the military-industrial complex. You're a sensitive, tough, competent, fragile, independent, and vulnerable human being who has to uproot herself from the security and comfort of home to travel for business. The very least you can do to make life livable for yourself is to be sure your philodendron hasn't died by the time you return.

Who's Going to Water Your Philodendron?

Living creatures, like plants, animals, children, husbands, lovers, and friends, are the ones who need the most consideration when you're planning to leave home on a business trip. After all, you want your personal world intact when you return.

If you're married and/or have a family, you've already solved two-thirds of the problem of how to keep your daily life rolling along in your absence. Surely your husband will water the flowers, bathe and feed the children, answer your phone calls, leave the bed unmade in your absence, and do it all with a grin, as you and he have already reached a solid mutual agreement regarding your respective responsibilities. If you haven't made this accommodation, you'd better do it now with a sense of fairness, humor, and compassion, not to mention mutual supportiveness. But this is not a marriage manual and your connubial arrangements are far beyond its scope.

If you're not married, if you don't have a roommate or a live-in house-keeper, if you live alone, who's going to water your philodendron? Most likely, family or friends.

Friends may be your extended family, your surrogate support group. Cherish them for the important role they play. Make friends with your neighbors. Make friends with your ex-husband. And ask him or her or them to come in once a week while you're gone to water your philodendron. While you're at it, give them a key to your mailbox and ask them to pick up your mail.

If you simply can't get anyone to water your plants, give them a good dose of water (with a little plant food) the evening before you leave. If you're going to be gone for a few days, they'll survive. For longer trips, buy some of those timed plant feeders that look like king-size thermometers and plug them into the plant soil. If you're really concerned, set your plants in the bathtub, water them well and cover them with a tall tent of transparent polyethylene to create an impro-vised greenhouse. If no air gets in, condensation will collect on the inside of the plastic tent and will drip down on the plants to moisturize them. Plants will stay alive in this environment for weeks, even months. Be sure they have adequate light; use artifical spots if re-quired. And be sure the plastic tent is completely sealed.

PETS, HUMAN AND OTHERWISE

First of all, consider your pet animals. Obviously, you can't seal your pets in a Baggie with a timer that drips down pellets of food. If you travel a great deal for business and have a menagerie ranging from canaries to guppies to Great Danes, you had better reevaluate your priorities. It isn't fair to animals to neglect them or abandon them, even temporarily, to no care at all or to the erratic care of strangers.

Since I travel a lot, I have never kept pets. In my view, animals are family and they need constant love and concern. I would feel awful to find even a goldfish flipped over in a tank as a result of my neglect while away from home.

The best bet in caring for animals is to rely on your network of friends. There are plenty of people like you who live alone, keep and love pets, and are required to travel occasionally for business. Find friends who have the same needs as you do, and for whom you can return the favor the next time they're out of town. Arrange to have your cat or dog stay with them while you're away. Or ask your friends to drop in daily to spend a few minutes caring for your pets.

If you can't find a friend to help take care of your animals, look for some new friends. In the meantime, check the yellow pages of your phone book for the names of animal care facilities. Try under ''Kennels'' and ''Pet Exercising and Feeding Services.'' Call your local ASPCA (American Society for the Prevention of Cruelty to Animals) and see what they recommend as a temporary home for your pet. Or ask friends who have animals what services they employ. Recently, some enterprising folks across the country have established ''pet motels'' for boarding pets (most of them restricted to cats and dogs). They aren't cheap, but the care is usually good and you'll be able to travel in peace knowing that your animals aren't hurt, hungry, or abandoned.

Your Family Misses You

If you have a family or a live-in companion, you won't have to worry about who's going to care for your budgies and gloxinia, but you may worry about who's going to care for them.

If your household includes a husband and some children, presumably you have already arranged for their care and feeding (Burger King *et al.*), and their transportation to ballet classes and football practice in your absence. But you may want to leave some special surprises for them, like goodies stashed away in the freezer, or tickets to a basketball game or the theater, just as a reminder that you love and miss them.

On the road, telephone them frequently. Tell your children what you're doing and how your business projects are progressing so they can share in your triumphs and setbacks. You don't want your job to stand as a barrier between you and your children.

If you're a divorced or widowed mother with a full-time career, you have perhaps the toughest job of all. Nobody is beside you to share the responsibility of caring for your children. After an exhausting, demanding day of business, I don't know how you manage to be as good at mothering as you are.

When business travel obligations come into the picture, the strain is tremendous; you must find someone to care for your children while you're away. If your job plus other support permits you to have a live-in housekeeper, your problems are solved. Your children will stay safe and confident at home with your live-in surrogate. If you aren't so fortunate, you'll have to look to your family and friends for support.

A good friend of mine who is the divorced mother of two children gives very specific advice on this subject:

I'm always on the lookout for people who can take care of the kids. For instance, I have a dressmaker, a lovely woman who lives nearby and happens to be a widow. I've been cultivating her for years. The children know her and seem to feel comfortable around her, and she adores spending time with them. Sure enough, when I asked her to come and stay in the house for a week to look after the children, she was delighted. The children had fun, and the woman received a little extra income and a lot of extra joy that she seemed grateful for.

Other people to cultivate are your mother, mother-in-law, ex-husband, and even your ex-husband's second wife or girlfriend. Luckily, my ex-husband lives in the same town as we do. I can't tell you how many times I've asked him to take the kids while I've zipped around the country on a business assignment. I've even sent the kids to his girlfriend's apartment. The children know her and like her and everything worked just fine.

Friends and Lovers

Theoretically, you don't have to keep your real friends on ice—they'll be there anytime you need them, in any circumstance, whether or not you bring them a present from Detroit. And don't worry about your lovers. If they don't want to be kept on ice, if they forget your name, address, telephone number, and favorite perfume in the short two weeks you're away, there's not much you can do about it. If you think about it, you really haven't lost much in the first place.

The idea behind maintaining links with people you care about is twofold: You want them to know you're thinking about them, and you want them to think about you. It really boils down to a problem of communication. You have to stay in communication with people when you're out of town and out of sight. It's the only way to maintain a dialogue.

The telephone is a very successful twentieth-century device for communicating. Call your friends. Call your lovers. Call them from your hotel room when you're feeling a little bit lonely and tell them something funny or awful that happened to you that day. Or seductively whisper good night into the ear of your favorite boyfriend or your husband and tell him how much you wish he were with you. Take advantage of the separation to heighten the excitement you'll feel when you see each other again, even if it's going to be tomorrow night.

Send a mailgram, a telex, or a telegram. A short story. An anecdote. A newspaper clipping. An offer. A request. A confirmation of some plans. Buy a ''creative'' card with a ''message for every occasion'' and send the wrong message to the right person.

The idea is to involve the people you love and care about in your life and be available for involvement in theirs. If you're going to miss a favorite friend's birthday, send him or her some hot tamales through the mail. Or send a singing telegram, a plant, or a birthday cake from a local baker who will deliver. Keep a list of your friends' birthdays, anniversaries, and other important occasions in your address book or daily calendar, and check frequently so nobody gets forgotten. Give your husband or boyfriend your itinerary, or have your secretary report it to him as it unfolds, then plan a secret, exciting weekend together in some remote corner of the globe.

Whatever you plan to do for your friends and lovers when you're away from home on a business trip, just remember to ask yourself what you would like them to do for you. Then do it for them. It's all about tender loving care and communications.

SECURITY IF YOU LIVE ALONE

One of the things many people worry about when they're obliged to make frequent or prolonged business trips is the vulnerability of their homes, left closed and untended for days or weeks at a time. If you live alone in a house or an apartment, especially in a high-crime city, how do you manage to protect your home and valuables when you're traveling?

Apartment dwellers should choose a building with a doorman or apartment manager and good security when selecting a place to live. If you don't have a doorman or security personnel, you might consider moving to a more secure building if you travel extensively. If there's no question of moving, make friends with your building superintendent. Give him a $10 tip every time you go away and ask him to keep an eye on things for you.

No matter where you live, be sure the locks on your doors and windows are the best available, and that no spare keys are hanging around with workmen or casual acquaintances.

Before you leave, partially draw your curtains or shades so no one can peer into your empty, dark rooms. Leave a light on somewhere, or buy a timing device that turns the lights on and off at appropriate times. Also, buy a cheap portable radio (you don't want to burn out a good one), and leave it on, turned to a station with a lot of talking, at medium volume.

Place your jewelry, stock certificates, loose money, bank checks, important papers, and other valuables in a safe-deposit box. Buy a homeowner's insurance policy to protect your home against theft, fire, and other damage. If you have a lot of good silver, furs, or other things of value that won't fit at the bank, hide them or at least place them out of sight.

Alert your friends and neighbors to your travel plans. Give one of them a complete set of keys, and ask him or her to check in occasionally. Be sure someone knows how and where to reach you at all times. If you live in a suburban or rural area, you might alert the local police to your departure (if it's to be a lengthy trip). Their patrols might make a special check on your home while you're away.

For trips of six weeks or more, you'll need someone to pay your bills. Leave a bunch of addressed and signed checks with someone you trust, and have him or her open your monthly bills, fill in the amounts, and mail the letters off, plus keep tabs on the expenditures for your records. Or have a friend collect your bills and deliver them to your office, then have your office forward them to you in the next correspondence or office pouch.

Rent checks can be paid in advance by postdating your checks and mailing them to your landlord with a cover letter.

If your have a trustworthy cleaning person who comes in once or twice a week, pay the person in advance to keep coming. It's good to have someone visiting your home just to let a little air in. It's even greater to find the tables shining and the floors waxed when you return.

A HOME THAT'S NICE TO COME BACK TO

Whether or not you have someone to help out, there are many things you can do to make your home pleasant to get back to.

First of all, leave it clean. I once went off to Europe in a rush and left some dirty dishes in the sink and old clothes strewed on the floor. The bed wasn't made. The place was a mess. And that's exactly how I found it when I returned six months later.

Even if you have to leave for the airport at 5 in the morning, prepare your house the night before and leave enough time before your departure to at least make your bed and rinse out your coffee cup. There's nothing more morbid than coming back into a world that has been frozen in time like an Egyptian tomb.

Don't leave a vase of fresh flowers to wither and die and depress you when you return. Throw them out or give them to a neighbor, unless you're sure they'll survive.

Clean your refrigerator and throw out all the food that will spoil. If you plan to be gone for months, empty the fridge altogether, defrost it, and leave it unplugged with the door ajar and a dish of baking soda placed inside. Throw out your garbage, too.

Always stock emergency breakfast supplies and something to nibble on when you arrive home. If your refrigerator is working, stash some croissants and fruit juice in the freezer. Keep some fresh milk and butter down below if your trip will be a short one. Store powdered cream substitute and coffee or tea in the pantry.

If you can, make a house-care swap with a neighbor or friend. Ask him or her to put some fresh eggs, milk, yogurt, fruit, and a bunch of daisies in your house on the day you're due home. Then return the favor.

Take advantage of the time you'll be gone to have some repair or cleaning work done on your home. Send your bedspread and curtains down for their long-overdue cleaning. Have your carpet cleaned (if it can be sent out, or if you can arrange to have your doorman or maid supervise). Or get your floors professionally waxed. A room painted. A chair reupholstered. Some throw pillows made for the sofa. Or take the pictures that have been sitting behind the bedroom door for the last three years out to be framed.

Before you go, check around the house to be certain everything is in order. Leave a window open a crack somewhere just for oxygen, even in winter. If you live in a house, lower the thermostat to 55° to 58° in the winter—just enough to keep your plants in good shape. During the winter, always leave a faucet running slightly to keep the water moving through the pipes so they don't freeze and burst. Close the flues of your fireplace to cut off drafts. And shut down the water heater if you'll be gone for a long time.

If you have an answering service, be sure to contact it before you leave. Tell your service how long you'll be out of town and ask them to hold your messages, or tell them that you'll call in periodically. (If you're going to be gone for several months, you may want to have your telephone temporarily disconnected to save the monthly charge.)

Before going out the door, make a fast but thorough check around the house to be sure that no appliances—the iron, toaster, air conditioner, electric typewriter, record player, television, coffee pot, hair curlers—are plugged in. Be extra cautious and unplug all appliances before leaving, including the air conditioner and fridge. Check the dials on the stove to be sure everything is safely turned off. Be sure all pilot lights are lit—if they're not, the gas will build up unpleasantly, even dangerously, in a closed environment.

Are the windows closed and locked, except one safe one for a bit of air? Are the doors all locked, even the door to the basement and the door to the garage? Is the fire out in the fireplace? Are your cigarettes all out? Is your electric blanket unplugged? Take time and the trouble to go back over the list. An ounce of prevention may save your home.

HOME CARE CHECKLIST

General
- Build a network of mutual support friendships to help you keep your world intact when you're away from home.
- Solicit help from maid, doorman, building superintendent; tip well.
- Alert family/friends/local police.
- Give keys to a friend.
- Buy plant feeders or build a plastic greenhouse in bathtub.
- Leave pets with friends or at kennels. Call pet feeding service.
- Leave itinerary with family or friends.
- Leave thoughtful treats for those you love.

Communications
- Send letters/cards/telegrams/telexes/mailgrams.
- Use the phone.
- Bring back gifts and mementos.
- Plan get-togethers on the road.

Home Security
- Be sure apartment has doorman/other security.
- Get locks on doors and windows.
- Draw the curtains halfway.
- Leave lights on or install timer.
- Leave radio on.
- Put valuables in safe-deposit box. Hide others.
- Clean out fridge/throw out garbage.
- Leave emergency food supplies.
- Arrange for home cleaning and repairs.
- Check furnace/hot water/pipes.
- Turn off or unplug appliances.

Part 4

ON THE ROAD

21

Timely Departures

Your bags are packed. Your documents are in order. Your plants are watered. You've been over your home care checklist at least once. And your travel clothes are laid out on a chair. You set your alarm for some ungodly hour in the morning and go to sleep, knowing that you've made every possible preparation to ensure a smooth-flowing business trip.

Getting to the Airport

If you're leaving for the airport from home without a husband or a friend to drive you, arrange your transportation in advance. Many cities have private limousine services that transport passengers from the main airline ticket offices and the leading downtown hotels for a fee that's at least 50 percent cheaper than a taxi, and just slightly more than most airport trains or buses. If your city has an airport limousine service, call in advance to book a seat and to learn the departure and arrival times. If the airport is immense, with departure buildings scattered over an area the size of Manhattan Island, be sure to allow enough time for the limousine to deliver you to the right terminal.

The same applies for airport buses or trains, which usually depart from in-city airline terminals, or from fixed stops on the train line. Advance reservations are seldom needed for these, but you do need to know when they leave, how long they take to get to the airport, and, once you're there, how much time it takes for the bus or train to make the rounds. Sometimes a train or bus will not leave you at the door of your departure terminal, but at some depot several miles away. Find out in advance if this is the case, and schedule enough time to make the transfer.

Taxis

Getting to the limousine, bus, or train pickup point from your home or office usually requires a taxi ride. Call in advance and arrange with a company you trust to pick you up at the assigned hour. The same applies if you're taking a taxi all the way to the airport, which sometimes costs only a dollar or two more than the combined taxi-and-limousine or taxi-and-bus ride. Add up the total and measure the difference; the comfort of being picked up at home and delivered directly to your departure terminal without having to load up and reload your bags may make a taxi worth the extra cost.

Finding a reliable taxi service is as essential as learning the names of your clients' secretaries. If your company has a business account with a particular taxi fleet, identify yourself as a frequent customer, explain the importance of your request, and be sure the booking operator and the driver understand the value of your company's business.

Even in a large city like New York where taxi drivers aren't generally disposed to treating passengers preferentially, you can solicit the help and support of individual drivers. Chrisjean Whitten, whose flights to Tegucigalpa and Timbuktu always seem to depart before sunrise, has a taxi driver named Max whom she has called on for years to take her to the airport. Max owns his own taxi and is a responsible businessman. He gets consistent business from Chrisjean, plus generous tips, and he has even offered to pick her up at the airport when she returns, if given advance notice.

If you have no taxi service to call but think it would be easier to pick one up in the street, don't leave it to chance. Be sure, in advance, that you can find a taxi when you need one, even at 5 A.M. in a sleet storm. Check the weather report the night before you go so you can allow extra time for difficult conditions. Then try going out on the street some morning at 5 A.M. to see if taxis run frequently at that hour.

No matter how you get to the airport, keep the receipts for your transportation, or record the amount in your expense diary. Most taxi drivers have receipt vouchers available upon request. If you work for yourself, transportation costs for business trips are deductible from your taxes. If you're employed by a company, the amount will probably be included in your travel expense allowance, or reimbursed by the company upon your return.

Driving Your Own Car

If you plan to take your own car to the airport, make sure it has enough gas, and allow enough time to reach the airport in the traffic conditions that prevail; if you'll be hitting the morning rush hour or leaving at the beginning or end of a high-season weekend, allow double the usual driving time. When you reach the airport, drop your baggage off at the curbside check-in station, or give it to a porter to deliver to the check-in counter to be held for you. Be sure the porter gives your bags to the check-in clerks to hold behind the counter and doesn't just dump them on the floor nearby. Take the skycap's number and pay him for his services when you return from parking your car.

Your car probably belongs in the long-term parking lot of the airport, which may be miles from the departure building. Allow time for this maneuver, especially if you are not familiar with the airport. You will have to find the lot, check your car in (usually through one of those ticket-issuing machines), park it, lock it, and then get all the way back to the terminal. Jot down the location of your car on your parking-lot receipt and put it safely away among your travel documents.

Many of the larger airports have buses or trams that will pick you up at the long-term parking lot and transport you, free of charge, back to your departure terminal. Find out in advance if such a service exists, how frequently it operates, and where you should pick it up. Also calculate how long it will take—as much as an hour is needed in some airports. Call your airline or the airport information number for details.

Returning Rental Cars

Turning in rental cars before a flight can be just as time-consuming as parking your car. Find out where the return station is located, how you will get to your departure terminal from there, and how much time is involved. This is especially important to know in the case of small, local agencies that may not provide comprehensive services.

Beating Traffic

Some seasoned travelers claim they can save hours by taking circuitous routes to the airport through obscure suburbs. I never seem to save more than a bit of getting-stuck-in-traffic boredom by racing around on lengthy routes that add dimes to the meter and miles to the ride.

In your own city, ask around and experiment yourself to learn the quickest (and cheapest) routes at different times of day—one airport route may be great in the morning but a disaster during rush hour. In cities you're visiting, ask the hotel concierge or your business associates for their advice on the best routes. Keep a city map marked with the shortcuts in your files for future reference. Specify the route you want the driver to take when you get into a taxi. Also, note the routes taken by the airport buses and limousines from different parts of town—they're probably the shortest and quickest.

As in most travel situations, the basic and most valuable commodity in home-to-airport planning is time. Allow enough time to accommodate the worst contingencies—massive traffic jams, flat tires, and missed turns. That way, you'll never need to feel anxious or miss a flight.

CHECKING IN

Most airlines request that you check in at least half an hour before domestic flights and at least an hour before international flights. If you try to board the plane less than 10 minutes before the scheduled departure, many airlines will disclaim responsibility for seating you.

If you're traveling during a peak travel season, you may want to check in even earlier than the airline suggests to be certain you get the seat you want. Also, be sure you're not the latecomer who gets bumped if the airline has overbooked.

You may also want to check in early if you're carrying an extra load of baggage or business-related materials and will need special assistance from the airline.

Curbside Check-in

Many domestic and some international airports provide curbside check-in facilities where you may dump your bags and have them tagged for your destination, never to see them again until your arrival. Curbside check-in is a great convenience, in theory, but it's also one more possible point of error in the risk-laden business of transporting your bags.

U.S. airlines lose almost three million pieces of baggage every year, although they claim that 95 percent of all lost bags are located within the first 24 hours, and 99 percent within 72 hours. Your chances are roughly 1 in 100 that your bags will be lost (the three million bags the U.S. airlines lose every year represent about 1 percent of all the bags moved annually). If you add on the statistics about robbed or damaged bags, your chances are roughly 1 in 50 that your bag will be temporarily lost, damaged, or looted.

With these odds in mind, it's discomforting to realize that there's not a heck of a lot you can do to protect your bags except to see that they're labeled properly, inside and out, with your name, home or office address and telephone number, and with an address for you at your destination. The bags should be locked, and no jewelry, money, negotiable securities, or other valuables should be packed inside. Old baggage tags should be removed, no matter how fond you are of the memories they recall, since they will just confuse the baggage handlers.

If you take advantage of curbside check-in facilities, watch the clerk tag your bag to be sure the tag indicates the city you're actually going to. In airline lingo, destinations are indicated in three-letter codes that refer to the airport and may or may not have anything to do with the name of the city. ORD, for example, is the code for Chicago's O'Hare Airport. (For examples of codes to some U.S. and international airports, see the Appendix.)

Baggage Liability/Excess-Valuation Insurance

If you're concerned about losing your bags and want to cover them above the airline's liability, do not check them in at the curbside check-in station. Take them into the ticket counter to purchase **excess-valuation insurance,** which increases the rate of the airline's liability. On domestic flights, normal airline liability is limited to $750 per ticketed passenger (not $750 per bag). On international flights, airline liability is pegged at $9.07 a pound ($20 a kilo), therefore the weight of your bags should be marked on the baggage check incorporated in your ticket (this is not the same as your baggage claim check). Airlines do not accept responsibility for carry-on luggage, since it is not checked.

The cost of excess-valuation insurance is usually 15 cents for every $100 of coverage over and above the airline's traditional liability. Airline ticket clerks aren't always keen to provide you with this time-consuming service, especially when the check-in line is crowded with demanding passengers. But most domestic airlines have this insurance, and you are within your rights to request it. According to the CAB, airline personnel may examine the contents of your baggage when you purchase excess-valuation insurance.

Excess-valuation insurance covers your baggage only during the time it is in the keeping of the airline, not before or afterward, and it does not cover items that are unusually fragile or perishable—photographic gear, money, jewelry, works of art, antiques, silverware, or negotiable securities—all good reasons never to pack your valuables in a suitcase to be checked. If you wish additional insurance coverage for your valuables—or for your baggage in general when it is not in the hands of the airline—purchase a personal articles floater from an insurance agent. Travel insurance is discussed in Chapter 7.

Excess Baggage

If you are traveling with a half dozen large suitcases filled with metal samples, you will undoubtedly get hit with overweight penalties every time you check in for a plane. Rates for overweight baggage are charged at a flat rate per bag and are governed by international agreements. When there's no inspector around, however, the rules seem open to personal interpretation.

This is to your advantage. The airline clerks processing your ticket at check-in can unilaterally decide to waive overweight charges for your baggage if they want to. This is where your charm, directness, and professional presentation come in. The way to convince the airline personnel to help you is by making direct eye contact, presenting your business card, explaining the nature (and difficulty) of your journey, and then telling them how frequently you and your co-workers fly on their great airline. You're a First Class or full-fare Business Class passenger, as they will surely note, and you should tell them that you have always been given special consideration by their airline on prior trips. You'll be amazed how often it works.

Check in early, by the way, if you plan to ask for special consideration. The airline personnel won't be able to waive the rules for you in a crush when there are a dozen other passengers watching.

Beating Check-in Lines

First, try to obtain your ticket in advance. If you have to pick it up at the airport, there's no escaping the line unless you're lucky enough to find a ticket-dispensing machine in the terminal.

If you already have your ticket, you can avoid the line by checking your bag in at the curbside check-in facility, and then proceeding directly to the departure gate. If the airlines offers one-stop check-in, you can pick up your boarding pass and seat assignment at the same time as you check your bags, thus eliminating the need to get in line again in the departure lounge. Members of some airline frequent-travelers clubs can go directly to the club lounge to check in and pick up their boarding passes and seat assignments.

Many U.S. and other airlines offer club members and full-fare-paying business travelers the privilege of checking in at the First Class ticket counter, or in the First Class departure lounge. This is an especially valuable service in airports that do not have curbside check-in facilities.

Some airlines, armed with fancy new computers, have recently offered advance seat assignments to passengers on round-trip flights or multi-leg trips. Presumably, after you check in and get your first seat assignment, you never have to check in again—your assignment is valid for every subsequent stage of your journey. Every time you arrive at an airport, you can proceed directly to the departure gate. To be on the safe side, confirm your seat assignment before each leg of the flight. This is one situation where carry-on luggage would free you completely from having to deal with checking in.

Keeping Track

No matter where you check in, be sure to keep tabs on the transactions that occur. For example, if your airline ticket is a multi-flight ticket with several coupons included, check to see that the airline representative pulls only the coupon needed for the current flight. One friend has yet to be paid back for a coupon good for a flight from Madrid to Nice that was pulled by error in Paris, almost two years ago.

Always check the tags put on your bags for accuracy, and be sure the numbers match the baggage claim tickets given you. Watch as the clerk puts your bags on the conveyor belt. Then pray. There's not much else you can do.

Always keep your baggage claim tickets in a safe spot, preferably clipped to your ticket envelope, or tucked securely in your passport case or travel wallet. In many airports in the world, you are required to show your claim tickets before you're permitted to remove your bags.

Departure Taxes

In many countries, embarking passengers are obliged to pay a tax or departure fee at the airline check-in counter or at customs control. The amount involved is usually $10 or under, which should pose no problem except when you've just unloaded the last of your Haitian gourdes or Pakistani rupees, and then discover you must pay in local currency.

The nomenclature for various types of departure taxes differs around the globe. In the United States, you'll find a $3 departure tax insidiously included in the price of your airline ticket, charged automatically when you pay for the flight; it's called ''international transportation tax.'' ''Passenger service charge,'' ''ticket tax,'' ''civil aviation tax," "embarkation tax," and "head tax" are some of the other terms used.

There are about a hundred countries that charge some kind of departure tax, among them the United States, Afghanistan, Israel, Jordan, Pakistan, Sri Lanka, Philippines, Thailand, Hong Kong, Japan, New Zealand, Australia, Mali, Guinea, Paraguay, Uruguay, Ecuador, Peru, Venezuela, Colombia, Costa Rica, Panama, and several dozen Caribbean islands. The highest departure taxes for noncitizens are levied by Australia (about U.S. $11), Pakistan and Peru (U.S. $10), and Israel (U.S. $8.50). The only country in Western Europe requiring a departure tax is West Germany, and then only on routes out of West Berlin direct to non-German cities.

To find out what departure taxes are required and how much they cost, check with your airline, travel agent, or a good guidebook before you leave, or ask at your hotel or at the airport when you arrive at your destination. If no one can inform you of the exact figure, make a last-minute check with the airline ticket clerk when you check in—you'll still have time to arrange your finances before going through customs.

GETTING BUMPED

Because passengers are permitted—on most flights at least—to reserve seats and then cancel at the last minute without penalty, the airlines never know how many passengers will or will not show up. To counterbalance this potential lack of revenue—a situation that has become most urgent due to the high cost of fuel and declining revenues—the airlines sell more seats than are actually available. If too many passengers show up for a flight, somebody—usually the last passenger to board—gets bumped.

What do you do if there's no seat left for you? Learn your rights now, then make a very big fuss and pull every trick in the book to keep from being the one to get involuntarily removed.

Once, when I had just boarded a flight from New York to Athens, overbooked Coach passengers were moved up to fill the First Class section. Suddenly, a First Class passenger arrived with a confirmed ticket, a boarding pass, and a seat assignment, only to find that his seat had just been given away. Justifiably, the man hit the roof, refusing to get off the plane and delaying the takeoff by almost an hour. A compromise was finally reached when another passenger agreed to leave the plane in exchange for compensation to provide a seat for the irate traveler.

Before discussing the rules and regulations in detail, here are a few things you can do to avoid being bumped:

1. Have a confirmed reservation, and reconfirm your flight at least 48 hours before departure (72 hours before an international flight).
2. Have your ticket in your possession and check to see that it is in order (your status should be OK, not RQ).
3. Arrive at the airport early to receive your boarding pass and seat assignment, or obtain an advance seat assignment, when possible.
4. Report promptly to the departure gate as soon as your flight is announced.
5. Board the flight at least 10 minutes before the scheduled departure; otherwise, the airline is not obligated to honor your ticket.
6. Do not contribute to the problem of overbooking by being a no-show; cancel all flights you don't intend to take.

If you've done everything you're supposed to do and you still get bumped, you may end up missing your flight, but you will be given compensation.

The Bureau of Consumer Affairs of the CAB produces a series of free colored sheets entitled *Fly-Rights: Guide to United States Air Travel*. It's obtainable from the Civil Aeronautics Board, Washington, D.C. 20428. The latest rules and regulations are clearly spelled out in these documents, and you should obtain them to be totally informed.

Denied Boarding Compensation

According to CAB regulations, a domestic airline or an international airline embarking from a U.S. gateway airport (with charters and some other types of flights excepted), must request volunteers to relinquish their seats when a plane is overbooked. In exchange for the inconvenience, the voluntarily bumped passenger may choose to receive a cash compensation or a voucher good as payment when applied against future airfare. The amount of the cash payment or value of the voucher for voluntarily bumped passengers is determined by the local airline representative. Most vouchers are good for one year on any class of travel on the issuing airline, but there are other restrictions that vary by carrier.

Involuntarily bumped passengers are even better protected by the CAB rulings. They can demand cash payment on the spot for the full amount of the fare, with a minimum of $37.50 and a maximum of $200, provided they can be placed on another flight that is scheduled to arrive at their destination within two hours of their original flight arrival. If the delay is greater than two hours (four on international flights), the airline must pay double the fare, with a minimum of $75 and a maximum of $400. In addition to the compensation, the passenger is permitted to use the original ticket for the later flight. The involuntarily bumped passenger has a choice of a cash payment or voucher and can bargain for the amount of compensation given. Airline personnel are instructed to offer the lowest possible amount, and the strength of your demands will have a lot to do with determining the final compensation.

Delayed boarding compensation is not paid on flights that are canceled or delayed, or in cases where the airline has to substitute a smaller aircraft for a larger one. On foreign soil, all foreign carriers have the option of paying denied boarding compensation on flights bound for the U.S. Check with the foreign carrier when making reservations to see if you are protected by CAB rules on the in-bound flight.

For your interest, the bureaucracy that came up with all these rules has not given an official designation to the participants, and so we are stuck with "voluntary bumpee" and "involuntary bumpee." Might we suggest "replacement-evaluated passenger" and "fly-rights objector"? Or "voluntary" and "involuntary relinquisher"? Or "paper tiger" and "capitalist snake"?

If you should decide to voluntarily give up you seat, be sure you negotiate for a confirmed future flight to be arranged by the airline. Don't settle for requested or standby status, as you may find yourself stranded. Also be certain the airline agrees to provide you with meals, transportation, a hotel room, and telegrams during your stayover, as required. Otherwise, the delay may cost you more than the compensation and you'll end up losing money for voluntarily relinquishing your seat.

Most overbooking situations occur during peak travel seasons, which, of course, vary by destination. You can protect yourself during these times by checking in early and boarding promptly.

In cases where you are about to be involuntarily bumped, don't give up without a fight. You don't want to get into a personal wrangle with the flight attendants; it's not their fault that the plane is overbooked. Besides, you want them on your side. But do speak firmly on your own behalf and refuse to get off the plane. Remind the attendants that you are traveling for business on a full-fare ticket—the airlines need passengers like you a lot more than they need those flying on discounted fares. If you're adamant in your resolve not to be bumped, the airline will be forced to find a voluntary bumpee and you'll probably end up getting a seat. If you've paid for a First Class or full-fare Business Class seat and end up in Coach, the airline must reimburse you for the difference. But if you hold a Coach ticket and are seated in First Class, you are not required to pay a surcharge.

If all arguments fail and you do not get aboard, do not leave the plane or let the plane leave before your luggage is removed from the plane's baggage compartment. It may delay the plane a half hour or more, but this is not your problem. There's no reason why, after buying an expensive full-fare ticket, confirming and reconfirming your flight and arriving on schedule, you should be forced to suffer the double indignities of being bumped and losing your luggage.

FLIGHT DELAYS

If you'd called the airport before leaving home, you might have avoided this. But you didn't, and here you are, stuck in an aimless mill of irritated people, all of whom have their eyes fixed on some imperceptible point of reference in the future, like Giacometti figures, isolated in some existential limbo. That's all right. It happens to the most experienced travelers, and as often as not, the delayed flight is announced after you've arrived at the airport and are about to check in. There's nothing you could have done to avoid it, you tell yourself as you stare at the announcement screen, listing to starboard to escape the sticky fingers of the toddler with the jelly Danish sitting in the lounge chair next to you.

The first thing you should do, if the delay looks like a serious one, is to whip out your copy of the *OAG Pocket Flight Guide* and check to see if there's another flight to your destination on another airline. If there is, go immediately to the second airline's ticket counter and book a seat. Your ticket will automatically be transferred to the new airline; you do not have to refund it with the original carrier first. Carry-on baggage gives you the flexibility to make a maneuver like this quickly and easily. If you have already checked your baggage in with the first airline, you may have trouble retrieving it.

If there's no alternative flight, and you'll be stuck hanging around the airport for hours, it's up to you to rearrange your travel program and find something of interest to do. First, look at your business schedule to see how it will be affected by the delay. If you will miss appointments in your destination, or if someone is planning to meet your plane, you must get on the phone to change your plans. All this is easily handled if you're in your hometown airport—merely call your office and ask your secretary or assistant to make the necessary notifications. But if you're not within whistling distance of your office, you can run into expensive long-distance calls trying to amend your schedule. With luck, you might convince the airline to permit you to use its phone.

People and places you should contact as a result of a delayed flight are:

- Your appointments at the destination
- A person meeting your plane
- Your hotel, if you will now be getting in past the normal check-in time (6 P.M. at most hotels, 4 P.M. at many resorts)
- The rental car agency to ask them to hold your reservation
- Your family and friends to let them know of your changed schedule, and to overcome any feelings of travel alienation and loneliness

The airlines are usually pretty good about caring for delayed passengers, especially in long holdups. If you're missing a meal during the delay, or if the flight cannot resume until the following morning, the airline will probably provide you with vouchers good for a meal and/or a room in the airport hotel.

Killing Time—Profitably

If you're stuck in the airport during the day, with no hotel room in sight, you'll be glad you joined the airline's frequent-traveler club. Go immediately to the club lounge, plunk yourself down in a comfortable couch or chair, order a drink or a cup of coffee, and dig out your business papers or a good book. Or pull out your miniature backgammon set and look around for someone interested in a game. Many airline clubs permit members to use their phones free of charge for local calls; this service may come in handy here.

No matter how long your delay, there are many ways to use your time profitably. First of all, don't get anxious. There's nothing you can do. Once you accept this fact, you're free to regard the delay as an entity in itself, a period of found time to be used for some agreeable purpose.

Catching up on your business papers is one productive way of using this time. Others are writing letters and postcards, reading, or just relaxing in front of the airline club's TV. With luck, the airport or a nearby hotel will have a hairdresser, manicurist, or other beauty service with an open appointment. Or you can sneak into the ladies' lounge in the departure terminal and give yourself a manicure there, in privacy and reasonable comfort. You can take a tour of the airport control tower (some airports offer this, although if you've got even a trace of aviophobia, don't bother—the chaos usually depicted on the radar screen would discourage the stout-hearted).

If you have enough time, leave the airport altogether and visit some nearby attraction. From the Dallas/Ft. Worth Airport, for example, you could go to one of the theme parks in Arlington. In Boston, you could make the 10-minute trip into town for a quick visit to the Isabella

Stewart Gardner Museum to see the magnificent Renaissance paintings collected under the tutelage of Bernard Berenson, or you could simply explore the Quincy Market, only five minutes away.

If you can't think of anything to do, go to the airport kiosk and buy a magazine that you'd never thought of reading before. Take the magazine to the airport coffee shop. Every airport coffee shop I've ever been in, in the United States, at least, has been decorated in shades of cadmium orange and has served cadmium orange hot dogs, cadmium yellow mustard, and watery coffee in orange-brown plastic cups with a sugar substitute and ''cream'' made out of soybean residue. Never mind. Read your magazine and pretend you're a foreign visitor getting your first taste of American culture. Be happy, you know from here it's all got to be upbeat.

No matter how you spend those endless hours waiting, there are a few timewasters you should assiduously avoid. One is the airport gift shop. You and your friends don't need coasters emblazoned with Day-Glo kewpie dolls. A second is the candy display at the kiosk—buying a Hershey bar with almonds and unwrapping it slowly while walking through the airport is not a useful way to spend your time.

CHECK-IN CHECKLIST

- Get up early. Be prepared.
- Book taxi/airport limousine in advance.
- Find out airport bus/train schedules.
- Find out about airport long-term parking/rental car return.
- Learn best routes to airport.
- Keep records of all travel expenses.
- Check in early during peak season and when carrying excess baggage.
- Use curbside check-in facilities/advance seat assignments/airline clubs/one-stop check-in to avoid lines.
- Buy excess valuation insurance from airline.
- Keep track of ticket/receipts/baggage stubs.
- Keep enough local currency to pay departure tax.
- Know passenger rights. Claim denied boarding compensation. Refuse to be bumped. Collect baggage if your are bumped.
- Look for alternative flight if delayed.
- Adjust business schedule to accommodate delay.
- Use waiting time productively.

22

Airborne

In the early days of commercial aviation, the first stewardesses were registered nurses who cared for the passengers almost as if they were hospitalized. Today, on a jumbo jet, with over 300 meals to serve, children racing up and down the aisles, 600 or so passenger trips to the lavatories, and unceasing requests for sodas and cookies and pillows and smiles, stewardesses simply cannot offer old-fashioned attentive service.

That's all right. You, like your stewardess, are a busy professional who doesn't need to be nursed, coddled, flirted with, soothed, or humored through the skies. However, you do need to be treated with courtesy and respect, and you need to be given the efficient services that the airline promises and that you've paid for.

Since the deregulation of the air fares by the CAB and the subsequent proliferation of promotional fares, the airlines have been flying more people and enjoying it less. Low-priced tickets plus high operational costs have caused the airlines' profits to shrink drastically. First Class and full-fare Business Class passengers are the only ones the airlines make consistent money on. As a business traveler, you're probably one of them, so don't fail to take advantage of any special business-traveler services the airlines provide.

Before you board, check to see if you have been assigned a seat in the Business Class section, if such a section exists, or at least in the area you prefer. If you are paying full fare, you are probably paying almost double what the majority of the other passengers are paying, and you should be given your preference.

When there's room, many airlines cater to the business traveler by promising a seat in an empty section, or with a free seat between you and the next person. As a woman, unfortunately, you may have to identify yourself to one of the flight crew as a business traveler and ask to be given this service.

Many airlines offer business travelers free drinks, free headsets for music and the movies, and better meals than those on the ordinary Coach Class fare. Often, you can also order special meals from a Business Traveler menu; these must be requested several days before the flight, and you should check before you board to see that the meal has been put on the plane for you. Some airlines also provide business passengers with booking and reservation assistance at the destination, most frequently for hotel chains owned by the airline. Ask your flight attendant or the purser. They might not be able to assist you, but then again, they might.

Getting Comfortable

As soon as you board the plane and find your seat, take down a pillow and a blanket from the overhead compartment—it will save waiting for the stewardess to get one for you later on. Airplanes almost always seem to get chilly, even in summer, and a small lap rug will help keep you comfortable, especially on a long flight.

The selection of magazines on planes is limited. If you want one, pick it up from the magazine rack when you're boarding the plane to be sure of getting one that interests you.

Stow your coat, scarf, and unneeded carry-on baggage overhead before you sit down, or, if the plane isn't too crowded, ask the stewardess if she can hang up your coat.

MAKING GOOD USE OF FLYING TIME

Some management experts claim that one hour of uninterrupted concentration time is worth three interruption-filled hours at the office for the average harassed executive. On planes, you have a great opportunity to work quietly and in privacy, and you'll be astonished at the amount of work you can get done on a two- or three-hour flight. If you really want to concentrate, fly First Class to ensure a wide, comfortable seat, a large table surface to work on, and a minimum of distraction from your neighbors. In Business Class or Coach, sit by the window to reduce the chances of being disturbed, and sit where you can avoid seeing the movie.

One good way to use travel time is to do business reports—those that accumulate as a result of your travel activities, such as call reports, sales records, and expense accounts. Be prepared when you board the plane to do prebusiness or postbusiness work by having the papers and materials you need in your carry-on bag. If you have a pile of letters to write, bring a portable microcassette.

If you don't have work to do, you can use your on-plane time to improve your mind or simply to enjoy yourself. Some frequent travelers I know carry their own headsets, cassettes, and tapes, and listen to their favorite symphonies or to a language lesson during the flight. Another worthwhile activity is reading a guide to your destination, or something special—a book on French philosophy, Easter Island, the fourteenth century, Beatlemania, the stars.

Or go to sleep. For people like me, the best way to improve the mind is through dreaming. Bring your own eye mask and a set of ear plugs if you're a serious snoozer, and perhaps even a mild sedative to knock you out during an overnight flight.

If you're on a long overseas flight, you can use your flying time for personal beauty care. I have seen well-dressed, efficient-looking women business travelers pull bottles of nail polish remover, cotton balls, nail files and other gear out of their briefcases and set to work as soon as the plane gets in the air. Actually, I think this kind of activity belongs in the bathroom. I once saw a model on a New York bus plucking her eyebrow. It wasn't pretty. If you didn't have the chance to do your nails before leaving, or if you'd love to give yourself a face mask, steal into the lavatory when everyone is asleep and do your beauty treatments there.

IN-FLIGHT EXERCISES

Flights of three to four hours or more require some physical activity if you are to escape the low blood circulation and the swollen extremities that so often occur. Most airlines advise you to get up and walk about the cabin from time to time just to move your muscles. You can also do quick isometric exercises while in your plane seat. A simple set of exercises good for every kind of sedentary situation, including your office, can be found in a booklet produced by SAS entitled *In-the-Chair Exercise Book*, and in a great little booklet published by Lufthansa, in conjunction with the German Sports Federation, entitled *Fitness in the Chair—Lufthansa Executive Traveler Services*.

The exercises in these two books seem to be simplified versions of the warm-up exercises you probably do in your calisthenics class, combined with some yoga movements and isometric principles. With a little bit of knowledge of these disciplines, you can develop your own series of in-flight exercises merely by going down your body from head to toes and finding an activity for each set of muscles on the way. Examples:

Head: Sit erect, then turn your head slowly from left to right, turning your eyes around as far as possible over your shoulder. Hold the position for a moment, then turn your head and eyes slowly back to the front, then around to the other side. Breathe deeply as you hold the twist position.

Eyes: If you've been reading a lot and want to relax your eyes, hold your head erect and roll your eyes from left to right, very slowly, extending your range of vision in as wide a circumference as possible. Reverse the direction of the eye rolling. Then practice looking as far up, down, left, and right as you can. Open your mouth wide and stretch the muscles in your cheeks and eye sockets, then close your eyes and breathe deeply.

Neck: Sit erect, lean forward in your seat or chair to give yourself room, then roll your head around slowly from left, to the back, to the right, and then front. Repeat three times going from left to right, then reverse, going from right to left. Roll your head in long, luxurious circles, easing and stretching your neck muscles, never forcing or straining. Close your eyes and breathe easily. When you're finished, rest with your head bowed to the front, then slowly roll it back up to an erect position.

Shoulders: Sitting up, lift your left shoulder close to your left ear, hold it up for 30 seconds, then release it so it drops back into place. Then work the right shoulder up to the right ear. Do this five times, alternating shoulders. Follow this by lifting both shoulders up to your ears simultaneously and pulling them backwards as far as possible in shoulder rolls, down as far as you can, then forward, then up again to your ears. Roll them forward three times, then reverse the roll and go backwards. Your muscles should stretch easily, and feel deliciously relaxed.

Shoulders and Arms: Your seatmates may be staring at you by this point, but pay them no mind. Sit forward on the edge of your seat, back straight and head up, and lift your arms over your head. Clasp your fingers together and turn your hands inside out, pulling the muscles in your arms and shoulders up as far as possible in a long, languorous stretch. If you're giving a really good stretch, you should feel the pull all the way down in your diaphragm, almost as if you were lifting yourself out of the chair.

Keeping your arms erect over your head, release your fingers, hold your hands upright, and turn your wrists in toward each other, then

IN-FLIGHT EXERCISES

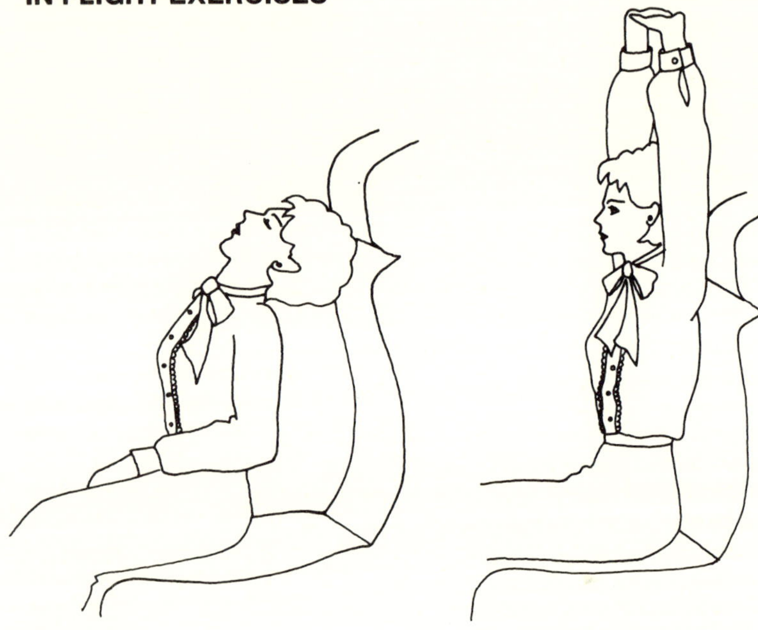

Back Arch

Shoulder and Arm Stretch

Hip Flex

away, to give your arms a bit of a twist all the way down into your shoulders. Extend your fingers up to the ceiling when you're doing this exercise, fingers stretched wide apart, to relax the muscles in your hands.

Back: Again, sit erect on the edge of your seat, head straight forward and shoulders relaxed, then arch your spine backwards from the shoulders, keeping your hands at ease in your lap. Pull your head back and bend your spine as if starting a backbend. Breathe easily and get the breath down into your diaphragm, loosening up the muscles along your spine. Keep pulling backwards, guided by the weight of your head, until you can feel a good pull in the lower part of your back. When you've had enough, slowly lift your head and straighten your spine to an upright position. Then breathe deeply and slowly three or four times.

To stretch your spine the other way (and thus prevent strain), suck in your stomach muscles as tightly as possible against your backbone and arch your spine forward, pulling your shoulders and arms around to the front. You are rounding your back like a hunchback here, stretching your upper back muscles in the opposite direction from the backbend. After holding this hunchback position for a minute or so, breathe deeply, exhale, and return to an upright position.

Another way to stretch your back muscles is to pull in your stomach, round your back, and lean forward until your head touches your knees. Relax in this position for a minute, then roll slowly up to a sitting position, head last. Repeat several times.

Stomach: As anyone who sits at a desk knows, stomach muscles respond to the ineluctable pull of gravity and end up, slowly but surely, in your lap. The way to correct this is through improving your bad posture and strengthening your muscle tone. Sit forward far enough so you can hold your back erect, keeping your shoulders relaxed. (A little trick to help you get a good spinal alignment is to pull up a piece of hair from the center of your crown, right at the top of your head, until you can feel your neck and back align vertically.) Once you're sitting up nice and straight, breathe deeply, expanding your chest like a weight lifter, then exhale slowly, sucking in your stomach muscles as hard as you can until your stomach muscles feel pulled back against your spinal cord. Hold the muscles taut for a count of 10, then breathe deeply again, expanding your diaphragm so it fills with air. Do this exercise three or four times. Don't stop breathing. Your back should be straight—no hunchback position for this one.

Hips: The man sitting next to you on the plane might get the wrong idea from this exercise; if he does, laugh or shoot him dead with a hostile look. Sit back in your chair in a relaxed position, arms at your sides. Then squeeze the muscles in your fanny as tightly as you can. Hold the muscles taut for a count of 10, then relax, breathing in when you tighten the muscles, and out when you release them. Repeat the isometric tension of the muscles three or four times. You should feel your hips start to lift off the seat.

For a variation of this exercise, rest your head against the back of the seat with your body slouched forward in a half-prone position. Your hips should be at the edge of the seat, and your legs should be held together and stretched out straight, with your feet under the seat in front of you. Place your hands on the seat beside your hips. Then squeeze the muscles of your fanny as tightly as possible, rising off the seat an inch or two. Your weight will be on your heels and your palms. Repeat this exercise three or four times, breathing easily throughout.

Legs: Still stretched forward as in the last exercise, place your palms on the seat beside your hips for support, and keep your legs stretched out straight in front of you as far as possible. Pull in your stomach muscles, then lift your legs an inch or two off the floor, holding them up together. If you feel your stomach muscles forced outward in a convex curve from the strain of this exercise, release your legs and try lifting just one leg at a time instead. While lifting, point your toes and tense the muscles in each calf and thigh as tightly as possible. If you have enough space, repeat, lifting both legs together, then kick your legs in little butterfly kicks.

Keeping the same position, kick your shoes off (if you haven't already). Lift your legs again one at a time and make long, stretchy circles with your ankles and feet. Turn your feet clockwise three times, then counterclockwise three times so you get a good stretch through the ankles and calves. Be sure your stomach muscles are held taut during this exercise—any movement that forces your stomach muscles outward is working against you.

Another way to exercise your legs while seated is to sit upright with your fanny pulled back into the seat, knees bent, and your shoulders relaxed, hands at your side. Tense the muscles in your thighs and fanny and lift your legs, one at a time. If you don't really tense your muscles, this motion is useless. If you do, you'll create enough tension to force your muscles to really work.

When you get up from your seat to visit the loo, walk around the plane for 10 minutes or so. Stretch your hands upright over your head, breathing deeply and lifting up from your hips. Then lower your arms and twist your torso easily from side to side to stretch your lower back and waist. Press your knees together and do little—or deep—knee bends. Then touch your toes. You may look funny, but you'll increase the flow of blood to your legs and feet and you'll help eliminate fatigue.

JET LAG

It's real. It's debilitating. Jet lag interrupts your psychological balance and your biological stability. And it must be dealt with respectfully.

I remember once, when I lived on a farm in British Columbia, observing a field of grazing cows during a solar eclipse. As soon as the moon started to obscure the sun and the light grew dim, the cows all knelt down as they do at nightfall when they're about to go to sleep. Then, a few minutes later, when the sunlight returned, the bewildered cows all stood again and returned to their grazing.

Something similar happens in the case of jet lag. When you cross several time zones flying from east to west or from west to east, you upset your diurnal and nocturnal rhythms. Your biological and mental patterns of eating, sleeping, thinking, and performing bodily functions get disrupted. The symptoms are obvious. First, your eyeballs get dry as a result of prolonged exposure to the 2 percent humidity in the airplane cabin. Your mouth and throat become parched, and your body begins to dehydrate, affecting your kidneys, among other organs. Your extremities (hands, ankles, and feet) start to swell mostly as a result of poor blood circulation due to the prolonged inactivity. Once on the ground, you find yourself wide awake in the middle of the night and ready to topple over with a snore into your *moules marinière* at the lunch table. You tend to get constipated for a few days, and your brain isn't particularly lucid. Working your way through complex mental tasks and making important judgments seem particularly taxing.

The effects of jet lag are not psychosomatic and there's no reason to get angry or impatient with yourself for not being on your toes immediately after a long international flight. In fact, many multinational companies prohibit their employees and representatives from making any important decisions for at least a day after flights that cross several time zones.

There's little you can do to prevent the disorientation your body experiences during jet lag; you should also keep in mind that some of the body's systems may take different amounts of time to adjust to a new schedule. Most people seem to feel stronger jet lag symptoms flying from west to east against the progression of the sun (or, more correctly, the turning of the earth) than with it, from east to west. I find this to be true. On a trip to Europe, especially a long eight- or nine-hour flight to Athens or Istanbul, I need several days before I begin to function properly. But flying back to the States, even on a flight of equal duration, it only takes a good night's sleep to make me feel quite normal.

The hours of arrival and departure can also affect the way you feel after a long flight. Leaving for a long trip in the morning hours makes your adjustment to the new time clock easier than leaving in the middle of the night. Similarly, a late afternoon or early evening arrival makes your adjustment much easier than an early morning arrival—which obliges you to get through a new day without sufficient rest. (If yours is a particularly pressing schedule, it would be worth it to invest in a ''sleeperette'' reclining chair, available on many airlines for First Class passengers.)

The medical rule of thumb for jet lag recuperation is approximately one full day of recovery time for every five time zones you pass through. Try to take this recovery period into account when you plan your business schedule. If you won't have sufficient time to rest upon your arrival, try leaving a day earlier in order to give your body a full day to adjust to the new time clock. If you can't leave early, at least try to schedule your first round of appointments as lightly as possible to provide you with the maximum amount of time for recuperating.

The condition in which you leave for your trip also affects the degree to which you experience jet lag. If you're exhausted before you go, or sleep badly the night before, the effects of jet lag will be all the more pronounced.

To minimize them, take a few precautions. First, get a good night's sleep the night before your departure, and eat lightly both before and on the plane. Drink in moderation when in flight—alcohol increases the dehydration your body is already experiencing and it destroys vitamins (mostly the B vitamins) your body needs.

Try to relax on the plane and bring earplugs and a sleeping mask if you plan to sleep. Wear loose-fitting clothes and shoes for maximum comfort, and bring a light sweater or jacket even in the summer, as the plane cabin can be downright chilly. Drink at least four glasses of liquid (nonsparkling mineral water and fruit juices are your best bet). Note that carbonated beverages should be avoided; the gases tend to expand in your intestine as a result of the cabin pressure, which is lighter than the atmospheric pressure down on earth. Do some exercises in your seat, and move about the plane from time to time to get your blood circulating.

Perhaps the worst thing about long jet flights is what they do to your eyes and skin. Your eyes are usually the first parts of your body to feel itchy and irritated, which will add greatly to your general discomfort. Many knowing travelers carry a small bottle of eye solution, like Murine, and treat their eyes every hour or so during the flight. If you wear contact lenses, you're apt to feel acutely uncomfortable, especially on flights of three hours or more. To spare yourself eye strain, wear a pair of eyeglasses instead of your contacts during the flight, then put the contacts in just before landing.

On jet flights, your skin is also adversely affected by the dry atmosphere and it's likely to feel brittle and dry. Many stewardesses I've spoken to wear very little foundation during long flights and apply a light moisturizer to their faces every few hours. You can do the same by keeping a small bottle of moisturizer handy in your travel bag and applying it lightly to your face and throat before settling into your papers or going to sleep. At the end of the flight, sneak into the lavatory and repair your makeup, brush your teeth, comb your hair, scrub your fingernails, and use some hand cream. Change stockings if yours have a run or if they look baggy. Then squirt yourself with a refreshing spray of perfume.

AIRBORNE CHECKLIST

- Claim seating and service privileges accorded to business travelers.
- Pick up magazine, pillow, blanket before sitting down.
- Bring business papers, book, or cassette recorder for on-plane use.
- Do stretch exercises on long flights.
- Reduce effects of jet lag by dressing comfortably, eating moderately, and avoiding carbonated and alcoholic beverages.
- Moisturize skin and lubricate eyes.

23

Brief Encounters

You're on a morning flight to Cleveland, sitting by the window, staring at the editorial page of *The New York Times*, smudging ink all over your fingers, and wondering whether your toast ever popped out of the toaster back at 5:30 A.M., or got stuck and is burning your house down. From behind you can hear the stewardess loading the scrambled eggs onto the serving cart. All of a sudden, a man's leg encased in a waffle-patterned, rust-colored fabric appears in the seat next to yours. You keep your eyes down, catching a glimpse of white vinyl fake Gucci loafers. "Do you mind if I join you?" his voice twangs. "I hate to eat breakfast alone."

If you're polite and smile—even wanly—and defer and do all those dumb, obsequious things many women have been programmed to do, you're a jerk. His next question, after droning on interminably about his job selling drainpipes and his "great gal" of a wife, will be: "What are you doing this evening? I hate to eat dinner alone." Or, if he's got any chutzpah he may come right out and say it: "What are you doing this evening? I hate to sleep by myself."

What do you do?

1. You can speak to the man if you don't mind chatting over breakfast (I can't bear it myself).
2. You can have dinner with him and follow him to his hotel room (I couldn't; I'm too much of a snob to handle the waffle-patterned rust-colored pants).

3. You can start a nonstop monologue about your stuck toaster in hopes of driving him away.
4. You can look him straight in the eye and say politely but firmly, "Yes, I do mind," then turn back to your newspaper.
5. You can pretend to be a deaf mute or fluent only in Urdu by making strange noises and frantic signs, then collapsing hysterically.

Fake Guccis to the contrary, business travel on your own is a great opportunity for meeting interesting people outside the ken of your usual experience. On a long plane flight you can establish contacts that can turn into valuable friendships, even if they last for only a short while. The trick is to do the picking yourself by making yourself open to those who look interesting, and closing yourself off like a clam to those guaranteed to be bores.

It's amazing how correct your first perceptions can be. Learn to trust them. It doesn't take a behavioral anthropologist to know that the guy with the screaming plaid jacket, the waving cigar, and the loud, desperate voice is going to bore you to death proving his validity (to himself). Or to understand what the middle-aged guy with the paunch and the soup stain on his tie has in mind when he leers, drooling, at you. (It's always astonished me how so many unattractive men have such high sexual opinions of themselves.)

The same applies to women travelers, who can either nourish you by their insight and expressiveness, or bore you to tears with their trivia. I remember sitting on a plane next to a woman from the Bahamas not long ago who kept telling me how *charming* her last seatmate had been. They talked all the way across the Atlantic to London, she repeated, as she looked at me with an accusing expression in her eyes. Blackmail, this. I didn't buy it. My first instinct was to feel guilty for being rude, until I remembered that I had paid a lot of money for my plane ticket and was not on board for the purpose of entertaining her.

Business papers are the most obvious subterfuge when you want to be left in peace. Just the act of opening your briefcase is a turn-off for most women and all male lascivious types. When you pull out a report entitled "The Actuarial Basis of Reinsurance Treaty Planning," you can be sure you'll lose your remaining audience.

It's a little more difficult to preserve your peace and privacy when you simply want to tune out, as I often do, and not go through the charade of doing paperwork. I have devised a method (natural, no chemicals) of switching into automatic the moment I hop into the airport limo. From then on I manage to float in a travel-time limbo during which nothing can make me feel rushed or anxious. I do the same thing on elevators. It's almost like a state of lowered (or heightened) consciousness during which you exist only in the present tense, immune to pressures, changes, boredom, delays. My eyes glaze over. I daydream. I stare at the headrest on the plane seat in front of me, or at the clouds, for hours and hours. I have a great time. I enjoy waking dreams. I refresh my busy brain. And even if the plane gets stuck circling over O'Hare for three and a half hours, I am not desperate. I am relaxed. I am spaced.

Fortunately, being spaced is almost like being ridden with the plague. When you've got it, everybody knows it, and no one bothers to get too near. The problem here is that you isolate yourself and may miss out on the interesting person sitting next to you or three seats away. It's great to float through the sky on a plane to Great Falls, Montana, but maybe the guy in aisle 12, who just glanced your way, is the prototypical Marlboro Man whose ranch lands run as far north as Moose Jaw in Canada.

Meeting People

Which brings us to the next point: Once you've escaped the bore sitting next to you, how do you talk to the attractive guy seated on the other side of the plane? It's all within your control. Unless he is immersed in his business papers or asleep with a newspaper over his face, the man is most likely open, receptive, and available. Maybe not for an enduring romance that will lead to marriage, 2.4 children, and a house in the suburbs, but for a friendly word or two, a chat, a shared drink, a little human contact.

You can ask to borrow the copy of *Barron's* on the seat beside him. You can follow the spoor of his boots back to the stewardess station and hang around while he finishes his drink. You can trip him as he walks past your seat, then leap up, smiling, to apologize.

There's no formula. There's nothing I can recommend doing that will help you if it isn't true to yourself. Use your resources. Be imaginative, friendly, good-humored, outgoing. Make a joke. Smile directly at him. If you can do it naturally, go up and tell him that you're flying into Great Falls for the first time and does he know it and would he like another drink.

The key thing to remember is that almost everyone else on the plane is caught in the same kind of colorless, travel-time limbo that you are, and most would welcome a bright smile, a bit of conversation, a pleasant respite from the humdrum plane experience. One friend suggests, very simply, that you twinkle. Radiate energy. Show some sparkle in your eyes, a light touch, a sense of fun. Some life. If you're heavy, if your eyes project that spongelike absorbency of melancholia, or the blank two-dimensionality of boredom, or the uptight self-concern of the busy business person, nobody's going to read them any other way. But if you have the gift of being able to project your own relaxed enjoyment—about nothing, if there's nothing else to be joyful about—you'll help the people near you feel relaxed as well, and they'll respond positively to your influence.

Being a good listener is another golden nugget of advice. It's easy to start the conversation. Just ask the simplest, most obvious question, like: "Do you live in Great Falls?" This can be amended to: "Do you *really* live in Great Falls?" Or: "Do you *have* to live in Great Falls?" Or, more simply: "*Why* do you live in Great Falls?"

Anyway, questions like these are not as stupid as they sound. You get the conversation going, and through your own attentive attitude and thoughtful responses, you encourage the other person to open up a little and share something about himself or herself. It also doesn't cost you anything to listen. You might actually learn something you didn't know before.

If the conversation should take on a nice balance, you may experience one of those precious conversational encounters that happen only in enclosed time-capsule situations, such as on a plane. They seem to happen most frequently on long international flights when you know you're going to be strapped in your seat for six or seven hours. Sometimes, in that enforced stillness, when you turn to the person sitting closest to you and find him simpatico, you manage to establish a level of honesty and openness in talking about your lives that usually exists only between the oldest and dearest friends.

I remember one conversation I had not long ago on a flight from London to New York. My seatmate was a businessman from the British Midlands whose firm manufactured some kind of sealant used on ships. Not the most intriguing subject in the world. And he was by no stretch of the imagination Jean Paul Belmondo. But he was a sensitive, honest man and for five hours, we spoke, with only a short break for a nap during the movie. By the end of the flight we had managed to reveal some of our deepest thoughts and feelings to each other. There was no hint of a flirtation. But there was a feeling of camaraderie more than a little akin to love. Like those five-second, intense eye communications you share occasionally with complete strangers on the street, we had touched something profound and universal in each other, in a moment, in the flash of a jet through the stratosphere. It was direct, honest, and evanescent, and could never have survived the atmospheric pressure down on earth.

What do you do when you're 40,000 feet in the air and there's a feeling more than a little akin to sex? The answer is simple: Take it. Or leave it.

In *Fear of Flying*, Erica Jong described what is probably a universal feminine (and probably a masculine) fantasy in her enticing chapter about the brief encounter she refers to as ''zipless.'' If you haven't read the book, zipless does not refer to trousers with buttons. It does refer to an intense erotic event that occurs quickly and anonymously on a train or, for our purposes, a plane.

The basic idea of a zipless encounter is that in the protected anonymity of a moving vehicle, with no one looking, you act your fantasy without ever compromising your reputation. You don't exchange names. You don't even have to exchange words. The idea is that one of you gets off, never to be seen again, at the next stop. Plane travel makes this a little more awkward since you probably have to go through customs together, or at least hang around the baggage carousel. You might even end up sharing a taxi into the city. Staying at the same hotel? Who knows, the zipless encounter might turn into a love affair. (Be careful on this one when flying into a small city—your anonymous partner might turn out to be your next business antagonist.)

Before you initiate an anonymous encounter, you first have to assess the possibilities. If the person making the suggestion with the bold, insistent penetration of his eyes is the guy with the belly and the soup stain on his tie, you simply refuse to pick up the message. Best bet: Keep your head turned permanently the other way. But if the guy is hard-edged and sexy, wearing a Rolex, and looks as if he'd know what to do in a clinch, you can test your own sense of adventure by meeting his eyes head on.

Sometimes you don't even need words. An extremely handsome friend of mine once told me of an encounter he'd had on a flight across the Pacific with a beautiful Malaysian woman who met him silently in a darkened corner of the plane. He remembers the encounter as one of the most erotic he ever experienced, and cherishes the memory of the woman's delicacy and straightforwardness.

Unfortunately, there's a flip side to the poetic and brief encounter and that is, quite simply, danger. You just can't know at such short notice whom you're getting involved with. You can't know what he will do to you or whether he will be discreet. And you can't know if he's going to give you some god-awful disease. That's enough to turn most sensible women away from the fantasy of the brief encounter.

There's also the danger of assault, especially in those parts of the world where men aren't accustomed to women traveling on their own. An acquaintance of mine, the daughter of a famous and wealthy man, carries millions of dollars' worth of diamond jewelry with her when she travels as the representative of an international jeweler. She was on a train from Barcelona to Madrid a few years ago, sitting alone in her compartment, when suddenly the conductor came in, shut the door, and tried to kiss her. She struggled against him, not knowing whom to call for help since, theoretically, the conductor was the only one to call. The burly man pressed his hand over her mouth and was trying to run his other hand up her skirt when she managed to bite him, then scream. For a moment he was stunned, and she jumped up and headed for the door. But her concern for her own safety was compounded by her concern for the cache of jewelry in her bags, and she was reluctant to abandon the compartment. Her hesitation cost her dearly. The conductor pushed her down on the seat and started to rough her up, hissing *puta* (whore) as he slapped her face and tore her hair. She finally managed to scream again, this time causing a commotion in the next compartment. Just as suddenly as he had arrived, the conductor fled down the corridor. She never saw him again, and was unable to get the other passengers or the authorities in Madrid to believe her story.

OTHER WORLDS, OTHER WAYS

In many parts of the world, there still prevails a rather dated attitude toward women traveling on their own that can get you into trouble—on the plane or off—and we might as well discuss it here.

In most parts of the United States women traveling alone for business can expect to be treated with equanimity. Other than the usual, extremely irritating, business of being looked at strangely by pasty-faced little desk clerks and winked at by the bellboys, or being seated under a steampipe behind a potted palm on the far side of the men's room in restaurants, women traveling alone in almost every U.S. area don't risk outright danger just by being there. But in some other places in the world, women doing business and traveling on their own are more than suspect. They invite overt aggression. Without a husband or a father to protect them, they're considered, like Victorian-era actresses, little better than prostitutes. This is most often true in the more conservative countries of the Mediterranean (Spain, Portugal, southern Italy, Greece), all Arab countries, and most Moslem countries (with special kudos to Turkey, Iraq, and Afghanistan), and a good bit of the Orient and Latin America.

Although things have changed in the last 10 or 20 years, it's useful to understand where many of the values in these countries are coming from. In the Mediterranean and most of Latin America, for example, the prevailing attitude has always been that the woman belongs in the home and if she were a decent sort she wouldn't be out in the world exposing herself to the crude advances of the very men who condemn her for being there.

This may seem outdated and patently untrue to those of you who have traveled recently through the Mediterranean or Latin America with nary a dirty look. But it's still worth remembering that until the middle or late 1960s the sexual codes in most of these countries were so repressive that unmarried men of all but the upper classes had almost no access to women until they married in their late twenties or thirties. Even if they were engaged for five or more years, as many were, the girls they were engaged to risked outright rejection and public scandal if they gave in to their fiancé's entreaties. And just a little over a decade ago, in the same part of the world, most of those same men who waited until their thirties before marrying and mating had little or no access to prostitutes. In one part of Spain I once witnessed the men of the town, wearing faded blue jackets and black berets, lining up in the fields to wait their once-a-year turns with prostitutes brought in for three days during the town's annual fiesta.

Then came the tourists, those thousands and thousands of smooth browned bodies prancing through the cities and seaside resorts with their breasts unfettered and their derrières hanging out the backs of their miniskirts. The local men went berserk. A social revolution took place. In a fraction of a generation, all the old taboos were broken down as the sexually repressed males suddenly got unrepressed. The tourists went home happy. A new cottage industry was born. It actually got so out of hand a few years ago that a young Greek man and a Swedish tourist were arrested for copulating in front of the police station in the town square of Rhodes at 5 o'clock in the afternoon.

Situations to Avoid

As a business traveler, you're not as likely to be overwhelmed by the attentions of the local talent as you would if you were a bikini-clad vacationer negotiating the cobblestones in high-heeled sandals. Nevertheless, the attitude of the locals toward single women foreigners has penetrated to the business centers, to the extent that many men in the conservative countries continue to regard single women travelers as fair targets for their advances. In a short period of time, a handy dual standard has evolved, one for the still-protected and respected local women, and another for the foreign *putas*.

Between us, Chrisjean and I have traveled alone on business in

Egypt, Turkey, Lebanon, Greece, Spain, Portugal, Italy, Tunisia, Morocco, Brazil, Colombia, Peru, Argentina, Bolivia, Paraguay, Venezuela, Panama, Guatemala, and half a dozen other countries that, technically, belong to or have recently emerged from that old-time *puta*-madonna ethic.

We have also been accosted, solicited, invited, insulted, cursed, shoved, pinched, and, occasionally, amused. The way we usually deal with the problem is to ignore it. Quite correctly, we have deduced that it is impossible in one brief conversation to educate an obdurate population of hirsute males about the righteousness of women's lib on a street corner at dusk in some Mediterranean city with a red moon rising and a few bats darting over the rooftops.

However, we do remind ourselves, with a deep sigh and a forward glance, that we are upright, well-bred, polite, independent, responsible, and self-respecting individuals. We don't need to feel insulted by some blithering little macho who has gotten it into his noggin that we have arrived in his country for the sole purpose of consorting with the likes of him.

However, we are also extremely careful not to put ourselves in situations, anywhere, at any time, from which we cannot escape to safety. We don't walk around the streets at night. We don't loiter on corners. And we don't flirt with people for the hell of it in unknown situations unless our intuition tells us we should take the time to talk (cautiously) to them. We also stay almost entirely to ourselves in places where women are not normally seen traveling—for business or other purposes—on their own.

Several years ago, I had just arrived in Casablanca after a flight from Lisbon and was due to catch a train to Marrakesh the following morning. I checked into my hotel, then decided to take a walk, since I hadn't been in Casablanca in several years. It was only about 7 o'clock in the evening and the sun was just setting behind the date palms in the square in front of the hotel. I walked through the shadows, passing a group of men in white djellabas, then continued down the central avenue toward the shopping district. Suddenly I noticed that I was the only woman on the street: no tourists, no Western-dressed Moroccan women, not even veiled and robed local ladies rushing home to their co-wives and couscous. My first thought was to keep on walking. It was still light and I wanted to stretch my legs. But I was aware that the passing cars were all slowing down and the men walking by were murmuring suggestive comments, and suddenly there seemed to be a lot of them and only one of me. I felt stupid to feel so precautious and I felt angry to be so confined, but I also realized that the Levantine world didn't subscribe to the same values as my culture—at least not regarding women—and there was nothing I could do to alter the fact. Reluctantly, but realistically, I walked back to my hotel.

Chrisjean and I have each been sexually molested only once in years of travel and, strangely, it happened to both of us at the same time. By chance, we were both on business assignments in the small Greek resort of Navpaktos, an old fortified town on the Gulf of Corinth, with battlements encircling its harbor. When we both found ourselves with a free afternoon during the long Greek siesta, we walked down to the local beach to have a swim. Since it was crowded, we followed the curve of the bay around to a lonely promontory surrounded by tall reeds. We seemed to be completely alone as we lay on our towels talking idly, when suddenly a crazy-looking man with his pants half open ran out of the reeds and threw himself down on top of me. Chrisjean screamed in Greek for him to go away. I stood straight up with an unexpected surge of strength and the man fell off me backwards, then regained his footing and lunged for Chrisjean. He turned to me again and I tried to fight him off while Chrisjean hurriedly gathered our belongings, dropping a wallet in the process and unloading a thousand drachmas into the sand. She shouted the Greek word for ''police'' and the man suddenly backed off, making only halfhearted attempts to catch us as we ran down the beach trailing our paraphernalia behind. Our knees were shaking as we finally slipped through the reeds onto a dirt road and at last emerged onto the outer edge of the public beach.

Afterward, we viewed the whole event almost with humor, especially the absurd spectacle of the man jumping around and of us racing down the beach in disarray. The man was probably a local loner, horny and desperate, provoked out of control by our perceived availability. The old double standard again. He probably never would have attempted to molest a local girl. The Greek police didn't find the story the least bit amusing, however. They reminded us how lucky we had been that the man was alone and hadn't been carrying a knife.

I believe you can control the space and events around you. You invite danger or repel it by the manner in which you handle yourself. In the case of Chrisjean and me on the beach, we were alone, foreign, and practically naked, and we had made an innocent but potentially harmful error of judgment.

In dealing with the world you have the choice of behaving in one of three ways. You can respond openly and enthusiastically to all the energy and activity you encounter with an assertiveness that says you're in control. You can respond openly, but with a receptive, vulnerable, and passive manner that says you're waiting for the world to act on you (which it will). Or you can insulate yourself from all energy and activity merely by keeping your own energy (and eyes and attention) to yourself.

If you choose the first or third way of behaving, there's no reason, ever, to be timid or afraid. Except for war and acts of nature (which can usually be avoided), each country is just another place to visit and do business, no matter how exotic or remote. Just be certain you maintain a cautious attitude until you know your way around. Learn something about the local customs. Modify your own behavior just enough to keep you from inviting unwanted interference. (For more on this subject, see Chapter 27.)

I don't want to leave you with the impression that the woman business traveler is constantly confronted by danger (masculine or otherwise). With this in mind, let me introduce you to my friend Cynthia Moss, whose business travel experiences throw yours and mine into a different perspective.

Cynthia, a five-foot-four-inch blond with soft curly hair and delicate skin, is a zoologist who travels alone for business most of the year, primarily to and from her camp in the African bush. For the past half decade she has been studying a population of elephants in Amboseli, a game reserve in Kenya just north of Kilimanjaro. She spends many of her days in her Land Rover among the elephants (one of whom, I'm proud to say, is named Penelope after me). At nightfall, Cynthia returns to her camp and her cat, now on its eighth life after having spent the last seven avoiding the stomachs of the predators. After dinner, Cynthia retires to her tent and goes to sleep. During the night, lions—real live lions—frequently wander into her camp and brush up against the tent canvas just inches away from my dear friend Cynthia's head! When I asked her if she wasn't afraid, she answered nonchalantly, "Oh, not really. Only when they roar and wake me up."

If Cynthia can handle the animals with the orange manes and big teeth in the course of her business travels, you and I certainly ought to be able to handle the ones with orange doubleknit suits on a flight to Cleveland at 40,000 feet.

BRIEF ENCOUNTERS CHECKLIST

- Control interactions with others.
- Be aware of local attitudes.
- Do what you want to do—with forethought.
- Don't, if you have second thoughts.
- Respect local customs.

24

The Airport Escape

Some people always manage to be the first off the plane and the first through customs control. It's not always luck—there's a method to their speedy escape that has to do with being prepared.

When the plane starts its descent for landing, get your coat and baggage down from the overhead compartment before the "fasten your seat belt" sign comes on. Have your landing card, passport, immunization card, other documents, and luggage keys available in an easy-to-get-at pocket or compartment of your travel bag so you won't have to fumble for them when you get to the customs counter. As soon as the plane comes to a full stop and the seat belt sign goes off, step right out into the aisle and move up as far as you can toward the exit, without being rude to the other passengers, of course. If you're sitting in a window seat and the person on the aisle is not a fast mover, sit down and relax—there's nothing you can do but wait.

Once you reach the baggage area, find a handcart for your luggage—some airports offer these in lieu of porters, and there never seem to be enough to go around.

While waiting for your bags to appear on the airport carousel, make sure you have some change handy for tips and transportation. If not and you are traveling abroad, see if there is a foreign exchange window nearby, and go to it as soon as you collect your luggage and get through customs. Most airports have a choice of booths, some for returning nationals and others for foreign visitors. Don't waste time in the wrong line. Hand the customs officer your landing card, if one is required, and be ready to open your bags.

If you are entering a foreign country as a business traveler and have no suspicious samples or goods, the chances are that you will not be asked to open your bags. If you are carrying suspicious-looking or bulky samples, the customs inspector may insist on taking a look unless you have an internationally recognized registration form. The form should state the nature of the goods and the purpose for which you are carrying them, and declare that they are not intended for resale.

Finding a Helping Hand

Sometimes when you're traveling, the man sitting next to you on the plane will make a generous offer to carry your bags. I don't know about other women, but I'm almost always flattered and grateful when this occurs. Other times you have to travel with more bags than you can possibly carry, and there's no polite gent around to help. Sometimes there aren't even porters or luggage carts. In circumstances like this, go immediately to the airline's public relations director before your bags show up on the carousel. If you speak politely, explaining that you've got a problem you can't solve yourself and that you would greatly appreciate some help, a solution will almost always be found. I've even had an airline director of public relations carry my bags for me himself—his name was Rodriguez and he worked for Iberia.

If you stop at the foreign currency exchange counter in the airport, change only what you'll need for the moment. The exchange rate at the airport, even at a bank branch, is almost always less favorable than the exchange rate at the banks in town.

If you're not too loaded down and there's a branch of the local tourist bureau, or a kiosk with a promising array of local literature, stop to pick up a city map and interesting guide material. You may find the same publications available in your hotel later on, but then again, maybe you won't. It's always to your advantage to have local information handy.

Lost Luggage

It could happen that instead of rushing through customs and making a beeline for the airport limo, you find yourself alone, staring forlornly at the empty baggage carousel going around and around. Your suitcase didn't arrive.

Don't panic. As I have already mentioned, 95 percent of all baggage shows up within 24 hours, and 99 percent within 72 hours, and there's no reason the fates should punish you by making you one of the losing 1 percent.

Don't leave it to the fates to find your bag, though, and don't leave the airport until you have reported your loss to the airline. You will be asked to complete a complaint form describing your lost suitcase and its contents, and to indicate where you can be reached locally. Be sure to give an accurate assessment of the bag's contents, as this will be used later as a measure by which to establish a repayment fee if the bag never shows up. Keep a copy of the form for your records, and ask the airline rep what telephone number you should call to check on the airline's progress. Plan to call at least once a day until the bag is found. You should also expect a daily report from the carrier.

Many airlines will partially reimburse passengers for purchases made to replace necessary articles of clothing or toiletries packed in lost luggage, although there is no official ruling on this matter and the airlines may disagree with what you deem necessary. For example, the airline will probably reimburse you for a modest supply of toiletries and cosmetics, if these have been lost, or they may provide you with an emergency toilet kit containing a few essentials like soap, razor, toothpaste, and toothbrush. Some travel experts advise you to go right out and buy fresh stockings and underwear, a clean blouse or dress, or even a new evening gown if your first night in town includes a black-tie affair.

As a general rule, the airlines will reimburse you for half the cost of replaced garments or equipment on the assumption that you will be able to use them again. If you put up a fight and demand total reimbursement, the airline may agree, but they may also insist that you return the new purchases in exchange for complete payment. If your lost luggage contained sports gear or other equipment, the airline will usually pay for the rental of replacement equipment until your own is returned.

If your suitcase arrives damaged and it's the fault of the airline, the carrier will usually reimburse you for the cost of repairs. If the bag cannot be repaired, they will negotiate a repayment sum based on the depreciated value of the bag.

When Your Bag Never Shows Up

If your luck runs out and you never see your suitcase again, you will have to press a claim against the airline. As we have mentioned, the airline's liability per ticketed customer is $750 on domestic flights and $20 per kilo of luggage weight on international flights.

Even though their maximum liability is fixed, the airlines won't always pay you the maximum amount for lost luggage. They will review your claim, using the information you provided on the complaint form, and they will place an evaluation on the lost items based on the depreciated—not replacement—value.

There's virtually no way to get the real value of what you lose reimbursed by the airline, and it's always a good idea to forestall this kind of wrangle by buying excess valuation insurance before the flight. At the current rates, a meager few dollars will buy you $2,000 worth of excess valuation insurance. It's money out the window if your bags don't get lost, but money in your pocket if they do.

Another worthwhile precaution is to keep receipts for clothing and other personal items that get packed in your bags so you can make a solid case for your claim if you have to fight the airline. This is especially important if your packed belongings are unusually valuable. The airline will probably take from six to twelve weeks to reimburse you for your claim. If you can't reach a satisfactory agreement with the airline personnel handling the case in the destination, get in touch with the airline's consumer affairs office when you get home. Prepare a thorough, documented, and forceful presentation of your demands, keeping in mind how much the airlines dread public criticism.

Changing Planes

If you're passing through an airport and have to change planes or airlines, report immediately to the airline public relations representative and tell him or her where you have to go. Airline personnel are usually extremely attentive in helping passengers make connecting or interline flights, and usually they will help speed you on your way.

If your baggage is tagged for an ongoing destination, it supposedly will be forwarded automatically from one plane to another. Unfortunately, on some international flights, you have to collect your baggage from the carousel and take it through customs before racing across the airport to check in at another departure gate. A friend of mine had to take her bags through customs in Taiwan, where everything gets opened, and was about to miss her connection. To expedite the transfer, she got hold of a Cathay Pacific Airline representative, who helped her get through customs without delay and delivered her on time for the second leg of her flight.

Even if you have to tip generously for service of this sort (not usually permissible, but in some countries the only way to get action), do it. Request airport assistance from the airline in advance, perhaps when you board the plane in the departure city, or from the purser on the plane when you're in the air.

GETTING TO YOUR HOTEL

Now that you've negotiated the Scylla and Charybdis of the airport, you have to get yourself and your baggage into town. If your hotel is a large, center-city establishment that caters to business travelers, it may provide a courtesy car for arriving passengers. Look around the airport departure area for a direct-line phone to your hotel—you may be able to call for free transportation.

If no hotel service exists, you have the option of taking a taxi, bus, train, airport limousine, or rental car. If you decide on a taxi, ask someone with a responsible position at the airport, such as the airline rep or the customs inspector, what the average cost of a taxi ride should be. With metered taxis, there will be no question about the rate. Otherwise, determine a price with the driver before you get in the cab. Some negotiating may be in order.

Many large city airports have limousines with seating for eight to twelve passengers, or more. These usually make the rounds of the leading hotels in the center of the city and cost half or a third of what taxis cost. Some limousines require booking in advance; when you plan your trip, ask your travel adviser to reserve a space for you.

Airport buses and trains are perfectly functional ways of getting into a city from the airport, but they can be a false value. If you're familiar with the city and know that the bus or train will let you off in front of your hotel, then take it. But if you don't know the city and might end up being dropped off at some godforsaken bus station with all your luggage piled around you, save yourself the trouble and splurge on a cab.

Picking Up a Rental Car

If you have made a reservation for a rental car, you should find the rental car counter conveniently located in or near the arrivals terminal. If you have a fast-booking account with the car rental firm, you need only show your card and your driver's license, and then sign the agreement. Have your reservation form (or the reservation number, at least) handy in case there is any confusion regarding your reservation. Sometimes car rental firms are not able to provide you with the kind of car you reserved. When this happens, they almost always give you a car in a more expensive category at the original price.

If you are eligible for a corporate discount with the car rental company, or if your corporate membership entitles you to some kind of free insurance, check your rental agreement to see if these discounts have been included. Most car rental companies will deliver your car to the airport terminal where you are waiting, although occasionally they will transport you and your baggage to their station somewhere in the airport complex.

If you are driving in unfamiliar terrain, be sure to get a good local map from the rental car company before leaving the airport, and study it for a few minutes before taking off. Ask one of the rental clerks to trace the quickest route to your destination on your map, and ask about local driving habits or hazards.

Before taking off, spend a minute or two checking out the various functions of the car, making sure you know how everything works. Check the lights, dimmers, flashers, windshield wipers, emergency brake, reverse gear, ignition key lock, seat adjustments, air conditioning or heat control, and so on. Ask the clerk how to open the gas tank if it is locked, and check to see that the car has a full tank of gas.

If your business appointments and hotel are in a town 80 miles from the airport, you probably have no alternative but to rent a car to drive there. If you are staying in a nearby city, however, why not take the courtesy car or a taxi to your hotel, then have the rental car delivered there the following morning? I try to arrange rental cars in this fashion whenever possible. It saves me the anxiety of having to wrestle with an unfamiliar car or unfamiliar roads after a tiring flight when I'm burdened with a lot of luggage.

AIRPORT ESCAPE CHECKLIST

- Begin preparing to deplane before plane touches down.
- If flying abroad, have important documents handy at all times. Be ready to open bags for customs check.
- Always have a small amount of change or low-denomination bills on hand. (When traveling internationally, arm yourself ahead of time with foreign currency for tipping or paying for transportation to your hotel.)
- File a complaint for any lost baggage. Follow up with progress reports to the airlines.
- If renting a car, weigh the pros and cons of having the car delivered to your hotel.
- Before driving a rented car, check lights, horn, windshield wipers, etc. Ask for directions and driving tips before leaving rental agency.
- Negotiate unmetered taxi fare in advance.

25

At the Hotel

A lot has been written about the rude treatment frequently accorded women business travelers when they check into hotels. In a typical bad scenario, the desk clerk looks at you with a sideways glance, clearly implying by his smirk that he regards you as a suspect female. He will then assign you a mean little room off in a forgotten corner of the hotel, overlooking the air shaft or the garage. The bellboy, who leads you up to the room, gives you a lascivious grin as he shows you the bed. "If you need anything, sugar," he mumbles, "just call."

Things like this do happen, but the times are changing.

Many of the larger chain hotels catering to business travelers are finally becoming sensitive to this type of situation. They have recently learned that almost 30 percent of their lucrative business traffic comes from businesswomen. This awareness has done a lot to break down the old behavioral patterns, and, as often as not, you will now run into polite, efficient, and passive acceptance of your erstwhile threatening presence.

One way to encourage a good reception at the hotel is to make a confirmed reservation, through which you agree to pay for your room even if you never get there. For this, the hotel promises to hold your room for you until the next booking day, even if you arrive at 4 o'clock in the morning.

For a business traveler, a confirmed (also called "assured" or "guaranteed") reservation is a must especially in cities that are chronically short of hotel rooms. For a woman business traveler, this is doubly important. You don't want to get bumped and find yourself out on the street—the confirmed reservation will identify you and your purpose to the hotel staff, and will almost always elicit a correct, professional reception.

CHECKING IN

The best time for checking into a hotel is midafternoon. The hotel has had enough time to prepare your room, and you arrive early enough to calm any fears that you might be a no-show.

However, your business schedule and flight plans don't always conform to the hotel's convenience. Sometimes your plane gets into a city early in the morning before your room can be prepared. And other times, your plane delivers you long after dinner, hours after the time until which the hotel has agreed to hold your room.

The way to cover yourself on an irregular schedule is to keep the hotel informed of your plans, when possible, and offer them the assurances they need. Always ask for the hotel's assistance if your arrival and departure cannot correspond to the standard check-in and checkout times. If you arrive too early, the hotel may be able to give you a room anyway. Or they will at least be able to hold your bags.

When you arrive at the hotel, tip the doorman about $1 if he has helped move your bags. If he hasn't, tip him only when you leave. At the registration desk, give the clerk your name and show him your reservation confirmation slip, which has been given to you by the travel agent who did the booking. If you don't have the confirmation slip, at least have the hotel's own booking number (also given to you by your travel agent), as verification that the reservation has been made.

Ordinarily, you will be given a registration card to fill out with your name, address, and telephone number, and your driver's license and license plate numbers if you are driving. At international destinations, you will also have to give your passport number, and in many countries, the hotel desk will keep your passport overnight in order to register you with the police.

If you or your company qualifies for a corporate discount, be sure this has been indicated on your room registration form. Often, hotel night managers are not equipped to verify discounts and you will have to straighten the matter out the next morning.

If you have a preference for the type of room you like (near the elevators or away from them, with a view, with a bathtub or a direct-dial phone), request it now if you have not already done so. You are perfectly within your rights to ask to see the room before agreeing to pay for it. Don't be intimidated into accepting anything you've been assigned.

By identifying yourself as a business traveler whose firm does extensive business with the hotel, you may be able to impress upon the reservations clerk the value of your patronage. This can be done politely, without abrasiveness, merely by presenting your business card and requesting precisely the kind of room you would like to have. I was once given a horrid little single right next to the elevators with a window overlooking the garbage cans. Since the hotel wasn't even half full, there was no reason for this selection other than the desk clerk's evident disdain for me. Calmly, but politely I refused the room. I explained that I required more space to accomplish my business objectives, and more quiet in order to sleep. I had made my confirmed reservation long in advance, I reminded the clerk, and on the second try, I was given a room more to my liking, with space and light and a pleasant view.

After you have gone through the paces of checking in, the bellhop will be given the key to your room and he will take you up to it, either bringing your baggage himself, or having it sent up by a porter on the service elevator. As soon as you are led into the room, be sure you like its location and facilities, and check to see if it has been sufficiently cleaned. Make a quick perusal before tipping the bellhop—if anything has been omitted, you want it replaced immediately.

What to look for:

- Curtains that close out the light
- Enough blankets and pillows
- Heating/air-conditioning control
- Ashtrays
- Light bulbs in all the fixtures
- Hangers
- Lock for armoire or desk drawer
- Writing paper and envelopes
- Radio/TV that works; ask how to operate it if you don't know
- TV program guide
- Working locks on the door
- Towels
- Soap
- Tissues
- Toilet paper
- Drinking glass
- Shower curtain
- Tub and sink stoppers

- Lights over the mirror
- Hot water
- Toilet that works
- Direct-dial phone

AT YOUR SERVICE: THE HOTEL STAFF

Your first introduction to the hotel staff will most likely be through the bellhops. If there are two bellhops attending you—one for the key and the other for your bags—you should tip them both. Being inclined to err on the side of excess on the premise that good tipping buys good service (which it often does), I would give the bellhop who brought up the bags $1 for a single bag or 75¢ per bag for two or more bags, and I would give $1 to the bellhop who brought the key.

Now and again a bellhop, in youthful enthusiasm, may overstep his position and try to flirt with you. The easiest solution is to ignore his overtures completely, provided they have been of a harmless sort. If you don't pick up his little signals, he will probably think you are stupid and/or asexual and will quickly lose interest. If, however, he should be more assertive or downright offensive, don't play the flustered, insulted lady. Look him straight in the eye, ask him for his name, and report him to the management.

Making Friends with the Staff

There are several people in the hotel hierarchy whom you want on your side. One is the concierge or bell captain, who can provide great assistance, advice, and information, and is potentially one of the best travel-acquired friends you can have.

First of all, a good concierge will become a personal point of contact who will make you feel that you've got someone on your side when you're alone on the road. Secondly, the concierge can prove indispensable when it comes to recommending a good restaurant for entertaining your business guests, or reserving a good table for you as a solo business traveler. He can book theater tickets and get you a seat on the airport limousine. And he can tell you where and how to find the best shops, the best nightclubs, the hidden-away restaurants, and the quickest, cheapest routes to the airport.

Do make friends with the concierge. The simplest way of soliciting his attention is to explain that you're traveling on your own and will need his assistance for the next few days. So there's no question of the honor of your intent, slip him a neatly folded $5 or $10 bill, depending on how often you will require his services, and pay him in advance, never on a piecemeal basis. The objective in paying him before he performs any service is to show your good faith and to overcome any nagging doubts he may have about the generosity of women travelers. Another way to do it would be to slip him $5 at your first meeting, and then give him another $5 on your departure if you feel he has earned it.

You should also become acquainted with the housekeeper, who will get your clothes pressed quickly and your hem mended, and might even manage to get an ironing board and iron into your room so you can touch up a few things by yourself. Since the housekeeper probably will not be needed on an ongoing basis, plan to tip her for each service. A tip of 50¢ per service would probably be adequate, but it won't earn you undying devotion. I'd give $1.

If your hotel does not have direct-dial phones in the rooms, you will be dependent on the good will of the switchboard operator. One friend of mine goes to the trouble of finding this behind-the-scenes person, introducing herself to him or her, and explaining how important her phone calls will be. My friend then encourages good service by discreetly handing the *telefonista* a modest tip of $3 or $4. She makes a friend of the operator, a comrade in arms, so to speak, and gets her calls through promptly when she needs to.

Taking Advantage of Hotel Facilities

Almost all hotels have a visitor's booklet that describes the various services provided by the hotel and informs you how and where to obtain them. Typically, your hotel or motel will provide room service (although perhaps not 24 hours a day), and many hotels provide breakfast order forms that get hung on the doorknob the night before. A call to the switchboard can probably produce a morning wake-up call—set your travel alarm anyway in case there's a snafu. Housekeeping and concierge services have already been mentioned—these usually take care of your personal and social requirements. If your hotel caters primarily to business travelers, it also may provide conference rooms, photocopy machines, secretarial assistance, typewriters, and other facilities. And, if you're lucky, you might even find a resident masseuse, a sauna, or a pool.

USING HOTEL ELECTRICITY OVERSEAS

You may be in for a surprise when you try using your hair drier or curling iron in some foreign hotels. Electrical outlets and currents differ around the world. Some countries have both 110- and 220-volt currents; other countries have only one or the other. You may even discover mysterious ratings like 150, 230, or 200 volts.

You're likely to find two rectangular-pronged plugs, like the ones common in the United States; two round-pronged plugs, like those found in most of Europe (in the U.K. they're round but often of a different size); and occasionally, round and rectangular prongs on the same plug. If you have a pretechnological brain, as I do, all of this is confusing beyond words. The solution: Buy a travel pack containing a transformer that will convert 110 volts to 220 volts or vice versa, plus three or four plug adapters that will let you attach anything to anything. Sets of this kind are available from many hardware and notions stores, luggage stores, and department stores. It's a worthwhile—no, necessary—investment. (When buying transformers, be aware that most travel-size devices have only the capability of transforming current for low-voltage appliances, such as an electric razor. A travel iron or other more demanding appliance would probably burn the transformer out.)

You can also buy appliances, such as hair driers, hair stylers, and electric hair rollers, in travel-sized editions with the capability of adapting to either 110 volts or 220 volts.

Then there's the business of AC (alternating current) and DC (direct current). In the States, electricity runs on AC, as it does in most population centers around the globe. You will run into direct current, however, in isolated parts of South America, Australia, and a few other destinations, as well as in special cases in which a hotel or a resort has its own generating station. If there is any doubt whatsoever, be sure to inquire before plugging anything in. The DC will burn out any appliances made for AC outlets. Refer to the appendix for information on electric current usage around the world.

WHAT TO DO IF YOU GET BUMPED

If you arrive at your hotel armed with a confirmation slip and a guaranteed reservation and find there's no room at the inn, what do you do?

What you don't do is give up easily. And what you don't do is metamorphose from a polite, well-mannered, and controlled business professional into a screaming harridan.

If you have a confirmed reservation, every hotel that honors this system agrees in advance to provide you with equivalent accommodations, plus transportation there and back, in a nearby hotel of the same standard. Hold the hotel completely to this promise if they have not held a room for you, and feel free to stay on in the substitute hotel if you prefer it to the original. If you like your first hotel better, make sure the hotel agrees that the substitution will last only until a room in the original hotel opens up.

Sometimes, when you have an unconfirmed reservation, the hotel claims to have never received word of your booking or your deposit. When this happens, and the clerk insists that there's no room available under any circumstances, don't give up and walk away. Insist that your reservation was made and your deposit sent. Produce the hotel's own booking number to prove it. If you aren't armed with this documentation, the fate that befalls you is partially your own fault.

If you still get no for an answer, ask to see the manager. Calmly introduce yourself and hand the manager your business card. Explain the importance of your business assignment, the respect you and your entire firm have for his hotel, and your complete trust that he will find a solution for your problem. If you have visited the hotel before and have the good sense to make yourself known to the manager as a regular, grateful customer, you have a better chance of being bailed out. Even if you're not known, you stand a much better chance of finding a solution if you *solicit* assistance rather than demand, threaten, insult, or make a spectacle of yourself.

One acquaintance of mine, a well-known public relations woman from Chicago, checked into the Regency Hotel in New York only to find that her reservation had never gone through. The hotel was jammed—in fact, the entire city was jammed. My acquaintance went directly to the manager, whose friendship she had made several years before. She explained that she was planning to conduct important business with some key people in the city government and was expecting a number of phone calls, including one from her young son. She simply had to have a room. The manager confirmed that he had no rooms available, but he asked her to come back in an hour so he could try to find something for her. She came back and found unusual but comfortable accommodations set up in what was normally a banquet office. It was better than nothing, and she had been taken care of because she was polite, insistent, and a valued customer.

Here's another solution. A friend of mine on a long business trip through South America once flew into La Paz, Bolivia, at 3 A.M. after her plane had overflown La Paz and gone all the way to Santiago, Chile, and back because of a wild snow storm. She arrived freezing and exhausted and tried to check in, only to have the desk clerk imperiously inform her that she was too late to get a room. A man standing near the desk suddenly leaned over the counter and grabbed the clerk by the collar. "Find the lady a room," he said. The clerk did.

If you get bumped from a hotel or receive unacceptable treatment, there's no fixed guideline for the payment of compensation as there is for the airlines. Your only recourse is to make your complaint known to the hotel manager, the hotel's corporate director of customer services, or the national tourism association. In foreign countries, many government tourist boards monitor visitor complaints with an eagle eye, and they will act to rectify the situation.

In the United States, send your complaints to the management of the individual hotel, its corporate headquarters, and the **American Hotel and Motel Association,** 888 Seventh Avenue, New York, New York 10019. While you're at it, write to the AHMA and request a useful booklet entitled *Tips for Travelers,* available free of charge. (Western International Hotels also produces a free pamphlet, this one called *Tips for the Woman Business Traveler.* Western International deserves credit for being one of the first companies in the travel business to regard women travelers with the respect and concern they deserve. Write for the booklet to *Tips,* Western International Hotels, P.O. Box 1996, Seattle, Washington 98111.)

SAFEKEEPING: YOU AND YOUR VALUABLES

When you live in the bush in Africa, you learn to reach an understanding with a lot of potential dangers, not the least of which are poisonous snakes. You don't stay home out of fear or wear thigh-high boots made of thick cowhide. But you do develop an instinct about your surroundings and you always know where your feet go.

The same might be said for your personal safety out in the world when you're traveling for business and are in an unfamiliar area. Go where you want to go and do what you want to do, in freedom. Just be sure you know what's going on around you.

I have never encountered any problem I couldn't handle in a hotel, but safety is certainly an issue of great concern—and outright fear—for many women who travel alone. The most frequent problems are generally encountered in airport hotels and motel chains, where many women travelers report having to push the furniture against the door in order to guarantee a good night's sleep. Many women prefer to pay an additional $10 or $15 a night for a room in order to stay in a better hotel where the chances of being confronted with danger are less likely to occur, even if it means paying the additional amount from their own pockets.

Many hotel and motel chains, inspired by the fact that women business travelers now account for billions of dollars of annual revenue, are taking steps to improve the safety of their facilities. Better lighting in parking lots and public areas, and stronger bolts on hotel room doors are some of the measures being taken. Some hotels even report allocating certain floors of the hotel especially for women travelers and providing extra security for them.

Wherever you're staying and whatever you're paying for a hotel room, there are certain precautions that you should take automatically and that should become second nature when you're traveling. In, *Tips for Travelers* (mentioned above), the American Hotel and Motel Association provides a few useful guidelines. To paraphrase:

DO keep your hotel room door locked and double-bolted when you're inside. Use the chain closing or other secondary locks provided. Put the ''Do not disturb'' sign out to prevent a maid from barging in.

DO check your door when you leave to be sure the automatic lock has actually closed. Or lock the door with your key, then turn the knob to check it.

DO close and lock all sliding doors and windows with access to a patio or balcony, especially if they can be reached easily from the ground or a nearby roof or ledge.

DO place your excess cash, traveler's checks, documents, plane tickets, negotiables, jewelry, and other personal valuables in the hotel safe-deposit box, which is almost always provided free of charge.

DO preserve your anonymity by giving casual acquaintances only your first name—you don't want to invite unwanted attention by having someone call you in your room or pound on your door.

DON'T invite strangers to your room and then wonder what hit you when you wake up with a bump on your head and your valuables gone.

DON'T leave valuables lying out on the table or even hidden in your suitcase. Deposit them in the safe-deposit box. Keep your suitcase locked whenever you leave the room.

DON'T confront suspicious characters on your own. Avoid them by going quickly in the opposite direction, and then report them immediately to the management.

DON'T pull out a roll of $100 bills when you're buying a news-paper at the hotel newsstand. Use traveler's checks and credit cards for major purchases.

You should also take responsibility for your own safety by developing an attitude of pragmatic confidence. Use your judgment. Don't flash your room key, with the number clearly showing, in public places such as the hotel coffee shop or bar. And don't hand your key to the thoughtful stranger who offers to help you open your door—you might not get it back again. Don't hang the "Please make up this room" sign on your doorknob as a signal to passersby that you're not at home. And never leave your door unlocked or unbolted whether or not you're inside. Bolting the door is especially important in European hotels, where the room service waiters have the extraordinary habit of un-locking your door with a pass key and entering without bothering to knock first.

As you walk around the hotel, rank different areas of category ac-cording to their relative safety or lack thereof. Your room is safe, pro-vided the door is locked and double-bolted. The dark and lonely garage and parking lot are not safe. If you can avoid entering them late at night, do so, even if it means leaving your rental car there for the evening and taking a taxi instead. Back stairways, empty corridors, or unattended public rooms are places to invite unpleasant encounters. So are the hotel elevators, at times. Learn to trust your intuition. If there's only one man in the elevator when you start to get in and you don't like the looks of him, turn away as if you had forgotten something and wait for another elevator.

CHECKING OUT

When you're ready to leave a hotel ask the cashier to prepare your bill ahead of time so you can examine it thoroughly before paying. Sometimes, another guest will inadvertently—or advertently—charge a few drinks or bottles of champagne to your room. If your bill looks suspiciously high, you can ask to see the signed chits. If you check your bill during the day, you can complain to the daytime manager and have the bill amended. Often, night managers do not have the au-thority to correct room bills.

Most hotels give check-out times in the late morning or early afternoon, usually between 11 A.M. and 2 P.M. If your plane doesn't leave until 8 P.M. and you would like to keep your room until 5, this can often be arranged if you give the hotel advance notice and if they aren't crowded. When the hotel is full you may not be permitted to hold your room, or you may be charged an extra half day. Even if the hotel can't give you the room, almost always it will agree to store your baggage until your departure.

Hotel chambermaids should be tipped about $1 a day for every day of your visit, provided they have done a satisfactory job. Leave the money in the room, perhaps a bit out of sight so the bellhop doesn't get his hands on it first. Keep track of all tips you give—they're legitimate business expenses and belong on your expense account.

When you're ready to leave your room, ring the bellhop to take down your bags and be sure you have checked the room for forgotten items. The most frequent place travelers leave belongings is hanging on a hook on the back of the bathroom door. Also check the bathroom cabinet, the closets and drawers, and under the bed. Deliver your room key to the desk in the lobby, or give it to the bellhop.

Many hotels that cater to business travelers provide a fast check-out service that saves you the time-consuming business of waiting for your bill to be tallied up and paid for. With express check-out or whatever they call it, you merely sign the receipt and hand in your key. The bill will be sent automatically to your billing address. Even if you take advantage of this service you should still take the time to look at your bill before signing. You don't want to end up explaining someone else's Dom Perignon when your expense account is reviewed.

Hotel bills always seem to mushroom in uncountable ways: tourist taxes, state and city taxes, service charges, and sometimes in foreign countries absurd surcharges for outgoing telephone calls. If you're working on a strict budget and/or paying in cash, you can keep from being unpleasantly surprised if you find out in advance what additional fees will be charged. Don't hesitate to ask the hotel manager to explain any charges you don't understand.

HOTEL CHECKLIST

- Identify yourself professionally when checking in.
- Request room preference/corporate discounts.
- Ask to see room in advance. Check room for complete facilities.
- Tip bellhop fairly.
- Make friends with concierge/housekeeper/switchboard operator; tip when needed.
- Acquaint yourself with hotel facilities.
- Avoid getting bumped—have a confirmed reservation and documentation.
- Keep valuables in safe-deposit box.
- Lock luggage/doors/windows.
- Double-lock and bolt doors when you're in hotel room.

- Develop a sixth sense about avoiding danger.
- Check room for belongings when you leave.
- Have hotel bill prepared in advance of your departure; review all charges.
- Buy 220-volt appliances for travel to areas with 220-volt current, or buy appliances with 110/220-volt adaptability.
- Buy transformer with set of international plugs.
- Check local current (AC or DC) before plugging in.

THE BUSINESS
OF DOING BUSINESS

26

Getting Organized

There's not much difference between doing business in your office and doing business on the road except that you're operating on an improvised basis out of a hotel room and maneuvering on unfamiliar terrain. You still have to schedule appointments, make sales calls, follow up on your contacts, entertain, keep track of your records, and report back to your office.

The way to overcome the disadvantages of being without office support in an unfamiliar town is to compensate by allowing extra time. With sufficient time built into your schedule, you can do anything on the road as well as you can at home.

Local Sources of Information

When you first arrive at your destination, scout through the bookstores in your hotel and in town for weekly visitor's publications, special guides, and other local information. The more you know the easier it will be to schedule your itinerary. If you should need extra assistance, also call the local convention and visitors bureau, the chamber of commerce, or the government tourism board to see if they provide any special services or information for business travelers.

If you're traveling abroad and need advice on local business procedures, research material, or information on local companies, contact the U.S. Embassy or Consulate in your destination and ask to speak to the commercial attaché or the economic officer in the commercial section. If you have obtained a copy of the brochure entitled **"Key Officers of Foreign Service Posts"** before leaving, as recommended in Part 2, "Travel Abroad: Planning for the World," you will be able to ask for the correct foreign service officer by name.

Confirming Appointments

After you've done your preliminary research, get on the hotel room phone and confirm your business appointments. You should have a direct-dial telephone in your hotel room to save the tedious business of going through the hotel switchboard. This is especially important if you have a lot of business calls to make. If you forget to ask for this facility when checking in, do it afterward. The convenience of having a direct-dial phone would make the disruption of changing rooms worthwhile.

If you haven't made any advance appointments, consult a local street map before calling so that you'll know where each of your clients is located and how much traveling time you'll need to schedule to get to them. Whenever possible, make your appointments several days in advance, and as much as a week in advance on multi-city trips. When you're in the first city on your itinerary, call ahead to the next city to make or confirm appointments there. Time permitting, send a follow-up letter to each contact after you've made the appointment, stating briefly the nature of your business and that you're looking forward to the meeting. The more you do to solicit the interest and good will of your potential clients before you see them, the better reception you're likely to receive.

Conversely, it's a bad idea to try to see a client without an appointment. The odds are against your getting to see the right person on the spur of the moment, and even if you are admitted, you won't receive nearly as good a reception as you would if you had made the nature of your business known in advance.

International Phone Calls

If you're traveling outside the United States, check with the hotel management to find out what kind of surcharge the hotel levies on outgoing calls. You may be given the runaround, which you should read as bad news. If you are given an answer, you may be very unpleasantly surprised. In some countries, most notably France, Germany, and Switzerland, hotels may impose a surcharge as high as 300 percent over and above the standard phone company rate. This can add up to a fortune on expensive overseas calls.

A way around this unnecessary expense is to stay in a hotel that subscribes to **Teleplan.** Teleplan was begun by the Bell System a few years ago in an effort to get hotel chains and countries to guarantee that any hotel telephone surcharges would be restricted to a limited, uniform rate. To date, Teleplan is in effect in all Hilton International and Marriott International Hotels, Trusthouse Forte Hotels in the United Kingdom, Golden Tulip Hotels in the Netherlands, and all hotels in Israel, Portugal, and Ireland. Since Teleplan is expanding, check with each hotel when you book a room or when you check in.

If Teleplan is not guarding your telecommunications, there are other ways you can keep your hotel telephone costs down. Direct dialing is one; a direct-dial phone in your room permits you to dial your international calls yourself, thus saving time and any extra charges for operator assistance. If you're calling your office back in the States and have a lot of talking to do, call collect so that the call will be billed to your company at the U.S. rate.

Your telephone credit card is a useful device in foreign countries; it will be accepted nearly everywhere (Portugal, Malta, and West Germany are some exceptions). Be sure to read the instructions on the back of the card before placing the call. As a last resort, you can beat exorbitant hotel surcharges by phoning from a special telephone center or from public coin booths. If you're not fluent in the local language, this method can be most challenging, not to mention inefficient. Telephone systems—the sounds of the dial tone, ringing, and busy signal—all differ drastically in various countries. In London, for example, you may be baffled by rapid short tones followed by a pause, indicating a "ringing" telephone. Likewise, in Stockholm you may not know what to make of the long tone followed by a long pause—another "ringing" signal. Try a few local practice calls from your hotel room phone to get acquainted with the local sonorities.

When calling from Europe to the U.S., take advantage of reduced rate periods that permit you to reach the U.S. during business hours. Reduced rate periods are determined by the time the call is made.

TAKE TIME TO PLAN YOUR TIME

I know a lot of busy executives who think it's a waste to spend time ordering their work schedules. If they aren't out making contact with potential clients every moment of the day, especially when they're on business trips, they chide themselves for not being productive.

Wrong. Most business-management firms tell their executive clients that the time managers spend planning their work and giving priorities to different tasks is the most valuable time of all. An hour or two spent organizing a work plan can save hours, even days, of effort in the future. And a carefully worked out plan gives the busy executive a clear idea of both long- and short-term goals.

Lists as Extensions of Logic

It may sound simplistic, but the easiest way to organize your time is to make lists. The benefit of lists is that once you write something down on a piece of paper, you are no longer required to carry it in your head. You don't have to feel anxious about remembering your responsibilities if they're listed chronologically or in order of importance in your daily planner.

Keeping lists isn't an end in itself, however, and there are good and bad ways to make them. Typically, the things you have to take care of in a day, week, or month do not fall into a perfectly linear pattern with a natural, logical organization. Most likely, the things you list will have different values in terms of when they must get done, and in how important they are in relation to your overall objectives.

The easiest way to organize the things you have to do on a business trip is to break down each item by category. If it's sales calls you have to make, group together in one column all those things that relate to the preparation of your materials for the calls. In a second column list all the things that relate to the calls themselves, such as confirming an appointment or getting your suit back from the hotel cleaners in time for a 3 P.M. meeting. In a third column, write down everything that pertains to follow-up activities, such as sending out letters, placing orders, preparing a report of the meeting for your employers, or other after-the-fact obligations. In a fourth column, list all your personal projects, such as getting your hair done, calling home, taking time out to see a museum, or inviting a friend out to dinner.

The next step is to rearrange your lists by priority, first on a column-by-column basis, then on a cross-column tangent. If your most important sales call in the morning will take you to the southwest corner of the city, and you know you can find a typewriter and a photocopying machine at an associate's office nearby, plan to do some of the follow-up letters from column 3 immediately following your appointment. Plot all these moves in your daily planner.

On a business trip, rarely can you get everything done when it's supposed to be done. This means you will have to go over your lists a third time to see which activities are the most crucial in terms of timing. If you have to write two cover letters for an important sales call at 9 A.M., they take priority over the equally important task of rearranging your business presentation for a later appointment.

The idea of lists is not to provide an excuse for procrastination. A list is not a substitute for action, but rather a game plan that makes future activity easier, as well as more efficient and productive.

When I'm on a business trip, I've always found that an hour or two in the evening spent organizing the things I've accomplished during the day, and setting out the things I have to do in the morning, gives me a sense of control that guides all my activities. I leave my ''To Do'' list on a table in my hotel room and study it when I'm having my room-service breakfast. I can get dressed quickly and out for the day with a sense of purpose—and without having to search my sleepy brain for clues as to what I'm supposed to be doing.

Organizing your time and planning your activities for a business day can take as little as 15 minutes or as much as one-third of your working time. When I was preparing a guidebook to one of the Greek islands and had an enormous amount of local research to do, I spent as much as three hours every evening working over my notes, organizing the information I'd acquired, and figuring out my schedule for the following day. I worried about the time I was spending just pulling things together, until I realized that I couldn't research efficiently or write convincingly until I had my data and future requirements under control.

Making lists that relate to reality takes a bit of practice and the exercise of ruthless, unsentimental logic. If you hate writing letters and put two letters you'll need immediately at the bottom of your list in the pretense of avoiding them, your list-making has served as nothing but a subterfuge. But if you organize your lists in a straightforward, logical manner, refer to them constantly, and *follow* them, you will impose a meaningful order on the free-form character of your business days.

ORGANIZING YOUR BUSINESS PAPERS

Every time I have stood at the window of a New York skyscraper and looked out across the city to the towers of other skyscrapers, I have been overwhelmed by the realization that all those offices on all those floors of all those buildings are filled with millions of people who do nothing but move papers from one desk and office and building to another, make copies of them, and move them back again.

Unfortunately, the paper mountain goes with you on a business trip, and if you don't control it, it will quickly bury you. When you're traveling for business, it's just as important to impose systematic control over the flow of your papers as it is to make your ''To Do'' lists. This means, simply, organize.

Allot whatever time you need during your trips to manage your papers, no matter how boring it might be. Devise a simple, logical system for keeping them. Organize them by client or category and keep them separate in envelopes, file folders, or in a portable paper file. Or group them with paper clips or rubber bands. Mark each group of papers so you know what it contains—it's a big waste of time to have to go back into a pile of papers and read them to find out what they say. If you fail to organize your papers, they'll quickly disorganize you; the order form for your biggest sale of the trip will end up stuffed between the mattress and the headboard of your bed and it will get left behind when you check out of your hotel.

To keep your papers under control, go through them every day or every few days and keep your organization up to date. Throw out those papers you no longer need, and consolidate scattered information. If you can, mail the papers and samples you don't need back to your office for filing or your attention when you return. Carry some pre-stamped manila envelopes if you're traveling in the United States to simplify the procedure. For bulky packages, ask your hotel to recommend a local freight service. Federal Express is a company I hear good things about, and many of the airlines offer fast-delivery service, with guaranteed delivery within 24 or 48 hours.

If you're traveling abroad, it's usually safe to send packages home through the mails. Remember to put air-mail postage on packages and mark them clearly or they'll end up on a slow boat to China. However, I have heard horror stories about the mail service in some countries. If there's any doubt about the reliability or efficiency of the local mails, call the American Embassy or Consulate for advice, or ship your parcels directly with an international airline.

T & E: YOUR EXPENSE ACCOUNTS

Another vital category of on-the-road business management is the organizing of your expense accounts. It's to your benefit to keep careful records of your business-related expenses when you're traveling, so you'll either get your money reimbursed by your company, or be able to claim the full amount as a tax deduction.

The tax law is explicit about expense account record-keeping. You must have a receipt for all your travel and entertainment expenses, with the sole exception of cases when it's difficult to get a receipt, such as for taxi rides. Canceled checks are partially acceptable as evidence of business expenses, but the Internal Revenue Service is much happier if the checks are accompanied by sales receipts. Credit card slips are well received by the IRS; each should be marked with the nature of the expense and, if it involves entertainment, the name(s) of the person(s) you entertained, their company, and your business purpose. If you're entertaining a group of five business associates for lunch, you must provide information about all five, unless the group consists of a principal guest and his or her subordinates. In this case, only the name and title of the main guest are needed.

Don't forget to itemize theater and sports tickets on your expense account if they have been used to entertain clients. You'll have no trouble claiming them if the event or entertainment took place within a day or two of business contact with the same people. If there's a gap of time between the meeting and the event, however, the IRS might question the legitimacy of the deduction.

In addition to keeping receipts of all travel and entertainment expenses, it's just as important to keep a written record of all minor expenses. Keep a daily planner or record book handy in your briefcase or travel bag and fill in the expenses as they occur, or at least at the end of every day. Remember to include things as petty as 10¢ for a phone call from a public telephone and $1 for a new ballpoint pen. Taxis, tips, tolls, parking, gas, postage, and official documents are all legitimate expenses. Record them all; you'll be astonished at how quickly the numbers add up.

Your hotel bills can be itemized specifically on your expense account records, or they may be summarized as part of your per diem expense allowance. If you claim a standard per diem amount, no receipts for your accommodations are required. (For more thoughts on expense accounts, turn back to Chapter 6.)

ORGANIZING CHECKLIST

- Do local research.
- Make/confirm appointments.
- Avoid hotel phone surcharges.
- Plan activities. Give priorities to tasks.
- Make "To Do" lists. Follow them.
- File and label all business papers. Send home unneeded materials.
- Keep receipts and careful expense records.

27

Business Conduct

Anywhere in the United States you can assume that most business is conducted at familiar times and in a familiar manner, with a few minor variants. (It's slower and less formal in most southern and southwestern cities than it is in the Northwest, the Midwest, and the hyperkinetic Northeast.)

When you're traveling abroad, however, you may have to make substantial changes in your ordinary way of doing things. With so many places in the world and so many possible styles of business behavior, you have to learn to adapt to local habits and personalities without losing your identity.

The simplest way to get to know a city or country that's not your own is to go slowly at first. Take the time to observe how others act, and gauge how they react to you. To take the most difficult examples, the majority of businessmen in the Orient and in many Arab countries have little or no experience in dealing with women in business and they're still in a state of shock at having to do so. This is unfortunate, but there's precious little you can do about it. For now, your concern is the fulfillment of your business objectives, not the raised consciousness of the local males.

What do you do? You behave in a completely professional, neutral manner to make encounter as easy as possible for your stricken male hosts. Don't threaten, don't be aggressive, and don't confuse the issue by flirting. Come directly to the point in a gentle and refined manner once the introductory niceties have been exchanged. Soft-pedal your cherished independence for the moment. This is at no cost to your self-respect, by the way; only a person with a secure sense of her own self-worth can adapt her behavior to compensate for the insecurities and limitations of others.

THE ARAB WORLD

If you are sent on assignment to one of the more conservative Arab countries, you may run up against a strict religious conservatism regarding the inherent threat of females that may be almost impossible to counterbalance. In Saudi Arabia, for example, local women are never seen alone on the streets. They huddle against each other, shrouded in black, or sit like stones in the backs of purdah cars (women are not permitted to drive). *The Wall Street Journal* reports that in public places, such as the market in Riyadh, even Western women improperly dressed by local standards are likely to be attacked by ''Committees for the Encouragement of Virtue and the Elimination of Vice.'' These ''vice squads'' are made up of old men who serve as morals judges, hitting women's bare legs and arms with sticks and spraying them with green paint. (The solution: Wear long-sleeved tops and full-length skirts.)

Ironically, many Arab government officials and leading businessmen are sophisticated internationalists with Oxford or Cambridge accents who regularly slip over to Bahrain to enjoy the favors of exotic courtesans from France, or attend secret baths populated with prepubescent boys. But even in private business meetings with these worldly types you should behave conservatively. Wear long-sleeved blouses and mid-calf skirts, and don't cross your legs. Lighting up a cigarette is a no-no, unless your host explicitly invites you to. Even Prime Minister Margaret Thatcher deferred to local custom when she visited Saudi King Khalid in Riyadh. She wore a long-sleeved ankle-length dress and a veil over her face.

Most of the Arab world is not as conservative as Saudi Arabia and the other feudal kingdoms of the Persian Gulf, although the underlying feeling about women is basically the same. Egypt, Lebanon, and Jordan are among the most Western in their attitudes; Afghanistan, Syria, Turkey (outside of Istanbul), and most of the desert kingdoms of North Africa are fairly restrictive. Morocco, which has seen a lot of half-naked female tourists roaming through its bazaars and cavorting on its streets, still retains a very restrictive attitude toward the conduct of its own women. Most men there will be uncomfortable at having to deal with you as an equal.

MISOGYNY IN THE ORIENT

In the Orient, the effect of the misogynistic attitude of the men takes a slightly different turn. Many Oriental women I've met are highly intelligent, thoroughly educated, and brilliant in the management of businesses and careers. Yet they conceal their steel-trap minds behind a façade of utter delicacy and helplessness, never preempting any masculine modes of behavior and never, ever, appearing threatening.

In Japan, where the traditional code of behavior indicates a prescribed response for virtually every type of human encounter, the excessive politeness and deferential treatment extends not only from men to women, but also from men to men. To keep from offending your Japanese business associates or presenting them with some sort of behavior they won't have a predetermined response for, modify your behavior according to local standards. This doesn't mean you should get involved in prolonged bouts of bowing or dress like a geisha, but you should come on softly with as much politeness as seems called for.

In spite of the apparent Westernization of Japan, you should keep in mind that the underlying culture remains bound in the old traditions, part of which includes the custom of entertaining business associates. In the Japanese language, the word *okyakusama* means both "customer" and "guest." You may find yourself invited to expensive dinners and other entertainment as an integral part of business life. Japanese businessmen have elaborate expense accounts to use on their guests' behalf. Traditionally, part of their entertainment would include an evening in a geisha house; but since this is a form of amusement ordinarily reserved for men, it's questionable whether you would be included. The Japanese also expect their guests to reciprocate, especially if the guest is the one soliciting business. For a woman, a geisha-house foray is out of the question, but an expense-account lunch or dinner at one of the better restaurants is an appropriate way for you to entertain.

In Japan, as in many parts of the Orient where traditional standards prevail, always remember to address people by their surnames, even when referring to your Western associates. Use the prefix "Ms." or "Mr." and the Japanese suffix -san, or other appropriate titles. You should also pay attention to the status and age of your business counterparts. Equals speak to equals, young people show deference to their elders, and everyone exchanges basic courtesies and pleasantries before getting down to the business of business. Also keep in mind the ingrained Oriental concept of saving face. As a woman in a man's world, you may have to be twice as careful as a man not to give cause for real or imagined offense.

The social codes in the rest of the Orient are never quite as restrictive or formal as they seem in Japan, especially when it comes to the acceptance and treatment of women. Other Oriental men, such as the Taiwanese, Koreans, and Indonesians, may hold basically misogynistic views by our standards, but their cultures are flexible enough to permit them to accept you without apoplexy, perhaps as "honorary males." (Not an impossibility. Some years ago, the race-obsessed government of South Africa bestowed the status of "honorary whites" on Japanese businessmen so they could stay at whites-only hotels.)

In China, you may be happy to hear, women are accorded equal status with men, do not take their husbands' names upon marriage, and receive equal pay for equal work. The Republic of the Philippines enjoys an almost Western style of culture (and is the only Christian country in the Orient). In Malaysia, people are generally so friendly that it's unlikely you would ever feel the least discomforted.

However, the Oriental style is clearly different from our own and there are hundreds of local customs dictating social behavior. A few rules to remember: Never point with your left hand, touch anyone with it, or hand something with it—in Moslem cultures (which include Indonesia and parts of Malaysia and Singapore), the left hand is thought unclean. Some countries in the Orient also think that pointing with the forefinger is rude, and in Thailand, crossing one's legs so that one's foot is pointed at someone is considered the height of bad manners (keep both feet flat on the ground, especially when facing someone).

Since most Orientals tend to be more subdued in public than Westerners, always remember to speak in a soft voice; you need only hear a fellow Yank or his wife bellowing in a shop or restaurant in the Orient to know how overbearing a big voice is in a soft-spoken culture. (The same is true by the way for many parts of Europe—Americans generally seem to speak much more loudly than other people.)

For more information on the Orient, get a copy of Japan Air Lines' *Executive Guide to the Orient* (mentioned in Part 2). Also ask business associates who have traveled to the countries on your itinerary, or inquire at the destination—the hostess in your hotel is a goldmine of good advice.

LOCAL CUSTOMS

In most parts of Northern Europe, business is conducted in the same punctual, to-the-point manner as it is in the United States. There are far fewer local idiosyncrasies to worry about than in an Oriental country, and far fewer restrictions against females. One thing I have heard Europeans, both male and female, point out, is that too many

American women are brash and unpleasant in what the Europeans feel is a mistaken identification of liberation with toughness. Why can't women be independent, equal, competent, and successful and still be women? they ask. As far as I'm concerned, this is a valid question.

Whether you agree or not, remember that when you're dealing with European or South American men in business, you'll get what you want a lot faster and more easily if you don't hit the locals over the head, in words or manner, with a women's lib karate chop.

No matter where you're traveling for business, give yourself time to pick up the nuances of local business life—in terms of individual personalities as well as culture. If your business associates seem wide open and informal in their dealings with one another, you should feel free to follow suit in a discreet way. Conversely, if the people are buttoned up tight, call each other by their patronyms after having sat in adjacent offices for 16 years, and make little bows while clicking their heels, you won't want to come charging through the door shouting ''Howdy, pardner!'' Keep to yourself at first until you have the chance to intuitively feel out the rhymes and rhythms of local etiquette.

One of the first things you'll discover in international business is that most people in the world operate on a much more relaxed schedule than we do. In fact, many people think American businessmen and women are off their rockers for running around at such a hectic pace, with no time off for laughter, a few jokes, a convivial hour spent getting acquainted, or other civilities. They have a point. Once you experience a more relaxed way of doing things, you may question the validity of our manic methods.

With the exception of Northern European countries and Japan, appointments around the world are seldom kept on time and no one really seems to care. When you're building your schedule, leave enough time in your planner to absorb delays of 15 minutes, half an hour, or even more before each business appointment. Your business contacts aren't necessarily being rude; they simply have a different perception of time from yours.

In countries not noted for their efficiency, schedule extra time for mundane projects like going to the post office or bank. A simple trip to cash a check can take several hours; I once spent three hours in a post office in Rome trying to mail a small package to my home office. A basic rule in countries where you expect delays (mainly those siesta, mañana cultures) is to cut your scheduled appointments down by about one-third.

Keep in mind that many cultures do not operate on a nine-to-five basis. Many Mediterranean, Latin American, and other countries with warm climates enjoy a long break in the middle of the day. All those aggressive businessmen you've been sparring with all morning go home to the bosom of their families to enjoy a huge midday meal, then climb into their jammies and go to sleep for two hours or more. Check a guidebook for general business and banking hours before planning your schedule. In Athens, for example, the second half of the business day doesn't get going until around 5 P.M. (The government keeps threatening to change all that, but so far, they've met with little cooperation.)

Consider the effect the pace of local life might have on the timing and success of your business pitch: Will your hungry client be paying attention to your speech about the benefits of the latest floppy disk, or dreaming of moussaka and his afternoon snooze?

Local holidays can also run counter to your business objectives and you should know before you go what you might run into. Most guidebooks include lists of standard national holidays, but miss such ongoing events as the Moslem month of Ramadan, or the general French exodus to the seashore during the month of August. Check with the national carrier of the country, or with the embassy, consulate, or tourist board.

Wherever you are, always be sure there is sufficient flexibility in your schedule to accommodate all the delays and inconveniences that can occur. If you haven't budgeted for local idiosyncrasies, you'll be forced to try to make the local world conform to your predesigned idea of how it ought to work; it never will.

In order to forestall problems and avoid *faux pas* when you're on the road, follow a few basic rules no matter where you are. First, always be on time for appointments, even if you don't know when your business contacts will show up. It's better to wait for them than to have them wait for you. Punctuality is especially important in most parts of the United States, Canada, Northern Europe, Switzerland, Austria, China, Australia, and Japan.

Be prepared to engage in some pleasantries—light conversation on nonpersonal subjects—before getting down to business. An American business contact might shake your hand when you enter his office, invite you to sit down, and then ask you directly what business you have come to discuss. Few other people in the world are quite as abrupt as this, especially in Europe, Latin America, and the Orient. Let your host be your guide in this matter. If you're perceptive, you'll know exactly when the right pause has occurred to indicate that you should now speak of business.

To make light conversation easy, know something about the economic and commercial activities of your host country, and what's going on locally. A quick scan of the local English-language newspaper will give you all the conversational leads you'll need. As a general rule, avoid comments about politics, especially in nondemocratic countries. Also, be prepared to proceed slowly. Your first meeting may serve only as a get-acquainted encounter, as a prelude to later negotiations.

In your behavior, be observant and receptive at first, rather than expressive. Give yourself a chance to see and pick up examples of local behavior; give your host the opportunity of offering his hand or bowing before thrusting your hand toward him. If you watch rather than act, you will be able to follow the other person's lead until you feel confident of what's expected of you. Your hesitation, by the way, can be timed only seconds after the other person makes a move, once you get good at it, so you'll never seem to be passive or afraid. Surprises you may encounter: Malaysians smile a lot and are reassured when you smile too; in Peru and Portugal, don't be alarmed if a courtly gent gestures to kiss your hand.

All over the world, always call business associates by their surnames unless explicitly invited to do otherwise. I have already mentioned the use of the suffix -san in Japan. In Malaysia, you may encounter *Inche, Che, Tunka,* and *Tun* as honorific titles for men and women, which should be used each time you address them. In China, your business contacts should usually be addressed by their professional titles, from Chairman on down. Most Oriental names give the patronym first and the given names last.

The business of titles applies equally in parts of Europe, mostly the Germanic countries. In Switzerland, Herr Doktor Professor Schmidt of the pharmaceutical company in Basel is called Herr Doktor Professor Schmidt by Herr Doktor Professor Kopf, who has worked beside him for the last 43 years, and there's no reason why you should call him Franz.

BUSINESS CARDS AND MATERIALS

Few countries in the world do not use business cards as a functional part of business procedure (China is one that doesn't, which adds to the problem of getting your business associate's name and title straight). In Korea, business cards are used almost like calling cards, and are handed to the receptionist upon entering an office, to be formally carried back to the person you have an appointment with.

To save yourself embarrassment, always have a supply of 100 or so business cards with you when you travel, and if you'll be in a country where English is not readily understood, or where a different alphabet is used, you should go to the trouble of getting bilingual business cards printed beforehand. As already mentioned, several international airlines, notably JAL, Lufthansa, and Pan Am, offer this service at a nominal cost. Allow from two days to a week to get the cards; in some places you can get them overnight for a surcharge. If you're traveling to China, get bilingual cards printed to give your Chinese associates, even if you won't receive cards from them.

Whenever you're doing business in a country where English is not the dominant language, you should try to make yourself, your mission, and the goods and services you're discussing as comprehensible as possible to your business counterpart. If you're sure Herr Doktor Professor Schmidt speaks fluent English and has no problem understanding the nuances of your proposal, feel free to deal with him in English and to use English documents. But if you're dealing with someone who is not secure in English or doesn't speak it at all, you should have the courtesy to deal with him or her in the local language or through an interpreter.

In this case, your business documents should be prepared in the language of your host, even if it means hiring a translator. If you are dealing with brochures or other marketing tools provided by your company, there's nothing you can do about replacing them on your own, but you should agitate for bilingual materials within your own firm. If you're in doubt about how to deal with a prospective client, reverse the situation to see how it feels. If a German manufacturer visited you in your Chicago office to try to sell you a line of hardware, and he spoke to you only in German and showed you a German-language brochure, and if you had taken two years of German in high school 12 years ago, how would you respond? You might admire the fine photography in his brochure, and note the expensive coated paper and the perfect binding, but you wouldn't have a clue as to how to evaluate the merits of what he was trying to sell. That's how the German manufacturer looks at you when you visit his office in Düsseldorf; although, being European, he's more apt to be fluent in other languages than you are.

If you have no alternative, hire a translator to translate your brochure or other printed sales materials on a page-by-page basis so your client can relate the translation to the actual brochure. You can find a translator through your hotel, an international airline, or by asking for advice from the American Embassy or Consulate.

You could also contact one of the new organizations springing up around the world for the purpose of assisting international business travelers. One such service in France is **France Contacts,** at 50 Avenue des Champs-Elysées, 75008 Paris. This useful organization helps independent entrepreneurs and businessmen from small companies find contacts, set up meetings, arrange travel and accommodations, and obtain the services of interpreters.

THE TOWER OF BABEL

If your business travel requires you to make repeated visits to a specific country or area of the world where a single language dominates, it's worth your while to learn that language. You may not have the chance to become fluent, but familiarity with the language will make it a lot easier for you to operate. There is an added bonus: you will feel like a native.

The Berlitz Schools, which have intensive and expensive crash programs for business people who need to learn a language quickly, apparently do a good job of forcing the language down your throat and getting you to speak some words. I have also heard the Berlitz method criticized for teaching phrasing only by rote, not building a basic understanding of the language. Language records and tapes are a good way to learn a language, if you can discipline yourself. Chrisjean Whitten learned Greek, Portuguese, and Spanish partly through the aid of Linguaphone records.

You can also find someone to tutor you privately, if you can afford it. Or, you can enroll in a language course at a university or an institution such as the Spanish Institute or Alliance Française. If learning a language is critical to the performance of your job, you might cajole your company into picking up the tab. And by all means, deduct the cost of business-related language lessons from your income taxes.

Even if you don't have the inclination or opportunity to study a language, do take the trouble to memorize a few key phrases. "Hello," "Good morning," "Thank you," and "Where is the ladies' room?" are always useful to know in a variety of tongues. Surprisingly, most people in the world respond supportively to your efforts to speak their language.

If you have to enter into delicate negotiations in a language that you're not totally comfortable with, ask your host to speak English, or hire an interpreter. In most business communities around the world the lingua franca is no longer French, but English. However, if your local business counterparts aren't completely fluent in English, or if there's any danger of a lack of understanding, it's your responsibility—and to your advantage—to hire an interpreter. Most hotels that cater to the business traveler can provide this service on one or two days' notice.

Some international airlines, such as JAL and Air France, can usually also help find an interpreter for you. If you're stuck and can't find anyone to help you, get in touch with the U.S. Embassy or Consulate and ask them for assistance.

ComputerSpeak

There's still another language tool: a magical little computer that can translate words, phrases, and sentences for you, including the right verb tenses. Small enough to fit into your pocket, there are several of these miraculous creatures on the market. The Craig M-100 Translator and Information Center has interchangeable memory capsules ($25 each at press time) that help you find your way in English, Spanish, French, German, Italian, and Japanese. The Craig M-100 comes with its own case, an AC adapter, a calculator, and has a metric conversion facility. The cost of the unit with an English language capsule is about $120.

A similar gizmo is produced by Texas Instruments, this one called the Language Tutor, which costs about $150. This machine will actually translate words, phrases, and sentences for you, and will speak to show you how to pronounce them correctly. If that's not eerie, I don't know what is. Tapes for this version cost about $50.

"Businessese"

Also, be aware that in foreign countries, even those locals who are fluent in English probably have been spared the gobbledygook of American ''businessese.'' Words and phrases such as ''time-frame'' (or ''windows in the time-frame''), ''prioritize'' and ''strategize,'' ''interface,'' and ''eyeballing the net-net'' most likely have not entered the international lexicon, and you will confuse the issue and baffle your associates if you use them. ''Massaging the alternatives'' is another one to look out for—someone might misconstrue your meaning and take you for the ''alternative.''

Written Communications

Some countries make a big deal of correspondence and expect to have letters promptly answered. Even when the response is negative, answer your foreign correspondents punctually, and have the letters translated into the recipient's language if you feel this would be helpful.

The same applies to phone calls. In my experience, the top executives who have the most authority and make the largest salaries almost always answer their phone calls. It's the middle managers harrassed by work and arrogant about their positions who fail to extend even this basic courtesy. No class, I say, and whenever business contacts fail to return my calls, I deduce something negative about them.

BUSINESS ENTERTAINMENT

We have already mentioned business entertaining in Japan, with its elaborate and expensive customs. You'll find the same attitude toward entertaining as a functional part of doing business throughout most of the Orient, with the exception of Hong Kong. In Thailand, Singapore, Indonesia, Korea, and the Philippines, entertainment is regarded as an integral part of the business procedure and is taken most seriously. In some countries, entertainment is thought of as supplementary to the business of doing business; Malaysia is an example of this category.

By custom, you will almost always receive the first invitation, either to lunch, dinner, cocktails, or other events, such as a day at the seashore, a game of golf, or a visit to someone's home. It is incumbent upon you to reciprocate in almost every country in the Orient, with the exception of China, where facilities for returning invitations are somewhat limited. Even there, if you have been wined and dined at an elaborate banquet by your hosts, try to book a table at the best restaurant you can afford and return the favor. In Peking, restaurants that cater to foreigners are few and in great demand—book as far ahead as possible.

The correct attitude to have toward reciprocal business entertainment is not that it's an unpleasant duty, but that it's a means of establishing civilized relationships and personal trust between you and those you plan to do business with. This may take time and effort, but most people in the world do not function with the cold efficiency that we do; they give more value to the human element. They don't like signing contracts with people they don't know, and believe that pleasant occasions shared on a personal level do much to enhance the chances of doing business.

The value of personal contact was brought home to me clearly by a Greek friend in the shipping business. Among the world's most hospitable people, the Greeks make a great effort to take care of their business guests; they think nothing of getting up at 4 in the morning to drive them to the airport, or of taking them to the best restaurants and bouzoukia clubs in Athens six nights in a row. As a result, they establish real friendships with their visiting associates. (They also often make a great effort, almost always successful, to fix their male business guests up with the best talent Athens has to offer—even to the point of participating in all-night sexual activities together in a bordello. One Greek I know told me frankly that the way to establish bonds with a business associate was to go whoring with him. Maybe he's right. I'll never know.)

This is neither here nor there as far as you're concerned, except that you should be aware that it occurs more often than you'd imagine, and any men you're traveling with may be party to such after-hours fun and games. In the all-male secret society, from which you will always be excluded, you are clearly at a disadvantage when it comes to using shared personal experiences of an intimate nature to establish bonds of friendship. There's not much you can do about it.

It's not unheard of for women traveling for business to use their sexual charms to establish bonds of another nature for the purpose of winning contracts. I can't believe that behavior of this kind would help anyone in the long run. It would also seem to be a backhanded way of functioning as a prostitute. If you're going to do it, do it and pocket the money. But what kind of misperceived selflessness could possibly persuade any woman to use her body to win profits for her company?

Entertainment Planning

Fortunately, the question of entertaining business associates usually concerns the much more prosaic problem of where to take your guests and how to pay the bill.

No matter where you are, when you're the stranger in town, it's usually the role of the local person to extend the first invitation. That makes your job of reciprocating easier, since you will have some foreknowledge of the best time and place to entertain. If you have been invited to lunch, extend another luncheon invitation a day or two later; the midday meal is universally acceptable as an appropriate time to entertain. Drinks after work are commonplace, breakfast is occasionally a meeting time (usually in crisp, northern countries), and dinner is almost always acceptable. With dinner, you run into possible problems regarding your guest's misassumption about the nature of your invitation, or difficulties regarding his or her schedule. If your guest lives in the suburbs, and has a two-hour commute and a wife waiting with dinner, he may not be willing to accept your invitation.

If you are inviting a male business associate for dinner alone, make it clear by the manner in which you extend the invitation that you're not making a subtle pass. If the person mentions his or her commute and a spouse waiting at home, why not extend the invitation to the husband or wife, too?

If you aren't sure where to take your guests, consult a good guidebook, perhaps one purchased locally that specializes in reviews of the top restaurants. Local business associates and your hotel concierge can also give you advice, or, if you're really stuck, ask your guest to recommend a restaurant where he or she would particularly enjoy dining.

A day or two before the occasion, ask around for the most popular mealtimes and find out how long you will probably have to wait in the restaurant before being seated. To assure a good reception in a restaurant where you're not known, arrange your party in advance with the maître d' and give him a $5 or $10 tip (depending on the number of guests and the category of the restaurant). Explain your preferred meal hour and seating arrangement to involve the maître d' in your project. If you know in advance what wines you wish to order (a risky business), or if you want it understood that you are the hostess and wish to be handed the wine list as well as the bill, make sure this is understood by the maître d', the waiters, and the sommelier.

Getting the Bill

Women entertaining business associates often have a terrible time getting the bill, as the general assumption is that women don't or can't pay. The way around this situation is to speak beforehand to the powers that be, as mentioned, and be sure everybody understands that you're the one who's supposed to get the bill. You can even have a credit card slip written up in advance, to be quickly completed as you leave. Another way to do it is to get up from the table toward the end of the meal and take care of the bill with your waiter, out of sight of your guests. I have seen many men do this. In my experience, it is the most discreet way of being the host or hostess, as you never confront your guests with the imposing reality of the bill, and you don't have to put up a fight about who is going to pay it.

A related problem is the occasional reluctance of some men even to accept an invitation from a woman in the first place. Consciously, or subconsciously, they seem to feel threatened that their masculine position of dominance has been preempted. A way around this kind of sensitivity (which you will have to ferret out with your intuition alone) is to suggest an engagement not in terms of ''I want to invite you . . .'' but the less threatening ''Please join me—as the guest of my company.''

Gifts

Gift-giving in the course of business activity is another aspect of international travel that you will have to adapt to. The first thing not to do is to give away a lot of free trade goodies, like cheap rulers or ballpoint pens with your company name on them. Unless you're bartering for cowrie shells with Trobriand Islanders, such trinkets will be deemed valueless and may even be considered insulting (as they probably would be in the Trobriand Islands, too).

The most formal in the business of giving gifts, as you might expect, are the Japanese. On first contact, you are not expected to give your host a gift, even though you may receive one (usually something hand-crafted locally, like a lacquered plate inlaid with mother-of-pearl). When you return home, you should acknowledge the gift with a hand-written note to the giver, and reciprocate with a gift of equal value upon your return to his country. Impersonal gifts, usually business related, are the safest. Leather desk calendars and fancy pen sets with engraved initials are standard and will be gratefully received, or give a bottle of imported liquor (you can pick one up duty free on the plane).

If you are meeting some high-level business or government executives in Japan, a ceremonial exchange of gifts on a corporate level may occur at the first meeting. Call the secretary of the person you will be seeing to find out if gifts will be exchanged. Ordinarily, your Oriental host will not open his gift in front of you, but he may ask you to open the one he has given you, which you should then do enthusiastically to show your appreciation. Hesitate before starting to open the gift, however, and if you're not encouraged to proceed, wait until later to open it in private.

In China, gifts are not given to business associates, except in the case of an official delegation to a government ministry, nor are gifts customary in Malaysia or Hong Kong. Gift-giving is frequently part of the business procedure in Singapore, Thailand, Korea, Indonesia, Taiwan, and the Philippines.

In Europe and Latin America, gifts are not normally a standard part of business practice, and many countries have laws governing the maximum value of gifts that may be legally received. Ask experienced business associates or find out locally what is expected. If you give a gift, do it on the basis of personal friendship, and be careful that it cannot be interpreted as an attempt to buy favor.

An exception to not giving gifts, anywhere in the world, is when you are invited to a business associate's home. Whenever this occurs, send a handwritten note of thanks to your host and hostess, and include a bunch of flowers, a basket of fruit, or some chocolates.

SURVIVING FELLOW TRAVELERS

Awkward situations can also arise when you are traveling with business associates of the opposite sex. ''What will my wife say when she learns

I'm traveling with a woman?'' squawked a male business associate of mine when we were making plans to attend a sales conference in another city.

''Whatever she thinks,'' I answered, ''is completely between you and her.''

Many men in business have nightmares—or fantasies—at the thought of traveling with women associates. One businessman of my acquaintance even asked me to wait before getting off the plane on our return flight so his wife wouldn't see us together. I refused, and told him that if he felt guilty by implication, then he could remain on the plane until the other passengers, including me, had disembarked.

Some men, usually the same bunch who fear that their wives will be waiting with accusing glances, assume that because you're sleeping alone in a hotel bed in a faraway city, you're available to them. I once had to make an overnight business trip with what I thought was the straightest, most moral, most married, most monogamous man I'd ever met—the last one I ever expected any overtures from. But when we said goodnight at the door of our side-by-side rooms, he tried to block my way and invited himself in. With a brief kick to the shins and a consoling pat, I sent him to his room alone. I ignored the incident altogether the following morning since I didn't want there to be any professional discomfort between us.

Isn't it a bore that the burden always seems to fall on women, both in rejecting (or accepting) the overture, and then in compensating for the man's reactions?

Another fear expressed by some corporate managers is that a sales conference attended by male and female employees will turn into an orgy. My answer to that is, so what? Over half the men I've met away from home on business missions, especially in the free-for-all of a convention, are on the make in any case. If the women on the trip decide to let loose and have a good time too, has some sacred business code been violated?

Some women do precisely that—have a good time. I know many women in prestigious positions in large corporation who behave just as wildly at conventions or sales meetings as their uninhibited male associates. However, it's the rare one who doesn't suffer opprobrium afterward in terms of her prestige and power. The danger here, as I have witnessed more than once, is that the woman concerned drinks too much, runs herself ragged, and destroys a substantial portion of her reputation. Forever after, she is subjected to the overt (unwanted) familiarity or the disdain of her sexual partner(s)—and all those who know about her behavior.

Women are not yet equal to men in this kind of situation. Although they are certainly free to do what they want to do, the double standard is still in force. When all is said and done, women are the ones who get punished. In the perception of others, they have acted cheaply and lost value and respect.

CONDUCT CHECKLIST

- Find out from guidebooks and experienced associates how business is conducted in your destination.
- Play down your independence in areas of the world where it might be threatening.
- Wear long skirts and long-sleeved blouses in Saudi Arabia.
- Metamorphose into an ''honorary male'' for business in the Orient.
- Address people by surnames unless invited to do otherwise. In the Orient, don't point; don't gesture with the left hand.
- Adapt to local pace; schedule for delays.
- Exchange pleasantries before getting down to business topics.
- Know about local holidays before scheduling your trip.
- Be prompt for all appointments.
- Use bilingual business cards and trade materials.
- Answer all phone calls and correspondence promptly.
- Take a language course or employ a tutor to learn the language of your foreign business associates.
- Take advantage of language cassette tapes.
- If you plan to participate in extensive negotiations, hire an interpreter.
- Claim the cost of language lessons, records, and books as legitimate business expenses.
- Avoid ''businessese.''
- Reciprocate when entertained.
- Arrange ahead to get the bill.
- Speak softly; carry a big gift.

28

Dining Alone

Everybody makes such a big issue of dining alone that it seems out of proportion to the reality. The biggest event in your life when you're on the road is not whether or not you have to eat alone—it's whether or not you accomplish your professional objectives.

The discomfort and social embarrassment associated with dining alone is not peculiar to women business travelers. Most traveling businessmen I've spoken to feel exactly the same way and are not ashamed to say so. As far as I can see, the only way to deal with the problem is to *deal* with it, just as you handle any life situation that at first seems intimidating, but that through experience quickly loses its power to threaten you.

Developing the poise to survive a meal on your own is not nearly as difficult as many other tasks in life, and you should force yourself to do it to overcome what is an exaggerated and unnecessary fear. What is behind this fear of dining alone? A sense of social failure? Or the horror of being perceived as a social failure for not having a friend, lover, family member, or mere acquaintance to sit beside you?

At some time or other, just about everybody has had to eat alone publicly. All those people in the restaurant who you think are staring at you have been in your boots more than once in the past. At the moment, they are the insiders, comforted by the presence of others at their table. You are the outsider, and the herd all turns to stare at you to confirm the difference.

Have you ever noticed how people on the street will stop to stare at someone who has caught his or her heel and tripped or fallen down? Why? Because the one who has fallen has committed a *faux pas*. She has done something out of the ordinary, something that does not conform to accepted behavior, even though it was an accident. The person who has stumbled has become suddenly vulnerable—reminding us of our own fragility.

Something similar happens when you walk into a restaurant alone. If the people concerned, from the maitre d' to the group at the next table, had any class or sophistication, they would either accept your presence without interest or extend a discreet but warm welcome. If they fail to do so, it's a measure of their own discomfort, lack of self-confidence, and plain bad manners. You should identify their behavior as such and not perceive it as bad feelings against yourself.

I personally think you can control most of the responses you get from others, even in a situation like this. If you slink into a restaurant alone, feeling lonely and like a loser, people will perceive you as precisely that. But if you're bright, breezy, and confident, self-contained in your solitude and straightforward in the way you look at and respond to others, people will almost always regard you with positive interest.

There's another possibility when you go into a restaurant alone: Nobody will pay the slightest bit of attention to you. That's all right, too. The only thing you're asking for is the right to function like an ordinary human being, without being forced into some mode of behavior that presupposes shame, embarrassment, or coquettishness.

Some writers on the subject advise women business travelers to use whatever subterfuge they can think of to keep the maitre d' from knowing that they're single females. Booking your reservation in the name of ''Dr. Smith'' is one such device; calling yourself ''Mr.'' is another. I don't buy this. The world has to learn how to deal with women as plain, ordinary people, and it's up to us to show them how. We won't succeed if we pretend to be other than what we are. What's wrong with what we are?

One of the most common complaints of women business travelers (or any solo traveler, for that matter), is that they are always given the worst table in the restaurant. I don't think you should feel too offended if you aren't given the best table in the house. Somebody has to sit at the least attractive table. As the single diner represents considerably less revenue per table than two or more diners, it makes economic sense as far as the restaurant is concerned to consolidate its losses.

That doesn't mean you should settle for something unacceptable, especially if there are many better tables unoccupied. ''I would prefer to sit here,'' you say to the maitre d' politely, indicating a small table against the wall. Most often, he will oblige you. If he doesn't, and there's no good reason other than his own prejudice, you might consider refusing the table and leaving the restaurant. If your reception in a restaurant you're offering your patronage to is ungracious or surly, why support the restaurant with your business?

Enough of the negatives. How do you control the situation so you get a good reception in the restaurant of your choice?

First of all, reserve in advance. You can't expect any kind of preferential treatment if you show up unannounced at the door. Plan to eat a little earlier or later than the main lunch or dinner hour when there won't be as much demand for tables. Ask the concierge at your hotel about the best mealtimes and restaurants for solo diners. Have the concierge do the booking for you, too. If the restaurant knows you're a valued guest of the hotel, it may well extend some extra courtesies.

Another age-old method of getting a table you want is to grease the maitre d's palm. The maitre d' usually looks so aristocratic in his fancy black suit that you are afraid of insulting him. Don't be—the man probably makes over half his income from gratuities discreetly passed on by male patrons who know from experience how to get service.

When you're tipping, have a $5 bill folded up in your palm, out of sight. When you approach the maitre d', introduce yourself, tell him you are in his city for business and are dining alone, and would greatly appreciate a pleasant, private table. These guys are pros when it comes to accepting tips, and before you can bat an eye, the man will have your money safely in his pocket. He probably won't look at you gratefully or thank you profusely for your generosity. Most likely, he will ignore it. But you'll get a good table.

Reading at the Table

Opinions differ about whether to read at the table when you're dining alone. Having been taught as a child that reading at the table was the height of rudeness, I still have a resistance to doing it. In a good restaurant that takes pains with the preparation and presentation of its food, reading at the table would seem inconsiderate of the staff. Can you read *Time* magazine and truly appreciate your fresh asparagus or *moules rémoulade?* Maybe. Maybe not.

Not bringing any reading material to the table is a good way of testing your poise and self-confidence. Can you sit alone, eating quietly and enjoying your meal, observing the goings-on of the restaurant without being obtrusive, and still feel comfortable with yourself? If you can, you've won the battle of dining alone. Just be sure you don't stare at your plate like a bad little girl from St. Trinian's. Do learn the subtle art of looking occupied while never staring or violating other people's privacy. The way to do this is to look at everything that goes on around you, but always before others are aware of you. This way, you can see everything and make your own appraisals without ever making direct eye contact, unless you want to. Look toward things, but not at them. It's amazing what your peripheral vision will reveal. The idea is to be a passive participant in what's going on, and still know everything you want to know.

Chrisjean Whitten, who is as poised a business traveler as I've ever met, plays a little game when she's alone in a restaurant. She eavesdrops on other people's conversations. She tries to determine exactly where the speakers are from and what their lives are all about. She doesn't let people know she's listening—she keeps her eyes and attention to herself. But she overhears some extraordinary things—like a spy—and she manages both to enjoy her meal and amuse herself.

If all these words are for naught and you still prefer to bring reading material to a restaurant, at least choose a book or magazine that will fit discreetly on the table. A large newspaper sprawled all over the fresh linen tablecloth will do nothing to endear you to the maitre d', nor will it add to the ambience of the restaurant. If you must read a newspaper, take only the section you need, and learn to fold it down into quarters as commuters do when they read *The New York Times* on the 7:53 from Greenwich. If you bring a book, don't choose one the size of an encyclopedia. Place it to the side of the table setting and read before and after you are served but not while you are eating.

Unless you are in a steak-and-beer joint or a coffee shop, business papers have no place at the table. Read a report, if you must, but don't bring out your pen and scrap paper and start working over your balance sheet. First, you'll get ulcers, and second, it isn't fair to other diners to impose the unappetizing, unrelaxing artifacts of business on a genteel, civilized environment.

Invitations and Free Drinks

Many women traveling and dining on their own have been confronted with invitations from people at other tables. If you like the looks of the people and they extend the invitation in a respectful manner, join them, or invite them to join you. Usually, this kind of table switching is awkward during the meal, and it's better to wait until you're having your coffee to make a move. If you don't like the looks of the people, or if the invitation is extended by a bunch of rowdy drunks, thank them directly and then ignore them.

Another thing that women sometimes face in restaurants is receiving unordered drinks at their table, gratis from another guest. Some hotels, notably those in the elegant Coleman chain, have made it an official policy not to deliver anonymous drinks to women diners. This perceptiveness is rare, however. Usually, the waiter will deliver the drink and indicate with a glance who has sent it. If you accept the drink, look up and nod politely to the man who sent it. Don't respond with coy gratitude. And don't feel in the least beholden to him.

If you really don't want the drink and/or don't like the looks of the sender, refuse it politely by asking the waiter to thank the giver for you, anyway. After that, keep your attention directed away from the person who sent the drink so there's no misunderstanding and so you don't make him feel belittled or embarrassed.

Maybe it's time to turn the tables a bit and provide women with the same kind of flexibility and initiative traditionally preempted by men. How would an attractive man feel if you sent a drink to his table via the waiter? If you see someone who looks as if he has a sense of humor plus enough self-confidence not to feel that his masculinity is threatened, try it. Do it lightheartedly, with humor, and see what happens. Don't be crushed if your drink gets rejected.

Travelers' Tables

Many large city restaurants are finally beginning to respond to the needs of business travelers, male and female, by installing large ''travelers' tables'' or ''captain's tables,'' with communal seating for a group of solo diners. Both Sheraton and Best Western Hotels offer this type of seating in their restaurants, and I hope it will soon be standard. I think this is a great idea. The restaurant doesn't lose money on single customers occupying a table for two, and the travelers get to enjoy one another's company. Ask your hotel concierge to recommend a restaurant that provides this type of seating, or request it yourself when you call for a reservation. Japanese sushi bars, by the way, are also good places for people dining alone, provided you like raw fish. Diners sit at a wooden bar in an informal setting.

DINING ALONE CHECKLIST

- Make reservations in advance.
- Tip the maitre d' if you want special attention.
- Don't settle for unacceptable treatment.
- Don't bring business papers to the table; if you must read, bring a small magazine or book.
- Accept invitations from other diners only if you want to.
- Ask hotel concierge which restaurants have travelers' tables.

Part 6

THE BUSINESS OF HAVING A GOOD TIME

29

Health and Beauty on the Road

Before getting on to the business of pleasure, let's review a few ways to keep you feeling and looking good so you'll be able to enjoy your free-time activities when you're on the road.

Taking care of your health is especially important on a business trip, since your system is under constant assault from the strain of doing business in a foreign environment with little or no back-up support. Travel itself contributes greatly to the stress your body experiences. Anxiety about missing flights or being late for meetings when you're stuck in traffic in an unfamiliar area are typical pressures business travelers must endure. On long trips, your biological clock also gets thrown off by jet lag, and you experience further stress if you go through a radical climate change.

AVOIDING STRESS

The most important thing to do to avoid travel-related stress is to give your body a break. Don't stay up all night before a long trip and then schedule a full day of activities as soon as you arrive. Give yourself a head start by feeling good before you go, and build recuperation time into your schedule. Don't drink too much or eat heavy foods en route or at a new destination—your system has to adapt to new microbes as it is and you don't want to compound the problem with indigestion.

When traveling to faraway destinations, you may have to allow extra adjustment time to adapt to dramatic changes in climate or altitude. For example, if you have to do business in La Paz, Bolivia (12,001 feet above sea level), or in Cuzco, Peru (11,444), beware of *siroche*, the local name for traveler's fatigue or altitude sickness. The symptoms are breathlessness, dizziness, and extreme fatigue; the cure is a nap of several hours as soon as you arrive to let your body adjust to the thin atmosphere. In Peru, you may be served tea brewed from the leaves of the coca plant as a remedy. Take it—you'll feel great and it's legal.

Traveling from northern climates to the tropics can also create a stressful situation. At first, you're apt to feel a great languor caused by the heat and humidity, which makes it extremely hard to get your work done. Try to schedule a free day, or half a day, to give your body time to adjust. Plan on a long nap, or, at the very least, a good night's sleep on the day of your arrival.

In hot climates you perspire more than normal. To avoid heat exhaustion, which results from excess water loss, increase your fluid intake and eat foods that are rich in potassium (including bananas, tomatoes, nuts, and orange juice). Alcoholic beverages can contribute to heat exhaustion, as well as dehydration, by speeding up your metabolism, raising your body temperature, and increasing the amount of moisture lost through perspiration.

If you're traveling from a mild climate to a very cold one, your body has the opposite adjustment to make, and this can be stress-inducing as well. To help your body adapt, wear layers of clothing (undershirt, vest, sweater, jacket, and coat), and add or remove layers according to the temperature. Eat well, perhaps slightly more than usual, to give your body enough fuel to maintain its normal temperature. Move around to keep the circulation flowing to your extremities—a brisk walk or other exercise is needed every few hours.

Until recent decades, heart attacks and other stress-related illnesses occurred mostly in the male domain. For the most part, it was men who were banging their brains out in the market place and enduring the intense pressures of competitive work. No more. Since women have started to enter the work force in great numbers and assume greater responsibility, heart attacks and other stress-related diseases are beginning to affect them too. There is no sex-related immunity.

The way to avoid stress during a business trip is to plan carefully in advance and schedule ample time to account for local variables. If you must, steal time for yourself even during working hours. Spend a few minutes in a coffee shop relaxing over a glass of orange juice and reading the local newspaper, or take a short walk in a nearby park. Even a brief respite will do wonders to clear your mind of anxiety and free your body of fatigue.

For lengthier escapes, sneak back to your hotel in the middle of the day or between appointments and lie down on the bed, shoes off, with pads soaked in witch hazel over your eyes. Or wash your face, splashing it with lots of cold water, and then apply fresh makeup, to give yourself a new start for the second half of your business day. Or go to visit an old friend. A stewardess friend of mine, who loves art, stops by to study the incredible *Garden of Earthly Delights* by Hieronymus Bosch in the Prado Museum in Madrid at least half a dozen times a year. And whenever I'm in Málaga, Spain, I return to see the great old baobab tree near the harbor, remembering every time the French contention that Africa begins at the Pyrenees.

FUELING UP FOR A BUSY DAY

Food is another category of on-the-road health care that deserves special attention, both in terms of adequate nourishment and your desire to stick to a beauty regimen.

Learn to love the foods that nourish you. If yours is a high-tension business with a lot of stress, for example, choose foods rich in the B vitamins (liver, yeast, whole grains), since the Bs are the vitamins most healing for shattered nerves. This is not yet another book on nutrition; get yourself one and learn which foods are the most valuable in terms of vitamin, mineral, and protein content.

Wherever you are, establish good eating habits. Don't skip lunch during the middle of a business day because you're too busy. Give your body good fuel to run on, and it will run—your increased energy will more than compensate for time "wasted" in a restaurant. Diet fads seem to change with each issue of the fashion magazines and most seem limited for long-term use by their excessive dependence on one category of food: one recommends high-protein, high-cholesterol foods to the exclusion of all others; another calls for massive doses of carbohydrates; and still another focuses primarily on fructose. A doctor friend of mine pointed out that nature never operates in excess, but rather in synergistic balance—a point to remember the next time you read about another lopsided diet or megadoses of one kind of vitamin.

The consensus regarding diet seems to be that the most fuel-efficient, nourishing, and least deleterious foods are poultry (without the fatty skin), fish, fresh fruits and vegetables, and modest amounts of whole grains, dairy products, seafood, eggs, and meat. Bacon, sausages, pork, ham, and most sandwich meats should be avoided, as should butter, cream, fats, salt, and sugars (even the natural ones). Avoid all processed foods; they have too much salt and sugar and too many suspect chemicals.

When you're traveling, stick to light, nourishing, simply cooked foods, which, if you try, you can find even on the worst menu. I have seen beautiful New York models refuse the menu and ask the waiter for a piece of fish, chicken, or steak, broiled, poached, or baked, with no butter, plus a salad with lemon instead of dressing, and maybe a piece of melon or a dish of strawberries for dessert. Even if broiled fish isn't on the menu, if the restaurant has a piece of fish, they can broil it.

Surviving the Business Lunch

The above guidelines work equally well when you're being wined and dined on a business trip. Stay away from the rolls and bread sticks. Forget about butter. Order simple foods without sauces. And skip dessert or limit it to fresh fruit. This way, you'll survive your business meals and still stay in shape. As far as drinks go, you can save calories by ordering a glass of mineral water with a squeeze of lime (zero calories), or white wine, a spritzer, or Kir (white wine mixed with cassis), all of which have about 80 calories a glass.

If you get stuck in a German restaurant with business associates and through some aberration end up with sauerbraten, baked potato with sour cream, cabbage, and lots of fluffy white bread, go ahead and do it all the way—a piece of apple strudel and a glass of beer would add nicely to your carbohydrate intake. In case of a disaster like this, the solution is simple: Eat very little for the next two or three meals. If your heavy meal is at lunchtime, have a piece of fruit or some yogurt in your hotel room for dinner. Or if the disaster takes place in the evening, have an orange for breakfast and a light salad for lunch the following day.

B.Y.O.

For plane travel, many women travelers I know go to great lengths to avoid the food served on most airplanes. One way is to order a special meal (which may or may not be any better); you can choose among vegetarian, low-sodium, low-cholesterol, kosher, and other varieties, and the meal should be ordered from the airline at least 24 hours before departure. Or bring your own. Before leaving home, prepare a little packet of fresh fruits (apples, pears, peaches, grapes, oranges) cut into fairly large wedges and wrapped in several layers of plastic (squirt them with a little lemon juice to keep the pulp from discoloring). You can also prepare vegetable *crudités* and bring a little container of your favorite salad dressing. Or you can bring yogurt, a banana, a delicious sandwich made with whole-grain bread and a touch of watercress, a container of cottage cheese mixed with cut-up fruits, raisins, and nuts—whatever quick-energy snacks or light meals you enjoy at home.

Pack your snacks in tightly sealed containers and plastic bags (use two layers to be sure they're moisture-proof). Bring a small spoon, and a packet of tissues. Place your goodies carefully upright inside your carry-on travel bag.

Vitamin Packs and Quick Pickups

If you're used to taking daily vitamin supplements, you should not forgo this preventative health care when you're on the road. Quite the opposite—in times of stress you need your vitamins most. If you take a separate pill for every vitamin, you might consider simplifying matters by taking a good multivitamin during your trip, with an extra 500 mg. vitamin C supplement. My doctor, who is unusual in that he is an internist who is also an expert on nutrition, recommends Solgar VM-75 extra potency multiple vitamins, which seem to be about the most complete multivitamin pills available.

Some people also swear by high protein powders, brewer's yeast, or torula yeast taken as a diet supplement, usually mixed in vegetable or fruit juice. The yeast powders are rich in protein and complete B-complex vitamins, which are especially valuable in times of stress. Check the powder you buy to be sure it has the complete B vitamins and does not consist primarily of milk products. The reason: lactose tends to contribute to water retention, rather than to its elimination.

EXERCISE

Exercise is every bit as important as diet when you're traveling, and it can do away with fatigue, even at the end of a strenuous business day. I know women who work like demons, rushing around unknown cities on business assignments, and then do 50 laps in a hotel pool or play a hard game of squash and come out feeling more energetic than they felt before.

There's no reason to sacrifice your health and beauty for business success. You should have some kind of exercise program that you follow at home, and you should keep to the same routine when you're on the road. If you're in the habit of doing exercises on your bedroom rug, use a hotel bath towel as a mat and do the same set of exercises when you're traveling. Use the dresser as a bar for stretches and the bed as an anchor for your feet during sit-ups. Jumping jacks, arm stretches, shoulder rolls, spinal twists, leg lifts, and yoga stretches can all be done as easily in a hotel room as anywhere.

If you're used to going to a health club to work out, ask the manager of your club if it's affiliated with the **International Physical Fitness Association.** If it is, your club membership will be honored in over 1,000 fitness centers from coast to coast and in 24 countries. Write to the International Physical Fitness Association, 415 West Court Street, Flint, Michigan 48503 or call them at (313) 239-2166 and ask them to send you a membership directory (the cost at press time: $3).

Jogging is another easy way to get exercise when you're traveling; every city has some kind of esplanade or park where it's safe and pleasant to run, even at twilight or in the early morning. Pack your sneakers and running clothes and take off before ordering your room service breakfast. Many business-traveler hotels have mapped out good jogging routes for guests, and you probably won't find yourself out there alone.

If jogging doesn't appeal to you, but you still want to make your heart work and get some oxygen through your system, bring a jump rope and a pair of sneakers and do a set in your hotel room or on the balcony, in the fresh air. Do your jumping before taking your morning shower, or before a long, relaxing bubble bath after work.

Also take advantage of whatever health facilities the hotel has to offer: a gym with bicycles and other machines, an indoor pool, saunas and steam rooms, massage—any exercise or relaxation treatment contributes to your health. In fair-weather cities, stay at a motel with a pool instead of a midtown hotel, and when traveling abroad, take advantage of any special local services: a real sauna in Scandinavia; a masseuse who will come to your hotel room in Japan and Brazil.

KEEPING BEAUTIFUL: FACE AND HAIR

For business travel, all you need to know is that the system you use at home is basically the one you should use on the road, with the only conditions being that you simplify and miniaturize. (For more on this subject, turn back to the section on cosmetics in Part 3.)

Water Changes

One of the few things that can happen when you're traveling that you won't experience at home is that the water will be harder than you're used to and you'll find your shampoo clinging like flotsam when you try to rinse it out. The same thing can happen with soaps and cleansing lotions, which are geared by the manufacturers to work in the areas where they're sold. This has happened to me in Athens, where the water is unusually hard and my American shampoos and conditioners were useless, and in the mountain town of Sintra in Portugal, where I walked around with my hair matted to my head for days until I finally had to go to a local hairdresser.

The solution to a water problem is to buy shampoos, conditioners, and face cleansers locally. Ask for assistance in the pharmacy or *perfumeria*—the salesperson should be able to guide you to the best products. If you have a problem getting beauty products that work, go to a local beauty salon and have your hair done there, then purchase shampoos and conditioners from them. Theoretically, you could also take along a supply of a water softener like Calgon, although you'd need to carry too much for this to be a practical solution.

Makeup for Hot and Cold Climates

Sometimes the makeups and hairstyles you're used to wearing at home refuse to work elsewhere. The best example is when you travel to a hot, humid city from a temperate climate. In most warm-weather areas of the world, the quality of the light tends to be much warmer and redder than the bluish light of northern environments, and you'll find that the somber colors appropriate in the north look dirty and downright sad in the south. When traveling to tropical or warm climates, pack your summer makeup. Lighter, softer-colored lipsticks and blushers in true reds and pinks look better in warm climates than brownish or purple tones. You may also need a darker foundation if you plan to get a tan (get a foundation with a built-in sunscreen). The bright light also makes makeup much more noticeable in the daylight—wear about half the amount you normally wear at home.

Many fashion magazines recommend water-based makeup for hot climates. Oil-based makeup, they say, tends to streak and turn orange. Yet, Chrisjean and I have found that a lightweight oil-base makeup works fine for us. Just rub off half of it with a tissue after you put it on. Or skip the foundation altogether and use a light powder or a bronzing gel. Avoid greasy blushers and caky powders in hot weather, but keep a compact of pressed powder handy to blot up any heat-induced shininess.

Waterproof mascara is another good bet in hot climates; so is a "wrinkle stick" for quick moisture touch-ups on your lips, eyelids, and under your eyes. Some women business travelers I know swear by Evian mineral water sprays, sold in purse-size atomizers, for quick, refreshing face pickups in hot climates. This doesn't work if you wear foundation, but if you don't, it's a delicious way to keep your skin moisturized. Astringents are also a must in hot climates to keep your pores closed and your skin fresh.

For cold climates, use a rich moisturizer and a moisturizing foundation in a warm tone to give a little life to your face. Avoid too-pale or too-yellow tones, and use warm, colored blushers and contour powders. The thing to overcome in cold climates is the ghostly blue quality of the light, which often is like that of a fluorescent bulb.

Not matter where you're traveling, plan your makeup procedure in advance and test it upon arrival to be sure it works in the local climate and with the local water. If you must, go through a practice run as soon as you arrive at your hotel. This way, you'll know in advance what local conditions you have to make accommodations for, and how much time it will take to get yourself together.

Hair Care

When you're traveling to a hot, humid climate, your hair may go berserk, especially if your hairdo is at war with your natural curl. The solution here is simply to let it curl. Find a way of drawing your hair back with combs or barrettes so it looks well groomed. You might even try braided or upswept hairstyles.

Conversely, if your hair is permed or naturally curly and you travel from a warm, humid climate to a cold, dry one, you may find your hair has suddenly turned into a halo of Brillo wired with electricity. The best solution in this case is to treat your hair with extra-rich conditioners and design a hairstyle, using hair rollers or a curling iron, which will smooth out the kinks and give your hair a better shape and some body.

For business travel, you should always have an emergency hairstyle in your repertoire in case you don't have time in the morning to do your usual tricks, or in case you get stuck in a wind tunnel when emerging from the plane. A small scarf carried in your travel bag may not be terribly chic, but it's an efficient way to avert wind disasters. Short hair will usually comb back into place without too many problems; longer hair can be held back with combs, or pulled into a discreet grown-up pony tail at the nape of your neck. A hairpiece (natural, no Dynel) is also useful in emergencies, especially if you're traveling to a warm area and might want to take your lunch hour at the beach. You can always make something out of even sopping wet hair by slicking it back and hiding the ends under a chignon or a twisted braid. Or take a wig. (In my opinion, these went out with Gina Lollobrigida and always look like wigs, but many women seem to disagree.)

HEALTH AND BEAUTY CHECKLIST

- Prepare to adapt to changes in climate and altitude.
- Schedule free time during business day to avoid stress.
- Eat fresh or simply cooked foods in modest amounts. Fortify your travel diet with vitamins and high-protein snacks.
- Bring your own health snacks to eat on the plane.
- Keep to the same exercise regimen when traveling that you follow at home.
- Simplify your regular beauty system for travel.
- Buy shampoos and conditioners locally if yours don't work in the local water.
- Use lightweight makeup for hot climates.
- Use rich moisturizers and warm-toned makeup for cold climates.
- Plan emergency hairdos.
- Don't be afraid to look your best.

30

A Creative Use of Time

Without looking and feeling good, you can't have a positive time on a business trip—your health and beauty are the prerequisites for all other activities. Once these are established and maintained, the next problem is to determine what you want to do, when, and with whom.

What does that mean? Quite simply, anything you want it to. It can mean a new friendship, a new love affair, a private afternoon in an art gallery musing over a Chinese jade, a wild, rugged day of white-water rafting with new friends, or a quiet weekend locked up in your hotel room with your favorite lover imported especially for the occasion. It can also mean a long, lovely nap with pads soaked in witch hazel over your eyes on your one free afternoon in a crowded week of business obligations. Or a brunch with a friend of a friend. Or a weekend-long R & R in a hotel with a heated pool, swimming laps, fasting on Perrier, and reading a great book while having a gooey egg-and-honey facial.

There's no excuse, ever, for being bored. If you feel bored on a business trip—or any other time—look no further than your own resources and take responsibility for the ennui you feel. If you're exhausted from the toll of business toil, then *feel* exhausted, with a purpose. Take some vitamin C and go to sleep. That's not the same as feeling bored.

The world is filled with interesting things to see and do on your own or with others. And it's filled with interesting people, some quite like you, others completely different, all of whom can contribute something of value—knowledge, humor, a point of view—that will widen your horizons.

In Part I, I mentioned some of the things you might do before leaving home to make your business trip more interesting. Such as asking every friend and relative whom they know at your destination. Or digging out information about the history of the area. Or learning about famous artists or politicians, museums, theater or sports activities, where to get the best crab cakes in town, or croissants, or Tex-Mex tacos. Where to listen to some low-down blues, or watch a Nō drama, or hear Mozart's *Abduction from the Seraglio.*

There is nothing to keep you from participating in life in any part of the world, except your own lack of enthusiasm. (Enthusiasm, by the way, comes from the Greek word *enthousiasmos,* which means "to be inspired.")

The simple fact about the world is that people are people. They all laugh, cry, love, wear some kind of clothing and ornamentation, and live in shelters, simple or elaborate. They all play music, dance, sing, create art and myths, tell jokes, cook food, and function in some kind of economic capacity.

Think of yourself as a visiting anthropologist. You're an observer—or a participant—with keen perceptions, enjoying the panoply of life. To be of interest, your destination does not have to be an exotic outpost somewhere in the middle of the bush. A plain old middle-class city is as potentially rich in observable mores and manners as any place.

For example, take markets (which I always visit on my business trips to stock up on fruit, yogurt, and mineral water for my hotel room). Recently, in a supermarket in Ocho Rios, Jamaica (like markets in Moscow and Sofia, Bulgaria a decade ago), I saw row upon row of one kind of berry jam arranged single file to fill the empty shelves. On another trip, I visited a market on the outskirts of Khartoum, where women in dusty skirts crouched behind small pyramids of dessicated melons, with trussed chickens squawking beside them in the sand. At a market in Guadalajara, Mexico, upstairs under the eaves I found a silent Indian woman selling colored powders and dried herbs for magic rituals. I bought a dried bat from her and air-mailed it to a friend. Each market was a fascinating study, and each one showed me a facet of local life that was valuable.

Heather Hanley, a good friend of mine who has traveled for business in virtually every country on the globe (she hasn't been to Madagascar or the Seychelles), gets up before dawn many mornings and goes out to explore the city, camera in hand. Photography is her hobby, a point of reference that not only fills her with a great sense of personal satisfaction, but also draws her out into the world. Even in the worst areas of the most unfamiliar cities, nobody bothers her at 6 o'clock in the morning. Heather says:

> At dawn the world is just becoming, the light is warm, and the threat of the night simply disappears. In Rio, for instance, I've gotten wonderful shots of fishermen bringing in the catch at dawn, and *macumba* roses and candles in the sand.
>
> The early morning is *my* time to get in touch with my own interests so I feel like a whole human being. By the time I show up for my first business appointment, I feel fresh and alive. I've been out in the world, and I've participated in the tempo of local life.

Heather, who is a first-rate travel writer as well as a successful sales representative, sometimes travels alone for six months at a time. She usually carries a small portable typewriter stashed among her business materials. On many evenings, she composes copious letters to her friends (which, someday, will make a fabulous book). She explains:

> One of the dangers of business travel, especially in foreign countries, is that you get overstimulated. You experience more than you can absorb. That's one of the reasons I use my typewriter. Many evenings, I sit on the hotel bed with the typewriter propped on my knees and type out my thoughts—impressions of the day, business situations—anything. It helps me assimilate.

Heather also travels with an ample supply of good reading material, and always haunts the bookstores in her hotel and in the city she's visiting. "You find wonderful books in the most unexpected places," she says. "I found *Pilgrim at Tinker Creek* in Manaus on the Amazon, and *The Tao of Physics* in Tegucigalpa."

Heather also usually carries a portable cassette player the size of a paperback book and her favorite tapes. With little additional weight to her baggage, she has the pleasure of listening to her favorite music, something she finds especially important when the local radio is less than soothing.

Claiming Time for Yourself

No matter how much or little free time you have on a business trip, you can make it work positively for you. The point here is to claim free time for yourself at every opportunity. When you're overloaded with work, the temptation is always to collapse on your hotel bed with your papers to mull them over for the twentieth time, when, in fact, a fast run around a park, a swim, a movie, or an excursion to the countryside would refresh you and make your professional tasks easier.

On most business trips you are not usually afforded the luxury of an entire afternoon or a full day to claim for yourself, but you can still be creative with the time you have. There are three basic categories of things you can do: (1) You can turn your spare time into a satisfying R & R that gets you in shape and on your feet for the next round of business sparring. (2) You can direct your energies toward participation of some sort in the outside world. (3) You can spend your energy finding other people to share experiences with. Or you can do all three.

Sources of Information

Where do you find out what's going on locally so you'll know what you want to see or do? The first places to start, obviously, are the local newspapers, magazines, and visitor's guides.

Check listings for plays, musical comedies, and experimental theater; painting, sculpture, and photography exhibits; museum shows; poetry readings; concerts; opera; circuses; rodeos; ball games; hockey; wrestling; roller derbies; dog, cat, or horse shows; TV shows; flower shows; street fairs; book fairs; auctions; antique shops; sales; city tours; famous landmarks and historical places; gardens, parks, and zoos; special performances such as church chorales, university programs, and on and on and on—the list of possibilities is endless. If you can't find something interesting to do, then there's something wrong with you.

Even a movie can be an unusual diversion. Years ago I saw *Cleopatra* for 75¢ in Mbabane, Swaziland, after spending the afternoon on a broad, barren field near King Sobuza's compound watching 100 nubile maidens performing a ritual dance as part of the Festival of the First Fruits. The country, my afternoon experience, and the erotic machinations of Liz Taylor and Richard Burton could not have been more zanily juxtaposed.

R & R

I'm a workaholic, but I'm also a hedonist. Basically, I like pleasure more than I like work, and I have always made a point of getting out of the skin of my professional persona at frequent intervals to lie on a beach (or the closest approximation) luxuriating in a physical sense of self.

I do the same, in miniature, on every business trip, even if only for half an hour. I steal time for myself for a facial, or a trip to the hairdresser, or a massage, or a pedicure, or an hour of meditation in front of Monet's *Water Lilies* at the Orangerie in Paris.

Heather Hanley is a business traveler who welcomes the privacy and relaxation possible at night in her hotel room. ''I adore room service dinners,'' Heather says:

> You don't have to bother getting fixed up to go out, you don't have to worry about finding a taxi, and you don't have to sit at the restaurant table waiting for your check and twiddling your thumbs. When you've worked hard all day, I think it's a treat to get into your robe, order up half a bottle of wine and a light supper, and curl up with a good book and some music. It's almost like being at home. Having a room-service dinner alone in your hotel room is not a cop-out. Don't look at it as a social failure.

If you do decide to spend the evening in your hotel room, make a point of turning your solitary time into something special that pleases you. Order something good from the menu: prosciutto and melon, for example, or a big dish of chocolate mousse, or a small bottle of French champagne. Or do the things that are necessary to take care of yourself (hair treatments, manicures, etc.), performing each ritual slowly and deliberately.

Your mind—as well as your body—needs refreshment, and the best way to refresh your mind is to turn your attention away from your business problems. Read a book. Catch a cable movie. Answer a pile of letters. Keep a diary. Type up your reminiscences. Study a subject. Or write 20 postcards to your friends.

Local TV can be diverting, even when you're in a foreign country. You can't always understand what's going on, but you can get an interesting view of the culture. I remember once seeing some French drum majorettes strutting their stuff on TV in Paris—a hokey bit of American madness no less absurd in Gallic translation. And Greek TV soap operas are a riot; the acting is straight out of the *Sturm und Drang* school that one suspects really originated with Sophocles.

SHOPPING

Shopping is always a distracting spare-time activity, whether you're in a foreign city packed with exotic goodies or prowling around a hardware store at home. When in doubt, local department stores and specialty stores are always good bets. Here are a few treasures to look for in random destinations at home and abroad:

New York: Discounted sheets and towels at Ezra Cohen on Orchard

Street; jewelry bargains at Fortunoff; gourmet items at Zabar's.

Dallas: Anything, but anything, from Neiman Marcus; packets of spices for Tex-Mex chili from most supermarkets or specialty food stores.

San Francisco: Great wines from the Napa Valley not available elsewhere; sourdough bread.

Paris: Perfumes bottled here are richer than French perfumes bottled in the U.S.A.—buy them at the duty-free shop at the airport when you're leaving.

London: A scarf from Liberty's; cashmere sweaters are still affordable at Marks and Spencer's.

Milan: Fashions and leather goods of any kind—go for the lesser-known names for great styling, quality, and value (Armani and Basile sometimes cost less in the U.S.).

Düsseldorf, Frankfurt, and other German cities: Bring home gallons of Badedas (Vitabath)—it costs a fraction of its import price in the U.S.

Hong Kong: Cashmere underwear, the tops cut like T-shirts. The sizes come in fat, fatter, and fattest, evidently on the premise that anyone rich enough to wear cashmere underwear will be obese.

Tokyo: Antique kimonos and Biwa (fresh-water) pearls. Ask your hotel public relations hostess to recommend a reputable wholesaler.

Singapore: Good Chinese antiques. Check the shops in Orchard Grove.

Kuala Lumpur: Antique wood and silver betel-nut boxes; brilliant batiks.

West Africa: Hand-woven fabrics, batiks, ornaments, and wood carvings. Don't spend any serious money on "airport art."

East Africa: Basketry, jewelry, and *khangas* (gaily printed cotton sarongs—buy them in the local shops, or *dukkas*).

Bogotá: Brilliant natural-dye rugs and blankets; copper antiques.

The above, obviously, is not intended as a comprehensive guide to shopping around the world—just as a few tidbits passed on from friend to friend.

If you plan to shop in foreign countries, you should familiarize yourself with U.S. Customs regulations, as well as the category of countries designated "GSPs," which is not a disease, but the Generalized System of Preferences (see Chapter 11).

GOING OUT ALONE

Let me add a word here about going out on your own to places usually attended by couples or groups (restaurants, theaters, concerts, and so on). For some reason, as I mentioned earlier, many women feel ashamed or embarrassed to be seen out on their own socially. They seem to have buried deep in their psyches a residual guilt about being alone, unclaimed, unattached, and, by implication, unloved. (This feeling, by the way, is not exclusive to women. I have many attractive, poised men friends who feel a similar discomfort, especially when they're traveling for business.)

The point here is that we are not necessarily unclaimed, unattached, or unloved—nor are we prostitutes. And we should never permit ourselves to be prevented from going out in a new city for fear of being embarrassed or compromised. Whenever I've been on my own and started to feel that foot-shifting discomfort at being alone, I've fixed it, on the spot, by reminding myself that what's important is not what the world thinks of me, but what I think of the world. I'm not there to be judged. I'm there to perform a legitimate function. I'm minding my own business. Why should anyone or anything make me feel ill at ease?

Nothing should.

Knowing Where You're Going

Whatever you choose to do alone in your own free time, be cautious, especially when you're planning activities at night. It's generally a bad idea in most cities in the world to put yourself in the street far from your hotel after a certain hour. If you plan an evening at the theater, for example, be sure you know before you go precisely how you will return. Find out if taxis are readily available on the street, or if you should telephone for one, or if the public transportation is safe and virtually door-to-door.

You must also consider the customs of the country you're in before planning any unescorted after-hours activities. In most of the Orient and the Moslem world, men are still shocked at having to do business with women, let alone having to deal with them as independent social entities after dark. This is not to suggest that you shouldn't go out. But be aware of local attitudes. Look and ask for guidance before you leap.

Attitude Counts

I have deliberately started this chapter with a random run through a few things you might do with your free time on a business trip based on *attitude*, not activity. My little excursion through the supermarket might be yours through the local museums, the local jazz clubs, or the local men.

I also have deliberately not started this chapter with a coy discussion of your sexual activities (or lack thereof)—which we'll get to in the next few pages—because almost every man I've spoken to on the subject of women traveling for business immediately assumes that the crux of the issue is sex.

I don't.

As far as the social part of your business-travel experience is concerned, it's much more important for you to feel confident, in control, and free to make your own choices—sexual or otherwise—than it is for you to worry one way or the other about seducing or being seduced. If you feel lonely, insecure, and vulnerable in your free time alone, you're ripe pickings for a liaison you may not really want and that will make you feel unhappy about yourself. But if you're interested in things, self-determined in your activities, and motivated to get out and participate, any choice you make will be to your pleasure and benefit.

CREATIVE TIME CHECKLIST

- Boredom is a state of mind that you control.
- Anything, anywhere can be interesting if you have a positive attitude.
- Find activities that draw you out into the world. Check local media for listings.
- Claim free time for R & R, and participate in local life.
- Overcome any social discomfort or fears about going out on your own.
- If you're in an area with archaic attitudes toward females, plan your solo activities so that they cause the smallest amount of local disruption.

31

Social Sustenance

A good friend of mine was once on a business assignment in Japan during the Christmas season, and she dreaded the thought of being stranded by herself on Christmas Day with no one to give a present to or celebrate with. So she got on the international wires and tracked down a favorite beau who by good fortune happened to be in Korea on business. My friend left most of her suitcases and all of her business materials locked up in a Tokyo hotel and jumped on the next plane heading west. She and her friend spent the Christmas holidays together blissfully ensconced in the Chosun Hotel in Seoul, locked up in their room and surviving on room service, indulging in generous helpings of what they came to call ''Seoul food.''

A NETWORK OF FRIENDS

Most women I know make a point of building a network of friends in the destinations they frequent. They carefully keep names and addresses of people they have met on previous trips, and they keep the friendships warm with occasional cards, letters, and phone calls.

Many of them also interrogate their friends and relatives before leaving home, asking for the names of people to contact at their destinations.

''Even somebody's aunt,'' claims one woman, ''is worth visiting. Call her before you leave, introduce yourself, and invite her for tea.

She may turn out to be perfectly charming or a Charley's Aunt character. And she may introduce you to other people.''

I think that's an important point. One of the most worthwhile rewards of any kind of travel is the opportunity to establish a wide network of friends from all kinds of backgrounds. If you open yourself only to people who are just like you, you necessarily restrict yourself to a narrow range of possibilities. But if you solicit the friendship of interesting, worthwhile, and different people, you may discover that their lives, jobs, and experiences can do a lot to help you develop yours.

Contacting friends of friends is a safe and easy way to meet good people, and you never know what surprises may turn up. One friend of mine met the man she married when she was on a business trip to Chicago and gave him a call. And it was through a friend that Heather Hanley met an Italian yacht manufacturer in Beirut who had three Rolls Royces and an unbelievable villa, where the cocktails were served on the first terrace, the caviar on the second, and dinner on the third, and who insisted the only way to see Beirut was from water skis. The next morning, before her first business appointment, Heather was zooming along the Beirut seafront in her bikini.

Whom to Befriend, Whom to Avoid

The art of making acquaintances on a business trip takes a little practice and the honing of your intuition. With a little exposure, you'll soon be able to tell the good guys from the bad, and you'll instinctively know whom you want to open up to and whom to avoid.

On a business trip, the two ways you're most likely to meet new people (other than through personal references) are through business contacts or at your hotel. Most thoughts here turn immediately to men, but don't neglect your compatriots—women business travelers. You may be lucky enough to find a kindred spirit and a potentially valuable long-term friend.

Regarding men, some women make it a rule to keep all their social activities on a business trip separate from their business associations. Casual dinners or drinks after work would seem harmless enough, but there have been many occasions when a business associate has had a few too many and has gotten overly attentive. This can get particularly sticky if the man involved is a potential client and any rebuff on your part might insult him and make your job more difficult. The best way to avoid this kind of situation is to have a third person join you, or skip the drinks altogether and suggest instead that you meet for breakfast the next morning.

There are two schools of thought regarding after-hours fun with business associates. From what I've seen in the business world, it usually is a big mistake to have anything intimate to do with someone you work with or for. Whether we like it or not, the old double standard is still in full force when it comes to business hanky-panky. There are exceptions to the rule, but as far as I can see, the loser is usually female.

The same double standard is even more flagrant in the business travel situation. I would venture to say that at least 70 percent of all the men I've ever met or observed who travel for business make it a point to pick up women (or purchase their services) as soon as they escape the scrutiny of their wives or girlfriends. At the same time, many of them will insult *you* by assuming you're sexually available merely because you're traveling on your own. If you sleep with them, they'll slander you with a vengeance, because you've just proved that their first opinion of you was right.

In businessese jargon, it's what's called a no-win. You're damned if you do and damned if you don't. The solution? Very simply, ignore them. Men with values as shabby as these are not worth your time or consideration in the first place.

Fortunately for love, life, happiness, and the propagation of the species, there are men out there who are worth knowing, and one of them may actually be staying at your hotel. How to meet them? You can't do it if you hide out in your room, which means you'll have to go down to the bar or restaurant on your own.

There seem to be two basic ways of approaching people or getting them to approach you. One is the pleasant flirtation, or, occasionally, the rare eyeball-to-eyeball dead-center read-out that happens when two people look into each other's eyes and discover unexpected fireworks. The second is a straightforward, friendly approach that is not a disguised sexual ploy but a genuine, open communication that says, ''He (she) looks nice. I think I'll say a pleasant word to him (her).''

Playing the Game

It's not men's attention that we should object to, it's the way it's offered. If somebody treats you nicely and makes you feel good about yourself, you have by no means been insulted. But if somebody treats you like a piece of meat, your only recourse (unless you want to be treated like a piece of meat), is to treat him like a piece of garbage.

That means restraining the impulse to retaliate in kind. It also means getting yourself away from him and maybe even putting him in his place. You have several options. You can turn and tell him directly that you don't wish to speak with him. (You're not being rude, by the way; you're responding with more civility than the man has shown you.) You can make an excuse and tell him you're waiting for someone, and then keep your eyes focused in the direction of the door. You can simply ignore him. Or you can get up and leave.

Most men are as sensitive to rejection as women are, and most won't make an overture to a woman unless they've had some kind of invitational signal. The exceptions, of course, are the drunken bores who look at you as filet—these will come on as soon as they spot the curve of your hips (they don't waste time with your face). With most other men, however, you have the choice of providing an opening or not, and you control this almost totally with your eyes.

You can use your eyes in a subtle range of ways, giving off a variety of signals that suggest a little romance, a big one, a casual flirt, a friendly conversation, or none of the above. It's up to you to project the message you want the person to pick up.

I have always found that I can protect myself from being bothered in almost every kind of situation by simply refusing to make eye contact with anyone. That doesn't mean I don't see people. I do. I look at everything. But I usually see them before they see me. When you don't want to strike up a conversation or have a little flirtation with someone, just don't give him an opening. Or, if you give him a first chance and he proves to be boring, you can turn off again by taking the interest out of your eyes and by failing to give him any conversational helpers. He'll get the message.

When you like someone's look and seem to pick up a little electricity in his expression, by all means return the look and make eye contact. Don't be coy and then wonder why the guy never came to talk to you.

HAVE IT YOUR WAY

Many guidebooks for businessmen contain snide references (or whole chapters) about where the best sexual services in town can be found: massage parlors, districts of the city where the hookers hang out, brothels, sex clubs, and so on. Unfortunately, there are no such travel aids for women, and, in fact, the only place I've ever heard about where there are establishments devoted to catering to women's pleasure (with male attendants in G-strings?) is Thailand. So, unless you're traveling to Bangkok on business, you're on your own.

On some occasions you may decide that the best thing you can do on a business trip is have a marvelous, fast, no-strings affair. You can do this with all the cool detachment of your male business-traveler counterparts, the ones who cruise the lobbies of the hotels. In fact, you most probably can have your pick of them. Meat for meat is the trade-off. If that's sufficient for you, and if you're not making the choice out of loneliness or social discomfort, who's to tell you not to?

If you share a drink or a meal with a stranger, or indulge in a little flirtation or a friendly conversation, just remember not to go to his room or invite him to yours unless you mean business. And, if you do mean business, be certain you understand what the nature of the business is really all about. The man could be carrying—wittingly or unwittingly—some undesirable social disease. He might be someone with problems whose solution will become your responsibility. Or he might be dangerous, sadistic, boring, or inept. And don't forget: There are a lot of kooks out there walking around in the guise of ordinary-looking people. As the madam of a midwestern establishment reported:

> You'd be amazed at the sexual proclivities of the most ordinary-looking men. The surprising thing is how these men walk around holding responsible jobs and maintaining normal family lives, and still secretly indulge in the most bizarre forms of sex. I always wonder how these people can get what they want whenever they want it and still keep the respect of society.

Take a word from a pro and be sure to have the forethought to assess the dangers before you get as far as the foreplay.

One would also assume that you have given ample consideration to the effect your little fling might have on your professional reputation. What chance is there that the man will turn out to be your next client? The brother-in-law of your boss? Or the head of the competition? Do you care if word gets around—to your associates, employers, or contacts—that you're sexually available? How would this affect your professional position and performance?

It is a surprisingly small world, as I'm sure you know, especially within a specific field of endeavor. The odds are with you in far away major capitals. They're definitely against you in small- to medium-sized U.S. cities.

Sometimes the best judgments regarding sexual activities when you're on the road are made not on the strength of a first impression, but after you have had the chance for a second appraisal. If you're staying in a city for several days, for example, and meet someone on the first night, you have the option of waiting to see what you think of him the following day.

A friend of mine once met a man in a hotel in Amsterdam, and they had a very pleasant dinner together. At the end of the dinner, the man asked my friend if she would like to come up to his room for a nightcap. ''No,'' she refused gently but firmly, and, being a grownup, the man accepted her refusal graciously. Instead, they spent another few hours talking animatedly in the hotel bar.

The following evening, my friend was in her room, bathed and dressed in her bathrobe, having not yet responded to the man's second invitation to dinner. When he called, she said, ''I'm going to stay in this evening and relax with a room-service dinner. If you'd like to join me, please do.''

He did.

That's called ''Have it your way.''

Where to Meet

A big question regarding where to meet Interesting People when you're traveling can really be answered only by you. What kind of people do you like to be with, and where do they usually spend their time? More importantly, what do *you* like to do? In my view, there's a definite psychological disadvantage to going out looking for someone. Most important encounters happen quite on their own, accidentally, and never when you expect them to. They also happen easily and naturally when *you're* genuinely involved in something you like to do.

Your options are as endless as your interests. The bar. A bookstore. The dining room at breakfast (a good neutral time to make easy acquaintances). A museum. A concert. An art gallery. Jogging. A health club. Sitting in a park. Sharing a taxi. Anything.

If you think about it, meeting people is not exactly the most difficult task in the world, given that there are nearly four billion of us inhabiting virtually every corner of the globe. All it takes is the desire to do it. And a healthy sense of self that permits you to go out alone, with confidence, into the world.

The Weekend Escape

The best way to make the most of your business trips from a social point of view is to plan your weekends and your amours together by arranging to meet your greatest love at a resort near your destination or at some point between. You can always find a mountain retreat, ski resort, dude ranch, beach, lake, or island to get away to, and if you plan your air travel right, you may be able to save most of the added fare on your own ticket.

The whole point of this chapter is to encourage you to turn your business-travel obligations into genuine travel experiences that put you in contact with the world and enrich you through the exposure. Whether you bring a mate or meet one along the way is really immaterial. What is important is that no matter where you are or what you're doing, you should be living in the present tense, not postponing your ''real'' life until some indefinite time in the future.

SOCIAL CHECKLIST

- Build a network of friends at all your destinations.
- Trust your instincts about strangers.
- Calculate advantages and disadvantages before entering into liaisons.
- Don't tolerate rudeness. Don't be intimidated or coy.
- Control all choices, plans, and activities. Always have it your way.
- Let people meet you through shared activities and interests.
- Plan to meet friends for weekend escapes.

Postscript

I hope this book has provided you with as much practical travel information as possible, and that it will help you benefit from the travel experiences of other professional women. Remember, there are no dogmatic rules to follow when it comes to business travel—there are only the varied and continuing experiences of individual women who have acted with resourcefulness, courage, and creativity.

Now, with millions of us out there on the road doing business, we are no longer unique. That, in itself, is one of our greatest achievements.

P.N.
New York City
June 1981

APPENDIX

A Glossary
of Travel Terms

AAA. Automobile Association of America.

Advance seat assignment. A seat on an aircraft assigned to a passenger before the day of the flight.

Affinity charter. A plane chartered by an affinity group (see "Affinity group").

Affinity group. An organization (club, school, etc.) with a preestablished association, that qualifies for group travel rates.

AHMA. American Hotel and Motel Association.

Alternate airport. A second airport in or near a city, sometimes used by major airlines. Check your ticket to be sure your flight returns to the airport where your car is parked.

AP. American Plan. A hotel meal plan with all meals included in the room rate. Often called "full pension" in European hotels.

APEX. Advance Purchase Excursion Fare. A discounted fare to international destinations, with advance booking and payment requirements.

ASTA. American Society of Travel Agents.

ATO. Airport Ticket Office.

Availability. Travel industry jargon for a free hotel room or plane seat.

Aviophobia. Fear of flying.

Baggage allowance. The permissible amount of luggage a passenger may take on a plane free of charge; usually determined by overall baggage measurement.

Baggage and personal effects insurance. Travel insurance, sold by travel agents and through airport dispensing machines, that covers a traveler's personal belongings and luggage during the time he or she is on a plane or en route to or from the airport in a limousine or airport bus. Some valuables are excluded.

Baggage claim check. The stub or receipt given to the passenger by the airline
clerk, which indicates the baggage identification number. The larger part of
the baggage claim check is attached to the luggage.

Boarding pass. A coupon listing the passenger's flight and seat number, given
at the time of check-in (or, sometimes, earlier).

Boeing 707. Jet aircraft with approximately 123 seats, a length of 145 feet, and
a speed of 590 miles per hour.

Boeing 727-100. Jet aircraft with approximately 108 seats, a length of 133
feet, and a speed of 590 miles per hour.

Boeing 727-200. Jet aircraft with about 145 seats, a length of 153 feet, and a
speed of 575 miles per hour.

Boeing 747. Jumbo jet aircraft with about 400 seats, a length of 232 feet, and a
speed of 600 miles per hour.

Bumped. Denied a plane seat when a passenger has a confirmed reservation.
In other words, "kicked off."

Business Class. Usually a separate section behind the First Class compartment, reserved for full-fare-paying Coach passengers and/or Frequent
Travelers. Not available on all airlines.

CAB. Civil Aeronautics Board. A federal agency with the authority to regulate
domestic air commerce, and international air traffic to and from the United
States.

Coach Class. The standard air fare with seating in the part of the plane behind
the First Class compartment (Economy on international flights).

Commission. The fee paid to a travel agent for his or her services, usually
taken as a percentage of the cost of the air fare, hotel booking, or tour
package. It is not paid by the consumer.

Connecting flight. A flight between two destinations on which a change of
aircraft is required at an intermediate point.

CP. Continental Plan. A hotel meal plan including a continental breakfast
(coffee or tea, rolls, butter, and jam) in the cost of the room.

CTO. City Ticket Office. Operated by an airline or a group of airlines.

Curbside check-in. Check-in stations provided by some airlines, located at
the passenger drop-off point at the entrance to the departure terminal.

Day rate. A hotel room rate based on daytime occupancy, usually between 6
A.M. and 5 P.M.

Denied boarding compensation. Reimbursement regulated by the CAB and
paid to a passenger with a confirmed reservation who is denied a seat by the
airline.

Departure tax. Also called "head tax," "tourist tax," "entry tax." A fee
paid by a passenger as a requirement for entry into or departure from a
given country.

Direct flight. A flight with no change of plane, but often with stops en route.
Also called a "through flight."

Double occupancy rate. A hotel room rate quoted on a per person basis, when
two people share a room.

Double room rate. The all-inclusive price of a room for two people.

DP. Demi-pension. See MAP.

Dysrhythmia. A fancy word for jet lag.

Economy Class. On domestic flights, a class of air service one category beneath Coach Class; on international flights, the equivalent of Coach Class.

Efficiency. A hotel room or other accommodation with some kind of kitchen facility.

EP. European plan. A hotel room with no meals included.

ETA. Estimated time of arrival.

ETC. European Travel Commission.

ETD. Estimated time of departure.

Excess baggage. The baggage carried by a passenger over and above the allowance permitted by the air carrier. A surcharge is usually made on the basis of size, or per pound.

Excess valuation insurance. Baggage insurance covering luggage for loss, damage, or theft during the time it is in the possession of the airline, over and above the airline's maximum liability. Purchased from the airline at the time of check-in at a fixed rate per $100 of coverage.

Excursion fare. Discounted air fare, usually round trip or ''open-jaw'' (see below), with minimum/maximum stay requirements.

FAA. Federal Aviation Administration. Part of the Department of Transportation.

Fare protector insurance. Insurance coverage purchased from an airline or travel agent to cover the cost of prepaid air fares or tour packages if the purchaser should have to cancel for medical reasons.

First Class. The most exclusive and expensive air fares, with seating in the front part of the plane. Some airlines are discontinuing First Class in favor of a more commodious ''Business Class.''

FIT. Foreign independent travel. A term used by travel agents booking independent itineraries for individual travelers.

Flight insurance. Insurance purchased from airport dispensing machines and some travel agents, covering the traveler for one trip only against ''loss of life, sight, or limbs . . . '' only during the time he or she is in the aircraft.

Flight status. A passenger's status, as shown on his ticket. See OK, RQ, and OPEN.

Fly/Cruise. A tour package involving a combination of an air fare and a ship cruise, sold as a unit.

Fly/Drive. A tour package with combined air fare and rental car, and often accommodations, sold as a unit.

Fly/Rail. A tour package combining air fare and train travel.

Frequent Traveler. A name introduced by Pan Am in 1973; generally, the business traveler; sometimes treated as a separate fare category.

Full pension. See AP.

GIT. Group inclusive tour. A package tour designed for a group, usually including discounted group air fares.

Ground arrangement. All transportation and porterage services at the destination.

Ground operator. A supplier of ground services—transfers, guides, sightseeing, etc.—at a destination.

GSP. Generalized System of Preferences. A list of goods from some developing nations admitted to the United States duty free.

Guaranteed reservation. A hotel reservation made with a promise of payment for the full price of the room even if it is not used. The room is usually booked through a travel agent who makes the guarantee for the traveler, or it is booked on the traveler's credit card. If the hotel fails to provide a room, most hotels promise to provide an equivalent room in a nearby hotel free of charge, plus free transportation there and back, and telegrams or long-distance phone calls.

Hire car. A British term for rental car.

HIT. *Hotel and Travel Index.* A hotel industry reference book.

Hospitality suite. A hotel room or suite rented for entertainment purposes, usually during a sales meeting or convention.

Hotel representative. Individual or firm that handles hotel bookings for travel agents and individual customers.

IAMAT. International Association for Medical Assistance to Travelers.

IATA. International Air Transport Association.

Incentive travel. Travel opportunities, usually tours, offered by corporate management often to sales personnel to encourage better performance.

Interline. Travel that requires the changing of planes from one airline to another.

Junior suite. A hotel room usually consisting of a double room with a large foyer and a seating area.

Lanai. A hotel room with a patio or a balcony, usually in a resort.

Leg. Part of an air journey; each segment of a journey between two points.

MAP. Modified American Plan. A hotel room rate including a full breakfast plus either lunch or dinner. Also called demi-pension.

Maximum allowable mileage. The area in which a passenger is permitted to make unlimited stopovers en route to an ongoing flight.

McDonnell-Douglas DC-10. Jet aircraft with approximately 300 seats, a length of 182 feet, and a speed of 595 miles per hour.

NA. Travel industry lingo for ''not available.''

NATA. National Air Transport Association.

Nonaffinity charter. Charter air fares available to individuals not members of an affinity group.

No-show. An airline passenger or hotel guest who makes a reservation but fails to appear and doesn't bother to cancel.

OAG. *Official Airline Guide.*

Off season. Also called ''low season.'' The period of time at a specific destination when the fewest travelers arrive and when the hotel rates and air fares are usually the cheapest.

OHRG. *Official Hotel and Resort Guide.*

OK. A status code written on an air ticket, indicating a confirmed reservation.

One-stop check-in. A service provided by some airlines, in which the passenger checks his or her bags and picks up a boarding pass and a seat assignment all in one stop, usually at the check-in counter or the departure lounge.

One-way flight. A single flight in one direction between two connecting points (*see also* Round-trip).

OPEN. A flight status code written on a round-trip or multi-leg air ticket, indicating that portions of the flight have not yet been booked.

Open jaw. An unfortunate travel industry term referring to a round-trip ticket in which a segment of travel is not accounted for: From Los Angeles to New York with a return flight back to Los Angeles from Washington, D.C. is an open-jaw flight.

Overbooking. A common practice among airlines and hotels: accepting more reservations than there are rooms or seats available.

Package tour. A travel product that includes transportation, accommodations, and other ground services such as sightseeing and meals at one or more destinations; sold in advance for a fixed, discounted price.

Peak season. Also called "high season." The most popular time of year for travel to a specific destination, usually accompanied by higher hotel rates and air fares.

Personal accident insurance. The same as flight insurance, except the insured is covered during the entire travel period, coming and going to and from the airport, as well as on the plane.

Personal articles floater. Insurance coverage purchased from an insurance company separate from or in addition to a homeowner's policy, covering specifically itemized and appraised possessions.

Porterage. The services of porters in an airline terminal.

Prix fixe. A fixed-price menu, with some restrictions as to foods provided. Also called "table d'hôte."

Promotional fare. Any fare below the standard, undiscounted rate, usually involving some restrictions and advance purchase.

PSM. Passenger service manager. An airline employee responsible for assisting passengers in the airport.

Reconfirmation. A confirmation of a prior booking made to an airline, hotel, rental car firm, or other travel service company.

Revaluation sticker. A sticker attached to an airplane ticket indicating a change or correction in the booking.

Round-trip. A flight or fare based on two-way travel to and from the departure and destination cities.

RQ. A flight status code written on an air ticket, indicating that a seat has been requested but has not been confirmed.

Service charge. A charge of usually 10 or 15 percent levied on some restaurant or hotel bills as a gratuity for the staff.

Shoulder. The mid-season between peak season and off season.

Single room. A hotel room leased to one person, with a single-sized, double, or queen-sized bed.

Single supplement. An extra fee charged for hotel accommodations for a single guest when the rates are given for double occupancy.

SST. Supersonic transport—the Concorde. Technically, a plane that flies faster than the speed of sound, and at an altitude of at least 45,000 feet.

Standby. A passenger without a confirmed reservation, kept on a waiting list for a specific flight, and frequently not boarded until the last moment.

Stopover. A 24-hour or longer stay in a destination partway between the departure and final destination points.

Suite. Hotel accommodations made up of several interconnecting rooms, typically one or more bedrooms with a sitting room.

Super Saver fares. A variety of domestic APEX-style fares, with discounts of 30 to 40 percent, plus restrictions regarding minimum and maximum stay, and advance purchase requirements.

Table d'hôte. *See* Prix fixe.

Through flight. *See* Direct flight.

Transfer. A ground service, usually indicating transportation for passengers and their baggage between the airport and a hotel, cruise ship, motorcoach, or other mode of transportation or accommodation.

Transit passenger. A passenger changing planes in an airport but not staying in the destination.

Twin double. A hotel room with two double beds, for two occupants.

Twin room. A hotel room with two single beds, for two occupants.

UATP. Universal Air Travel Plan. A credit card for air travel, honored by all IATA airlines.

Visa. An official document issued by a foreign country providing permission for noncitizens to travel or stay in that country.

Voucher. A coupon or other document good for hotel rooms or other services, given to the traveler by the travel agent or airline when the traveler pays for the services in advance.

Waitlist. The list of standby passengers waiting for seats to open up on a fully booked plane. Also, guests waiting for space in a prebooked hotel.

Toll-free Directory
(Area Code 800)

Auto Rental

Airways Rent-a-Car Systems

Florida only   327-2503

Avis Car Rental

Continental U.S.
  except Oklahoma   331-1212
Oklahoma   482-4554

Budget Rent-a-Car

Continental U.S.   228-9650

Dollar-a-Day Rent-a-Car

Continental U.S.
  except California   421-6868
California   262-1520

Econo Car Rental

Continental U.S.
  except Florida   228-1000
Florida   342-5628

Greyhound Rent-a-Car

Continental U.S.
  except Florida   327-2501
Florida   871-3220

Hertz

Continental U.S.
  except Oklahoma   654-3131
Oklahoma   654-3711

National Rent-a-Car

Continental U.S.
  except Minnesota   328-4567
Minnesota   862-6064

Olins Rent-a-Car

Continental U.S.   327-1202

Sears Rent-a-Car

Continental U.S.   228-2800

Thrifty Rent-a-Car

Continental U.S.
  except Oklahoma   331-4200
Oklahoma   722-3200

U.S. and International Hotel Chains

Americana Hotels
Continental U.S.   433-1776

Best Western Motels
Continental U.S. except Arizona   528-1234
Arizona   352-1222

Howard Johnson's Motor Lodges
Continental U.S. except Oklahoma   654-2000
Oklahoma   522-9041

Hilton Hotels   Contact 800 operator

Holiday Inns   238-8000

Hyatt Hotels
Continental U.S.   228-9000

Quality Inns
Continental U.S.   323-5151

Ramada Inns
Continental U.S. except Nebraska   228-2828
Nebraska   642-9343

Rank Hotels
Continental U.S.   223-5560

Red Carpet Inns
Continental U.S.   323-4444

Rodeway Inns
Continental U.S.   228-2000

Sheraton Inns
Continental U.S. except Missouri   325-3535
Missouri   392-3500

Stouffer's Inns
Continental U.S.   323-4455

Travelodge
Continental U.S. except Kansas   255-3050
Kansas   332-4350

Treadway Inns and Resorts
Continental U.S.   631-0182

Western International
Continental U.S.   228-3000

Airport Codes/Miles to Town

U.S. Airports

City	Code	Airport	Miles to Town
Albany	ALB	Albany County	5
Atlanta	ATL	Atlanta International	8
Baltimore	BAL	Baltimore/Washington International	10
Boston	BOS	Logan International	2
Chicago	ORD	O'Hare International	16
Chicago	MDW	Midway	10
Cincinnati	CVG	Greater Cincinnati	12
Cleveland	CLE	Cleveland Hopkins International	13
Dallas/Fort Worth	DFW	Dallas/Fort Worth Regional	17
Detroit	DTW	Detroit Metropolitan	17
Fairbanks	FAI	Fairbanks International	5
Honolulu	HNL	Honolulu International	4
Houston	IAH	Houston Intercontinental	20
Indianapolis	IND	Weir-Cook	7
Kansas City	MCI	Kansas City International	17
Las Vegas	LAS	McCarran International	7
Los Angeles	LAX	Los Angeles International	10
Memphis	MEM	Memphis International	10
Miami	MIA	Miami International	6
Newark	EWR	Newark International	3
New Orleans	MSY	New Orleans International	14
New York	JFK	John F. Kennedy International	15
New York	LGA	La Guardia	8

U.S. Airports (continued)

City	Code	Airport	Miles to Town
Oakland	OAK	Metropolitan Oakland International	10
Oklahoma City	OKC	Will Rogers	9
Omaha	OMA	Eppley Airfield	4
Ontario (Canada)	ONT	Ontario International	3
Philadelphia	PHL	Philadelphia International	7
Phoenix	PHX	Phoenix Sky Harbor International	3
Pittsburgh	PIT	Greater Pittsburgh	16
Providence	PVD	Theodore F. Green	8
St. Louis	STL	Lambert/St. Louis International	11
Salt Lake City	SLC	Salt Lake City International	7
San Diego	SAN	San Diego International	3
San Francisco	SFO	San Francisco International	16
Washington, D.C.	IAD	Dulles International	26
Washington, D.C.	DCA	Washington National	4

International Airports

City	Code	Airport	Miles to Town
Amman	AMM	Amman	5
Amsterdam	AMS	Schiphol	10
Athens	ATH	Athens	6
Bahrain	BAH	Muharraq	4
Bangkok	BKK	Bangkok International	15
Beirut	BEY	Beirut International	10
Belgrade	BEG	Surcin	10
Bogota	BOG	El Dorado	8
Bombay	BOM	Santa Cruz	18
Brussels	BRU	Brussels National	10
Budapest	BUD	Ferihegy	10
Buenos Aires	EZE	Ezeiza International	31
Cairo	CAI	Cairo	14
Caracas	CCS	Maiquetia	13
Copenhagen	CPH	Kastrup	6
Delhi	DEL	Delhi	9
Dublin	DUB	Dublin	
Frankfurt	FRA	Frankfurt	8
Geneva	GVA	Cointrin	3
Guatemala City	GUA	Aurora International	4
Hong Kong	HKG	Hong Kong International	4
Johannesburg	JNB	Jan Smuts	12
Karachi	KHI	Karachi International	10
Kuala Lumpur	KUL	Kuala Lumpur International	14
Kuwait	KWI	Kuwait	10
La Paz	LPB	Kennedy International	5
Lima	LIM	Jorge Chavez International	4

City	Code	Airport	Miles to Town
Lisbon	LIS	Lisbon	5
London	LHR	Heathrow	15
London	LGW	Gatwick	28
Madrid	MAD	Barajas	8
Manila	MNL	Manila International	8
Melbourne	MEL	Melbourne International	14
Mexico City	MEX	Mexico City International	3
Milan	LIN	Linate	6
Montreal	YUL	Dorval International	12
Moscow	SVO	Sheremetievo	19
Munich	MUC	Riem	6
Panama City	PTY	Tocumen	17
Paris	CDG	Charles de Gaulle	14
Paris	ORY	Orly	12
Peking	PEK	Peking	16
Prague	PRG	Ruzyne	11
Quebec	YQB	Ste. Foy	12
Rio de Janeiro	RIO	Rio de Janeiro International	13
Riyadh	RUH	Riyadh	5
Rome	FCO	Leonardo da Vinci (Fiumicino)	20
Santiago	SCL	Pudahuel	11
Sao Paulo	SAO	Congonhas	6
Seoul	SEL	Kimpo International	16
Shannon	SNN	Limerick	15
Singapore	SIN	Singapore International	7
Stockholm	ARN	Arlanda	27
Sydney	SYD	Kingsford Smith International	9
Taipei	TPE	Sung Shan	3
Tehran	THR	Mehrabad	12
Tel Aviv	TLV	Ben Gurion International	12
Tokyo	NRT	Narita	40
Tokyo	TYO	Tokyo International	12
Toronto	YYZ	Toronto International	18
Vienna	VIE	Schwechat	11
Zurich	ZRH	Zurich	7

Directory of
U.S. Government Services

Civil Aeronautics Board

**Bureau of Compliance and
  Consumer Protection**
Civil Aeronautics Board
1825 Connecticut Avenue, N.W.
Washington, D.C. 20428
(202) 673-5482

Field Offices:
Civil Aeronautics Board
701-C Street Box 27
Anchorage, Alaska 99513
(907) 271-5146

O'Hare Lake Office Plaza,
    Room 254
2300 East Devon Avenue
Des Plaines, Illinois 60018
(312) 694-2686

P.O. Box 92007
Los Angeles, California 90009
(213) 536-6297

90 Church Street, Room 1316-A
New York, New York 10007
(212) 264-1700

Western Regional Audit
2555 Flores Street, Suite 395
San Mateo, California 94403
(415) 574-3153

U.S. Passport Agencies

John F. Kennedy Building
Government Center, Room E123
Boston, Massachusetts 02203
(617) 223-2946

Kluczynski Office Building,
    Room 380
230 S. Dearborn Street
Chicago, Illinois 60604
(312) 353-7155

McNamara Federal Building,
    Suite 1900
477 Michigan Avenue
Detroit, Michigan 48226
(313) 226-3878

New Federal Building, Room C106
300 Ala Moana Boulevard
P.O. Box 50185
Honolulu, Hawaii 96850
(808) 546-2130

One Allen Center
500 Dallas Street
Houston, Texas 77002
(713) 226-4581

Hawthorne Federal Building,
    Room 2W16
15000 Aviation Boulevard
Los Angeles, California 90261
(213) 536-6503

World Trade Center, Room 183
350 S. Figueroa Street
Los Angeles, California 90071
(213) 688-3285

Federal Office Building, Room 804
51 Southwest First Avenue
Miami, Florida 33130
(305) 350-4681

International Trade Mart,
    Room 400
2 Canal Street
New Orleans, Louisiana 70130
(504) 589-6161

Rockefeller Center
International Building,
    Room 270
630 Fifth Avenue
New York, New York 10020
(212) 541-7710

William J. Green Federal Building,
    Room 4426
600 Arch Street
Philadelphia, Pennsylvania 19106
(215) 597-7480

Federal Building, Room 1405
450 Golden Gate Avenue
San Francisco, California 94102
(415) 556-2630

Federal Building, Room 906
915 Second Avenue
Seattle, Washington 98174
(206) 442-7945

Stamford Passport Agency
One Landmark Square
Broad & Atlantic Streets
Stamford, Connecticut 06901
(203) 327-9550

Room G67
1425 K Street, N.W.
Washington, D.C. 20524
(202) 783-8170

U.S. Embassies and Consulates *(Partial List)***

(Embassies are indicated by asterisks. For mailing, use P.O. Box addresses.)

Country/City	Address	Telephone
AFGHANISTAN		
*Kabul	Wazir Akbar Khan Mina	24230-9
ALGERIA		
*Algiers	4 Chemin Cheikh Bachir Ibrahimi	601255/603222
ARGENTINA		
*Buenos Aires	4300 Colombia, 1425	774-7611/8811/9911
AUSTRALIA		
*Canberra	Moonah Pl. Canberra, A.C.T. 2600	(062) 73-3711
Melbourne	24 Albert Rd. South Melbourne Victoria 3205	699-2244
Sydney	T&G Tower Hyde Park Square Park & Elizabeth Sts. Sydney 2000, N.S.W.	235-7044
Brisbane	141 Queen St. Brisbane, 4000	(07) 221-2338
Perth	264 St. George's Ter.	22-4466
AUSTRIA		
* Vienna	IX Boltzmanngasse 16 A-1091	(222) 31-51-11
Salzburg	1 Franz Josefs Kal, Room 302	46461
BAHAMAS		
*Nassau	Mosmar Bldg. Queen St.	(809) 322-1700 322-1181

**From *Key Officers of Foreign Service Posts*, May 1980.

Country/City	Address	Telephone
BANGLADESH		
*Dacca	Adamjee Court Bldg. (5th fl.) Montijheel Commercial Area	244220 through 244229
BELGIUM		
*Brussels	27 Boulevard du Regent B-1000 Brussels	513-3830
Antwerp	64-68 Frankrijklei B-2000 Antwerp	(031) 321800
BERMUDA		
Hamilton	Vallis Bldg. Front St.	295-1342
BOLIVIA		
*La Paz	Banco Popular del Peru Bldg. Corner of Calles Mercado & Colon	350251
BRAZIL		
Rio de Janeiro	Avenida Presidente Wilson 147	(021) 292-7117
Sao Paulo	Edificio Padre Joao Manoel 933 Rua Padre Joao Manoel	(011) 881-6511
BULGARIA		
*Sofia	1 Stambolilski Blvd.	88-48-01 to 05
BURMA		
*Rangoon	581 Merchant St. 71st St. & South Moat Rd.	18055
CANADA		
*Ottawa	100 Wellington St. 5335 K1P 5T1	(613) 238-5335

U.S. Embassies and Consulates (continued)

Country/City	Address	Telephone
Montreal, Quebec	Suite 1122 South Tower Place Desjardins P.O. Box 65 Montreal H5B 1G1, Canada	(514) 281-1886
Quebec, Quebec	1 Ave. Ste.-Geneviève G1R 4A7	(418) 692-2095
Toronto, Ontario	360 University Ave.	(416) 595-1700
Vancouver, British Columbia	1199 West Hastings St. V6E 2Y4	(604) 685-4311
CHILE		
*Santiago	Codina Bldg., 1343 Agustinas	710133/90 710326/75
CHINA		
*Peking	Kuang Hua #17 (Embassy)	52-2033 Guang Hua Lui 7
COLOMBIA		
*Bogotá	Calle 37, 8-40	44843
PEOPLE'S REPUBLIC OF THE CONGO		
*Brazzaville	Avenue Amitcar Cabral; B.P 1015	81-20-70
COSTA RICA		
San Jose	Avenida 3 and Calle 1	22-5-66
CUBA		
Havana	Swiss Embassy U.S. Interests Section Calcado entre L & M Vedado Seccion	320551 329700
CYPRUS		
*Nicosia	Therissos St. and Dositheos St.	65151/5

Country/City	Address	Telephone
CZECHOSLOVAKIA		
***Prague**	**Trziste 15-12548 Praha Amembassy, Prague, c/o Amcongen**	**53-66-41/8**
DENMARK		
*Copenhagen	Dag Hammarskjold Alle 24	(01) 42 31 44
DOMINICAN REPUBLIC		
* Santo Domingo	Corner of Calle Cesar Nicolas Penson & Calle Leopoldo Navarro	682-2171
ECUADOR		
*Quito	120 Avenida Patria	548-000
EGYPT		
*Cairo	5 Sharia Latin America	28211/9
Alexandria	110 Ave. Horreya	801911, 25607, 22861, 28458
EL SALVADOR		
*San Salvador	1230,25 Avenida Norte	25-7100, 25-9984
FIJI		
*Suva	31 Loftus St.	23031
FINLAND		
*Helsinki	Itainen Puisotie 14A	171931
FRANCE		
*Paris	2 Avenue Gabriel 75382 Paris Cedex 08	296-1202 216-8075
**Paris (USOECD)	19 Rue de Franqueville 75016, Paris	524-8200
Bordeaux	No. 4 Rue Espirit des Lois 33000 Bordeaux	56/52-65-95
Lyon	7 Quai General Sarrail 69454	24-68-491
Nice	3 Rue Dr. Barety 06000	88-89-55

**U.S. Mission to the Organization for Economic Cooperation and Development.

U.S. Embassies and Consulates (continued)

Country/City	Address	Telephone
FRENCH WEST INDIES		
Martinique	14 rue Blenac Boite Postale 561 Fort-de-France 97206	71.93.01 71.93.03
WEST GERMANY		
*Bonn	Delchmannsaue 5300 Bonn 2	885-452
Berlin	Clayallee 170 D-1000 Berlin 33	(030) 819-7561
Düsseldorf	Cecilienallee 5 4000 Düsseldorf 30	(0211) 49 00 81
Frankfurt am Main	Siesmayerstrasse 21 6000 Frankfurt	(0611) 74-0071
Hamburg	Alsterufer 27/28 2000 Hamburg 36	(040) 44 10 61
Munich	Koeniginstrasse 5 8000 Muenchen 22	(089) 2 30 11
Stuttgart	Urbanstrasse 7 7000 Stuttgart	(0711) 21 02 21
GERMAN DEMOCRATIC REPUBLIC		
*Berlin	108 Berlin Neustaedtische Kirchstrasse 4-5	2202741
GREECE		
*Athens	91 Vasilissis Sophia Blvd.	71295 or 718401
GUATEMALA		
*Guatemala	7-01 Avenida de la Reforma, Zone 10	31-15-41
GUINEA		
*Conakry	2nd Blvd. and 9th Ave. Boite Postale 603	415-20 through 24
HAITI		
*Port-au-Prince	Harry Truman Blvd.	20200

Country/City	Address	Telephone
HONDURAS		
*Tegucigalpa	Avenido La Paz	32-3121/22/23/24/27
HONG KONG		
Hong Kong	26 Garden Rd.	239011
HUNGARY		
*Budapest	V. Szabadsag Ter 12	329-375
ICELAND		
*Reykjavik	Laufasvegur 21	29100
INDIA		
*New Delhi	Shanti Path Chanakyapuri 21	690351
Bombay	Lincoln House 78 Bhulabhai Desai Rd.	363611-363618
Calcutta	5/1 Ho Chi Minh Sarani Calcutta 700071	44-3611- 44-3616
INDONESIA		
*Jakarta	Medan Merdeka Selatan 5	340001-9
IRELAND		
*Dublin	42 Elgin Rd. Ballsbridge	688777
ISRAEL		
*Tel Aviv	71 Hayarkon St.	654338
ITALY		
*Rome	Via V. Veneto 119/A 00187-Rome	(06) 4674
Florence	Lungarno Amerigo Vespucci 38	(055) 298-276
Genoa	Banca d'America e d'Italia Bldg. Piazza Portello 6	(010) 282-741 through 282-745
Milan	Piazza Repubblica 32	498-2241/2/3
Trieste	Via Roma 9	(040) 68728/29

U.S. Embassies and Consulates (continued)

Country/City	Address	Telephone
IVORY COAST		
*Abidjan	5 Rue Jesse Owens 01 Boite Postale 1712	32-09-79
JAMAICA		
*Kingston	Jamaica Mutual Life Center 2 Oxford Rd.	809-92-94850
JAPAN		
*Tokyo	10-5 Akasaka 1-chome, Minato-ku (107)	583-7141
JERUSALEM		
Jerusalem	18 Agron Rd.; Nablus Rd.	226312 282231/272681 (both offices via Israel)
JORDAN		
*Amman	Jebel Amman P.O. Box 354 Com. Off: Madi Bldg. King Faisal St. (2nd Flr)	44371-6 38930/38724
KENYA		
*Nairobi	Cotts House Wabera St. P.O. Box 30137	334141
LEBANON		
*Beirut	Corniche at rue Ain Mreisseh	366-538, 361-800
LIBERIA		
Monrovia	United Nations Dr.	22991, 2292-3-4
LIBYA		
*Tripoli	Shari Mohammad Thabit P.O. Box 289	34021/6

Country/City	Address	Telephone
LUXEMBOURG		
*Luxembourg	22 Blvd. Emmanuel Servais	40123-4-5-6-7
MALAYSIA		
*Kuala Lumpur	A.I.A. Bldg. Jalan Ampang P.O. Box 35	26321
MALTA		
*Valleta	Development House St. Anne St. Floriana, Malta	623653, 62024, 623216
MEXICO		
* Mexico, D.F.	Paseo de la Reforma 305 Mexico 5, D.F.	553-3333
Guadalajara	Jal.; Progreso 175	25-29-98, 25-27-00
Monterrey	N.L., Avenida Constitucion 411 Poniente	4306 50/59
MOROCCO		
*Rabat	2 Ave. de Marrakech P.O. Box 120	30361, 30362
Casablanca	8 Blvd. Moulay Youssef	22-41-49
NETHERLANDS		
*The Hague	102 Lange Voorhout	62-49-11
Amsterdam	Museumplein 19	(020) 90321
NETHERLANDS ANTILLES		
* Curaçao	St. Anna Blvd. 19 P.O. Box 158 Willemstad, Curaçao	13066, 13350
NEW ZEALAND		
*Wellington	29 Fitzherbert Ter. Thorndon, P.O. Box 1190	722-068

U.S. Embassies and Consulates (continued)

Country/City	Address	Telephone
Auckland	Old Northern Bldg., Society Bldg. (5th Fl.) Queen & Wellesley Sts.; or P.O. Box 7140 Wellesley St.	375-102, 30-992
NICARAGUA		
*Managua	Km. 4½ Carretera Sur	23061, 23881-7
NIGERIA		
*Lagos	2 Eleke Crescent P.O. Box 554	610097
NORWAY		
*Oslo	Drammensveien 18 Oslo 1	56-68-80
OMAN		
*Muscat	P.O. Box 966	745-231
PAKISTAN		
*Islamabad	Temporarily located in AID/UN Bldg.	24071
PANAMA		
*Panama	Avenida Balboa y Calle 38 Apartado 6959 R.P. 5	27-1777
PERU		
*Lima	Corner Avenidas Inca Garcilasco de la Vega & Espana, or P.O. Box 1995 Lima 100	286000
POLAND		
*Warsaw	Aleje Ujazdowskie 29/31 Am. Embassy Warsaw c/o AmConGen	283041-9

Country/City	Address	Telephone
Krakow	Ulica Storlarska 9 31043 Krakow	29764, 21400
PORTUGAL		
*Lisbon	Avenida Duque de Loule, No. 39	570102
ROMANIA		
*Bucharest	Strada Tudor Aughezi 7-9	12-40-40
SAUDI ARABIA		
*Jidda	Palestine Rd. Ruwais	670080
SIERRA LEONE		
*Freetown	Corner Walpole and Siaka Stevens Sts.	26481
SINGAPORE		
*Singapore	30 Hill St.	30251
SOUTH AFRICA		
*Pretoria	Thibault House 225 Pretorius St.	48-4266
Cape Town	Broadway Industries Center Heerengracht Foreshore	021-471280
Johannesburg	Kine Center Commissioner and Kruis Sts. P.O. Box 2155	(011) 21-2684/7
SOUTH KOREA		
*Seoul	Sejong-Ro	72-2601 through 72-2619
SPAIN		
*Madrid	Serrano 75	276 3400, 276 3600
Barcelona	Via Layetana 33	319-9550

U.S. Embassies and Consulates (continued)

Country/City	Address	Telephone
SRI LANKA		
*Colombo	44 Galle Rd. Colombo 3 P.O. Box 106	26211 through 26218
SWEDEN		
*Stockholm	Strandvagen 101	(08) 63.05.20
Goteborg	Sodra Hamngatan 53 Box 428	(031) 80-38-60
SWITZERLAND		
*Bern	Jubilaeumstrasse 93 3005 Bern	(031) 437011
Zurich	Zollikerstrasse 141 8008 Zurich	55-25-66
Geneva	80 Rue du Lausanne 1200 Geneva	32 70 20
SYRIA		
*Damascus	Abu Rumaneh Al Monsur St., No. 2 P.O. Box 29	332315, 332814, 330416
TAIWAN		
Taipei	U.S. Government no longer maintains embassy or consulate. Travelers should contact new organization that will represent American interests: American Institute in Taiwan (no address or phone available at press time).	
THAILAND		
*Bangkok	95 Wireless Rd.	251-9260/2
TUNISIA		
*Tunis	144 Ave. de la Liberté	282.566
TURKEY		
*Ankara	110 Ataturk Blvd.	26 54 70
Istanbul	104-108 Mesrutiyet Caddesi Tepebasi	43-62-00/09

Country/City	Address	Telephone
UNION OF SOVIET SOCIALIST REPUBLICS		
*Moscow	Ulitsa Chaykovskogo 19/21/23	252-00-11 through 252-00-19
Leningrad	UL, Petra Lavrova St. 15, Box 1	(812) 274-8235
UNITED ARAB EMIRATES		
*Abu Dhabi	Sheikh Khalid Bldg. Corniche Rd. P.O. Box 4009	61534/35
UNITED KINGDOM		
*London, England	24/31 Grosvenor Sq. W. 1A 1AE; or Box 40	(01) 499-9000
Belfast, Northern Ireland	Queen's House 14 Queen St. BT1 6EQ	(0232) 28239
Edinburgh, Scotland	3 Regent Ter. EH7 5BW	(031) 556 8315
URUGUAY		
*Montevideo	Calle Lauro Muller 1776	40-90-51, 40-91-26
VENEZUELA		
*Caracas	Avenida Francisco de Miranda and Avenida Principal de la Floresta	284-7111/6111
YUGOSLAVIA		
*Belgrade	Kneza Milosa 50	645655
ZAMBIA		
*Lusaka	P.O. Box 1617	50222
ZIMBABWE		
Salisbury		791586/7

Overseas Citizens' Services

Citizens Emergency Center
Room 4800, Department of State
Washington, D.C. 20520
(202) 632-5225

**Office of Citizens Consular
 Services**
Room 4800, Department of State
Washington, D.C. 20420
(202) 632-3666

Visa Office
515 22nd Street, N.W.
Washington, D.C. 20520
(202) 632-1972

U.S. District Directors of Customs

Anchorage, Alaska 99501
(907) 271-4043

Baltimore, Maryland 21202
(301) 962-2666

Boston, Massachusetts 02109
(617) 223-6598

Bridgeport, Connecticut 06609
(203) 579-5605

Buffalo, New York 14202
(716) 842-5901

Charleston, South Carolina 29402
(803) 724-4312

Chicago, Illinois 60607
(312) 353-6100

Cleveland, Ohio 44114
(216) 522-4284

Dallas/Ft. Worth, Texas 75261
(214) 574-2170

Detroit, Michigan 48226
(313) 226-3177

Duluth, Minnesota 55802
(218) 727-6692

El Paso, Texas 79985
(915) 543-7435

Galveston, Texas 77550
(713) 763-1211

Great Falls, Montana 59401
(406) 453-7631

Honolulu, Hawaii 96806
(808) 546-3115

Houston, Texas 77052
(713) 226-4316

Laredo, Texas 78040
(512) 723-2956

(Los Angeles) San Pedro, California
 90731
(213) 548-2461

Miami, Florida 33131
(305) 350-4806

Milwaukee, Wisconsin 53202
(414) 224-3924

Minneapolis, Minnesota 55401
(612) 725-2317

Mobile, Alabama 36602
(205) 690-2106

New Orleans, Louisiana 70130
(504) 589-6353

New York, New York 10048
(212) 995-7083

Nogales, Arizona 85621
(602) 287-4955

Norfolk, Virginia 23510
(804) 441-6546

Ogdensburg, New York 13669
(315) 393-0660

Pembina, North Dakota 58271
(701) 825-6201

Philadelphia, Pennsylvania 19106
(215) 597-4605

Port Arthur, Texas 77640
(713) 982-2831

Portland, Maine 04111
(207) 775-3131

Portland, Oregon 97209
(503) 221-2865

Providence, Rhode Island 02903
(401) 528-4383

St. Albans, Vermont 05481
(802) 524-6527

St. Louis, Missouri 63105
(314) 425-3134

St. Thomas, Virgin Islands
(809) 774-2530

San Diego, California 92188
(714) 293-5360

San Francisco, California 94126
(415) 556-4340

San Juan, Puerto Rico 00903
(809) 723-2091

Savannah, Georgia 31401
(912) 232-4321

Seattle, Washington 98174
(206) 442-0554

Tampa, Florida 33602
(813) 228-2381

Washington, D.C. 20018
(202) 566-8511

Wilmington, North Carolina 28401
(919) 343-4601

U.S. Government Publications Offices

General Publications Division
Office of Media Services, Room
    4827A
Department of State
Washington, D.C. 20520
(202) 655-4000

Office of Commercial Affairs
Bureau of Economic and Business Affairs
Department of State
Washington, D.C. 20520
(202) 655-4000

Superintendent of Documents
U.S. Government Printing Office
Washington, D.C. 20402
(202) 783-3238

Conversion Tables

Centigrade to Fahrenheit

F	C	F	C	F	C	F	C
23.0	-5	44.6	7	66.2	19	87.8	31
24.8	-4	46.4	8	68.0	20	89.6	32
26.6	-3	48.2	9	69.8	21	91.4	33
28.4	-2	50.0	10	71.6	22	93.2	34
30.2	-1	51.8	11	73.4	23	95.0	35
32.0	0	53.6	12	75.2	24	96.8	36
33.8	1	55.4	13	77.0	25	98.6	37
35.6	2	57.2	14	78.8	26	100.4	38
37.4	3	59.0	15	80.6	27	102.2	39
39.2	4	60.8	16	82.4	28	104.0	40
41.0	5	62.6	17	84.2	29		
42.8	6	64.4	18	86.0	30		

Lengths and Distances

Yards	Meters	Miles	Kilometers
1.09	1	0.6	1
2.19	2	3.1	5
3.28	3	6.2	10
4.37	4	9.3	15
5.47	5	12.4	20
6.56	6	15.5	25
7.66	7	18.6	30
8.75	8	21.7	35
9.84	9	24.9	40
10.94	10	28.0	45

1 foot = 0.3048 meter
1 meter = 39 inches
1 mile = 1.609 kilometers
1 kilometer = approximately ⅔ mile

Weights and Measures

Pounds	Kilograms	Gallons	Liters
2.20	1	0.26	1
4.41	2	1.32	5
6.61	3	2.64	10
8.82	4	3.96	15
11.02	5	5.28	20
13.23	6	6.60	25
15.43	7	7.92	30
17.64	8	9.24	35
19.84	9	10.56	40
22.05	10	11.88	45

Comparative Clothing Sizes

	WOMEN			MEN		
	U.S.A	U.K.	EUROPE	U.S.A.	U.K.	EUROPE
Dresses/Suits	6	8	36	38	38	51
	8	10	38	39	39	52½
	10	12	40	40	40	54
	12	14	42	41	41	55½
	14	16	44	42	42	57
Blouses/Shirts	6	30	36	15	15	38
	8	32	38	15½	15½	39
	10	34	40	16	16	41
	12	36	42	16½	16½	42
	14	38	44	17	17	43
	16	40	46	18	18	45
Shoes	5	3½	36	6	5	38
	5½	4	36½	7	6	39½
	6	4½	37	8	7	41
	6½	5	37½	9	8	42
	7	5½	38	10	9	43
	7½	6	38½	11	10	44½
	8	6½	39	12	11	46
	8½	7	39½	13	12	47
	9	7½	40	14	13	48

International Electric Current Chart

Country	Voltage		Country	Voltage
Afghanistan	200/220		Colombia	110/150
Algeria	110/220		Costa Rica	110
Argentina	220		Czechoslovakia	110/220
Australia	240		Denmark	220
Austria	220		Ecuador	110
Belgium	110/220		Egypt	110/220
Bolivia	220		El Salvador	110
Brazil	110/220		Finland	220
Bulgaria	220		France	110/220
Burma	220		Germany	220
Canada	110		Ghana	240
Chile	220		Great Britain	220
China	220/230		Greece	220

Note: 110-volt appliances will work in the 100-volt to 160-volt range; 220-volt appliances will work in the 200-volt to 260-volt range.

Country	Voltage	Country	Voltage
Guatemala	110/120	Panama	110
Hong Kong	200/220	Paraguary	220
Hungary	220	Peru	220
India	220	Philippines	110/220
Indonesia	110/120	Poland	220
Iran	220	Portugal	110/220
Ireland	220	Romania	110/220
Israel	220	Saudi Arabia	110/220
Italy	110/220	Scotland	220
Ivory Coast	220	Singapore	220
Japan	110/220	South Africa	220
Jordan	220	South Korea	110
Kenya	220	Spain	110/220
Kuwait	240	Sri Lanka	220
Lebanon	110/200	Sweden	220
Liberia	120	Switzerland	220
Libya	110	Syria	110/220
Liechtenstein	220	Taiwan	110
Luxembourg	110/220	Tanzania	240
Malaysia	220	Thailand	220
Mexico	110	Tunisia	110/220
Monaco	110/220	Turkey	110/220
Netherlands	220	Uruguay	220
New Zealand	230	USSR	220
Nicaragua	110	Venezuela	110
Nigeria	220	Yugoslavia	220
Norway	220	Zaire	220
Pakistan	220/240		

Business Travel Notes

ADDRESSES AND TELEPHONE NUMBERS

ADDRESSES AND TELEPHONE NUMBERS

RESTAURANTS AND HOTELS

NOTES FOR NEXT TIME

THINGS TO SEE AND DO

WHAT TO BUY AND WHERE

ITEMS TO BE DECLARED

ITEMS TO BE DECLARED

MISCELLANEOUS